FRANCHISING IN BUSINESS

RESEARCH AND INFORMATION
GUIDES IN BUSINESS, INDUSTRY, AND
ECONOMIC INSTITUTIONS
(VOL. 1)

GARLAND REFERENCE LIBRARY
OF SOCIAL SCIENCE
(VOL. 472)

RESEARCH AND INFORMATION GUIDES IN BUSINESS, INDUSTRY, AND ECONOMIC INSTITUTIONS

General Editor: Wahib Nasrallah

1. Franchising in Business: A Guide to Information Sources
by Lucy Heckman

FRANCHISING IN BUSINESS
A Guide to Information Sources

Lucy Heckman

GARLAND PUBLISHING, INC. • NEW YORK & LONDON
1989

Library of Congress Cataloging-in-Publication Data

Heckman, Lucy, 1954–
    Franchising in business : a guide to information sources / by Lucy
Heckman.
        p. cm. — (Research and information guides in business, industry, and
economic institutions : 1)
(Garland reference library of social science ; v. 472)
    Includes indexes.
    ISBN 0–8240–5648–5 (alk. paper)
    1. Franchises (Retail trade)—Bibliography. 2. Franchises (Retail
trade)—United States—Bibliography. I. Title. II. Series.
III. Series: Garland reference library of social science ; v. 472.
Z7164.C8H43   1989
016.6588'708—dc20   89–32272
                                                              CIP

Printed on acid-free, 250-year-life paper
Manufactured in the United States of America

SERIES FOREWORD

The new information society has exceeded everyone's expectations in providing new and exciting media for the collection and dissemination of data. Such proliferation has been matched by a similar increase in the number of providers of business literature. Furthermore, many emerging technologies, financial fields, and management processes have amassed an amazing body of knowledge in a short period of time. Indicators are that packaging of information will continue its trend of diversification, confounding even the experienced researcher. How then will information seekers identify and assess the adequacy and relevancy of various packages to their research needs?

It is my hope that Garland's *Research and Information Guides in Business, Industry, and Economic Institutions* series will bridge the gap between classical forms of literature and new alternative formats. Each guide will be devoted to an industry, a profession, a managerial process, or a field of study. Organization of the guides will emphasize subject access to formats such as bibliographic and numeric databases on-line, distributed databases, CD-Rom products, loose-leaf services, government publications and books, and periodical articles. Although most of the guides will serve as locators and bridges to bodies of knowledge, some may be reference books with self-contained information.

Since compiling such guides requires substantial knowledge in the organization of information or the field of study, authors are selected on the basis of their expertise as information professionals or subject specialists. Inquiries about the series and its content should be addressed to the Series Editor.

Wahib Nasrallah
Langsam Library
University of Cincinnati

CONTENTS

PREFACE

Franchises today range from fast food chains to health spas to income tax preparation services. Finding the most appropriate franchise to buy is often a complex task. After purchasing a franchise, the owner must be constantly aware of legal and business trends affecting the business. Success in both selection and operation of a business depends on the information available to both present and future franchise owners. Such information is found in books, periodicals, indexes, and online databases. Additionally, government and non-profit agencies and organizations provide assistance as well as facts about franchising.

FRANCHISING IN BUSINESS: A GUIDE TO INFORMATION SOURCES was written to assist present and prospective franchise owners who need to know what agencies and resources are available. It is also a guide to students of business interested in finding out about the franchising industry. FRANCHISING IN BUSINESS is an annotated bibliography of books, journal articles, pamphlets, dissertations, and an audio cassette. The appendixes list and describe indexes, periodicals, online databases, and organizations. Source materials are divided into the topics: How-to and Introductory Guides; Directories of Franchising Opportunities; Bibliographies and Source Books; Guides to Financing of Franchises; Legal Information Sources; Franchising in the United States; International Franchising; and Case Histories of Franchises.

This reference guide contains English language primary and secondary sources on franchising. Dates of coverage of materials range from 1956 through June 1988. It is a selective bibliography of sources on franchising. Materials were located through scanning periodical indexes, bibliographies, and online databases including RLIN, OCLC, ABI/INFORM, and LIBRARY OF CONGRESS MARC RECORDS. Additional materials were found in the annual editions of the FRANCHISE OPPORTUNITIES HANDBOOK, which includes an annual bibliography

of sources. Copies of these books and articles were examined
and reviewed at various research libraries and/or sent through
the Interlibrary Loan Department at St. John's University
Library.

Each item is assigned an entry number and items are
indexed according to these numbers by author, title, and
subject. Since some sources cover several subject fields,
cross references are included. Each chapter has a brief
introduction to the topic and to information provided in the
items listed.

Appendixes consist of compilations of Organizations and
Associations; Journals, Newsletters, and Newspapers; Abstracts
and Indexes to Franchising Literature; and Online Databases.
All materials in the appendixes are designed to guide readers
to further information about franchising. Items in the
appendixes are arranged alphabetically.

FRANCHISING IN BUSINESS was written to bring together the
various sources on this form of business. Before buying a
franchise, it is recommended that one research the topic
through review of the literature, contact government and/or
non-profit organizations, and seek accounting and legal
advice. FRANCHISING IN BUSINESS is designed to be a starting
point in the path to operating a successful franchise.

ACKNOWLEDGEMENTS

I would like to thank the administration, faculty, and staff of the following libraries and organizations:

St. John's University Library, Jamaica, N.Y.

St. John's University College of Business Administration

New York Public Library

Brooklyn Public Library

Harvard University's Baker Library

The Library of Congress

C.W. Post's Center for Business Research

Adelphi University

Hofstra University

International Franchise Association

Brownstein, Zeidman and Schomer Library, Washington, D.C.

Special thanks are due to William Cherkasky, President and Chief Operating Officer of the International Franchise Association for all his assistance on this project. I wish also to acknowledge all the support and help from Terrian Barnes and Wayne Byers of the International Franchise Association.

INTRODUCTION

Franchising, as defined by the International Franchise Association is "a method of marketing a product and/or service. Franchise arrangements have been subdivided into two broad classes: (1) Product distribution arrangements in which the dealer is to some degree, but not entirely, identified with the manufacturer/supplier and (2) entire business format franchising, in which there is complete identification of the dealer with the buyer."

In franchising, there is an interdependent relationship between franchisors and franchisees. The IFA defines a franchisor as "a legal entity which owns the patents, trademarks, methods and supplies that it allows others to use under its auspices. Also called franchise company." The franchisee or franchise owner is defined by the IFA as "the individual or individuals who own and operate a business under a licensing agreement granted by the parent company known as the franchise company or franchisor. Franchise owners are commonly entitled to: use the trademark or trade name; sell or market the product or service; have access to pertinent trade secrets; receive management and other training; enjoy marketing and/or advertising support; build equity interest in the business; and benefit from the good will of the franchise company." Much of the literature on franchising concerns the franchisor-franchisee relationship.

Through buying a franchise, an individual may run a small business, market and sell an established product such as a McDonald's hamburger, and receive assistance in training, advertising, and management from the franchisor. However, the franchisee is accountable to the franchisor and is required to follow procedures and meet certain standards of quality. Furthermore, royalties are required to be paid to franchisors for use of the trademark and for assistance in training, management, marketing, etc. Prospective franchisees need to consider both advantages and disadvantages of buying a business.

The past few decades have seen an increase in the number
of franchise opportunities available to entrepreneurs. FRAN-
CHISING IN THE ECONOMY, 1986-88, distributed by the U.S.
Department of Commerce's International Trade Administration,
estimates franchising sales of goods and services will reach
almost $640 billion in 1988. Projected also are growth in
sales, employment, number of units, and expansion overseas.

An early form of franchising was developed in the United
States in the nineteenth century by I.M. Singer as a method of
marketing sewing machines. In the early part of the twentieth
century, Rexall, the Coca-Cola Bottling Company, General
Motors, and Howard Johnson's marketed and distributed products
through franchising. The 1940s and 1950s in the United States
were decades of great expansion for franchises. During this
time period, the following franchises were founded:
McDonald's, Kentucky Fried Chicken, Holiday Inns, Midas
Muffler, Dunkin' Donuts, and H & R Block. From the 1960s to
the present, the variety and number of franchises has
continued to expand. Industries represented by franchising
now include automotive products and services, beauty and
health aids, convenience stores, video sales and rental,
insurance, fast foods, health spas, and travel agencies.

Deciding what type of franchise to buy depends on an
entrepreneur's field of expertise and cost of the business.
For the franchise to be a success, the prospective franchisee
should have the willingness and persistance to invest time and
hard work in the enterprise. Details on how to investigate
and evaluate franchises are found in Chapters I and II. The
U.S. Department of Commerce's FRANCHISING IN THE ECONOMY, Info
Press's THE FRANCHISE ANNUAL, and the International Franchise
Association's DIRECTORY OF MEMBERSHIP provide listings of
opportunities currently available as well as facts about
franchising. Trade journals with up-to-date information on
new franchises are: BLACK ENTERPRISE, CONTINENTAL FRANCHISE
REVIEW, ENTREPRENEUR MAGAZINE, FRANCHISE LAW JOURNAL,
FRANCHISE LAW REVIEW, FRANCHISE LEGAL DIGEST, THE FRANCHISE
MAGAZINE, FRANCHISE WORLD, INFO FRANCHISE NEWSLETTER, JOURNAL
OF INTERNATIONAL FRANCHISING AND DISTRIBUTION LAW, NATION'S
BUSINESS, and VENTURE. The leading business newspapers and
magazines such as THE WALL STREET JOURNAL, BUSINESS WEEK, and
FORTUNE all feature items on franchising. Articles on
franchising may be located by scanning the indexes and
databases listed in the appendixes.

The next step in selecting a franchise is to write to
the companies and request a disclosure document which may be
termed: the Uniform Franchise Offering Circular, UFOC,
Offering Prospectus, Disclosure Statement, or Public Offering
Prospectus. The 1979 Federal Trade Commission rule requires

disclosure of all pertinent information to prospective
franchisees through this document. In addition, over twenty
states have their own disclosure regulations. The disclosure
statement is a means of protecting prospective franchisees
from fraudulent practices. In the disclosure statement, the
following facts should be included: names of franchisor and
officers in the company; the business experience of the
franchisor and officers and if any were involved in criminal
convictions, civil judgments, and administrative orders;
description of the franchised business; report of training
programs, management, and advertising programs offered by the
franchisor; number of franchised units currently in operation;
all fees that the franchisee is required to pay the franchisor; the franchisor's trade name and trade or service marks
to be licensed to the franchisee; description of financing
arrangements; financial information presented in the form of
the latest balance sheet and profit and loss statement;
conditions of purchasing goods or services; and conditions
under which the contract may be terminated or not renewed.
     Further data about a franchise may be found by contacting
federal government, state, and non-profit organizations. The
Better Business Bureaus located throughout the United States
maintain files of franchised companies. Problems with a
particular franchise that were reported to the Bureaus may be
discovered.
     The International Franchise Association is a non-profit
organization that sets standards for the industry through
preparation of a Code of Ethics to be followed by its member
companies, through presentation of conferences and workshops,
and through publication of books, pamphlets, and periodicals.
Its DIRECTORY OF MEMBERSHIP lists franchised companies which
have met IFA membership requirements involving length of time
in business, compliance with state and federal regulations,
and financial stability. The IFA Executive Committee
investigates franchised businesses and determines whether or
not they qualify for membership.
     The Small Business Administration provides assistance to
prospective entrepreneurs in the form of counseling and
financing. The SBA publishes guides to owning and operating
small businesses. Field offices of the SBA are located in
cities throughout the United States. For assistance to small
businesses owned by minorities, the regional offices of the
Minority Business Development Agency (MBDA) may be contacted.
     Addresses of the Council of Better Business Bureaus, the
International Franchise Association, the Small Business
Administration, the Minority Business Development Agency, and
other agencies may be found in the Appendixes.
     The investigation process is not complete without
professional consultation with an attorney. It is advisable

to go over provisions of the franchise contract and items in
the prospectus with an attorney. Many of the introductory
guides listed in Chapter I strongly recommend seeking
professional advice from an attorney. Discussion of business
terms with an accountant is also advised in some of the
introductory guides.

To buy a profitable franchise venture is a crucial step
for any entrepreneur. A critical factor in the success or
failure of a purchasing venture is taking the time to
investigate and evaluate opportunities. It is important to
review the literature and become familiar with franchising
history, its law and legislation, and its possible future.
Prospective franchise owners should examine the offering
circulars and compare opportunities. Additional facts may be
obtained through contacting members of government and non-
profit organizations. Before signing the contract,
entrepreneurs should seek legal and financial advice from
attorneys and accountants, respectively. After purchase of
the franchise, it is essential for franchisees to remain aware
of laws and trends in the industry through reading the trade
journals and being on the mailing lists of some of the
organizations and associations. Being knowledgeable about
franchising developments and trends is one of the
entrepreneur's best protections against business failure.

Franchising in Business

CHAPTER I
HOW-TO AND INTRODUCTORY GUIDES

In the literature of franchising for the general reader,
the how-to or introductory book is predominant. Whether
helping readers discover how to buy a franchise or instructing
experienced franchisors in expanding their businesses, these
books provide a wealth of information. Introductory guides
often furnish case histories of existing franchises and list
bibliographic references or agencies where readers may find
additional resources. This chapter provides an annotated
listing of book materials and one audio cassette tape. For
periodical literature, indexes and online databases may be
consulted.

1. Adams, John and Ken Prichard Jones. F IS FOR FRAN-
   CHISING. Designed and illustrated by Nick Tidman.
   New Revised Edition. Henley-on-Thames, Oxon,
   England: British Franchise Association, 1985.

   A reference work, in dictionary form, for
   prospective franchisees. Explains terms used in
   franchising such as "Franchisee," "Franchisor,"
   "Advertising," "Goodwill," "Operations Manual," and
   "Momma and Poppa Franchises." Emphasizes franchising
   in the United Kingdom and discusses role of the
   British Franchise Association.

2. Alexander, Sandy. FRANCHISING AND YOU: UNLIMITED OP-
   PORTUNITIES FOR SUCCESS. Los Angeles, California:
   Lawrence Publishing Co., 1970.

   Assists readers in finding the right franchise.
   Lists information sources of value including seminars,
   exhibits, and consultants. The "Master Franchise

Index" is a directory of franchised businesses. Case
histories of franchises described are: Pioneer Take
Out, Frederick's of Hollywood, Airline Schools
Pacific, B-Elegant Dog Salons, and Dolphin Clubs.

3. American Entrepreneurs Association. HOW TO FRANCHISE
   YOUR BUSINESS. IEA Special Report; No. 313. Los
   Angeles, California: The Association, 1981.

   A guide, written for the franchisor, to operating
   and starting franchises. Describes legal and managerial aspects of franchising a business. Covers the
   franchise agreement, the disclosure statement, training programs, fees, the Federal Trade Commission disclosure regulation, and the Uniform Franchise Offering Circular.

4. Boroian, Donald D. and Patrick J. Boroian. THE FRAN-
   CHISE ADVANTAGE: MAKE IT WORK FOR YOU. Schaumburg,
   Illinois: National Best Seller Corp., 1987.

   Donald D. Boroian and Patrick J. Boroian are the
   Chairman and President, respectively, of the consulting firm Francorp. Foreword is by Arthur Lipper
   III, Chairman and Editor-in-Chief of VENTURE MAGAZINE.
   Written as a guide on how to establish a franchise for
   entrepreneurs, prospective franchisees, general
   readers, franchisors seeking improvements, and corporate decision makers. Among topics covered are:
   franchising and the law, the franchisor-franchisee
   relationship, financing the franchise, and the future
   of franchising. Features case histories of the franchisors: Ray Kroc (McDonald's), Kemmons Wilson (Holiday Inns), Tom Monaghan (Domino's Pizza), Jules
   Lederer (Budget Rent-a-Car), Alan Hald (MicroAge), and
   Anthony Yniguez (Red Carpet Realty). "Up and Comers"
   or successful contemporary franchisors described are:
   Scott King and John Turnbull (Soup Exchange), Mark
   Dalen (Silk Plants Etc.), Merle Harmon (Fan Fair),
   Alan Levine and Vincent Powell (The Baby's Room), John
   Amico (Shear Genius), and Terry Fairbanks and Jim Hill
   (Copy Mat).

5. British Franchise Association. A COMPREHENSIVE GUIDE
   TO FRANCHISING. Henley-on-Thames, Oxon, England: The
   Association, n.d.

Twelve-page source with series of essays on what
franchising is about. Contents: "Meet the British
Franchise Association," by Tony Dutfield, BFA Director; "Get to Know Franchising," by Anton Bates;
"Finance and Franchising," by Mike Salinger; "Franchising and the Law," by Martin Mendelsohn; "Pros
and Cons: The Message of Franchising;" and "Franchisees' 'Top Fifty' Checklist (questions to ask
Franchisors)."

6. British Franchise Association. WORKBOOK: ESSENTIAL
   INFORMATION FOR DEVELOPING FRANCHISORS. Henley-on-
   Thames, Oxon, England: The Association, 1986.

   Defines terms of the franchising industry and discusses role of the British Franchise Association.
   Covers franchising industry in the United Kingdom, the
   United States, and Continental Europe. Appendixes
   provide lists of: BFA members, seminars and exhibitions, overseas franchise associations, and officers
   of the BFA.

7. Cameron, Jan. THE FRANCHISE HANDBOOK: A COMPLETE GUIDE
   TO SELECTING, BUYING, AND OPERATING. New York: Crown
   Publishers, 1970.

   Handbook for prospective franchisees from an author
   who has had extensive experience in franchising. Offers guidelines and questions to ask when investiga-
   ting a franchise. Lists publications and organizations to consult for further assistance. Provides
   information based on results of several hundred
   questionnaires sent to franchise operators.

8. Church, Nancy Suway. FUTURE OPPORTUNITIES IN FRAN-
   CHISING. Babylon, N.Y.: Pilot Books, 1981.

   Analyzes current trends and projects future op-
   portunties for prospective franchisees. Covers types
   of franchises available, a brief history of franchising, and some of the current laws affecting franchises. Designed to help prospective franchisees
   choose a business with the greatest potential for
   success.

9. Coltman, Michael MacDonald. FRANCHISING IN THE U.S.:
    PROS AND CONS. Self-Counsel Series. Vancouver,
    B.C.: International Self-Counsel Press Ltd., 1982.

    Written for entrepreneurs who wish to start their
    own businesses. Examines the history, advantages and
    disadvantages, laws, and financing of franchising.
    Features a Self-Test to measure readers' suitability
    to run a business, and a sample franchise contract.

10. Dias, Robert N. and Stanley L. Gurnick. FRANCHISING:
    THE INVESTOR'S COMPLETE HANDBOOK. New York: Hastings
    House, 1969.

    Written for prospective and present franchisees.
    Among topics covered are: where to look for franchise
    opportunities, evaluating the franchise opportunity,
    financing arrangements, advantages and disadvantages,
    and legal elements. Emphasizes the importance of the
    investigative process as a means of protecting the
    prospective franchisee from unfair practices and/or
    fraud.

11. Fels, Jerome L. and Lewis G. Rudnick. INVESTIGATE
    BEFORE INVESTING: GUIDANCE FOR PROSPECTIVE
    FRANCHISEES. Rev. ed. Washington, D.C.: Inter-
    national Franchise Association, 1981.

    Guide to evaluation of franchise offers. Advises
    investigation of past litigation, profit projections,
    cost, etc. Recommends consultation with professional
    advisors. Outlines role of the International Fran-
    chise Association and the Better Business Bureaus.

12. Finn, Richard P. YOUR FORTUNE IN FRANCHISES. Chicago:
    Contemporary Books, 1979.

    Guide for the prospective or established franchisee
    with information on contracts, financing, legal
    rights, location, record keeping, advertising, and
    insurance. Includes a directory of leading fran-
    chises with their addresses, telephone numbers, name
    of franchise director, and type of industry.

13.   Foster, Dennis L. THE COMPLETE FRANCHISE BOOK: WHAT
      YOU MUST KNOW (AND ARE RARELY TOLD) ABOUT BUYING OR
      STARTING YOUR OWN FRANCHISE. Rocklin, California:
      Prima Publishing and Communications, 1987.

      Explores franchising with special emphasis on the
      relationship between franchisors and franchisees.
      Describes various aspects of the franchise industry
      such as fees and royalties, how franchisors recruit
      franchisees, financing, how to evaluate a franchise,
      and the franchise agreement. Among appendixes are: a
      sample franchise agreement, a sample Uniform Franchise
      Offering Circular, and a bibliography.

*   Foster, Dennis. FRANCHISING FOR FREE: OWNING YOUR OWN
      BUSINESS WITHOUT INVESTING YOUR OWN CASH. Cited
      below as item 103.

14.   Fowler, Alan and Deborah Fowler. FRANCHISING: A SMALL
      BUSINESS GUIDE. Business Guidebooks. London: Sphere
      Reference, 1985.

      A source for both franchisors and franchisees that
      focuses on all phases of franchising from selecting a
      business to developing a training manual. Discusses
      pros and cons of franchising, financing the business,
      advertising and marketing strategies, and management
      techniques.

*   Friedlander, Mark, Jr. and Gene Gurney. HANDBOOK OF
      SUCCESSFUL FRANCHISING. 1981. Cited below as item
      87.

*   Friedlander, Mark, Jr. and Gene Gurney. HANDBOOK OF
      SUCCESSFUL FRANCHISING. 1985. Cited below as item
      88.

15.   Golzen, Godfrey, Colin Barrow, and Jackie Severn.
      TAKING UP A FRANCHISE. London: Kogan Page, 1983.

      Designed for prospective franchisees, this intro-
      ductory guide examines franchising opportunities in
      Great Britain. Covers various phases of starting a

franchise, among which are: evaluating the franchise,
the franchise contract, financing, legal and tax
considerations, advantages and disadvantages, and
training programs. Contains checklist of questions to
ask franchisors and other franchisees, advertisements
of franchise opportunities in Great Britain, and a
listing of books and organizations.

16. Gross, Harry and Robert Levy. FRANCHISE INVESTIGATION
     AND CONTRACT NEGOTIATION. Babylon, N.Y.: Pilot
     Books, 1985.

     Assists potential franchisees in selecting, ana-
     lyzing, and investigating a franchise and then nego-
     tiating the contract. Advises readers to also con-
     sult an accountant and attorney. Provides text of the
     Federal Trade Commission Full Disclosure Regulation.

17. Gunz, Sally, T. Regan, and Derek F. Channon. FRAN-
     CHISING. Centre for Business Research. Research
     Report. Manchester, England: Centre for Business
     Research in association with Manchester Business
     School, University of Manchester, 1980?

     Introduces the concept of franchising, highlighting
     the industry in Great Britain. Offers advice to both
     franchisors and franchisees on the franchise agree-
     ment, advantages and disadvantages, legal obligations,
     and methods of investigating a franchise. Discusses
     role of the British Franchise Association. Appendixes
     include legal documents for the franchised businesses:
     Kentucky Fried Chicken and Pronuptia & Youngs Ltd.
     Statistical tables illustrate trends for franchises in
     sales, numbers of establishments, and revenue growth.

18. Henward, DeBanks M. and William Ginalski. THE FRAN-
     CHISE OPTION: EXPANDING YOUR BUSINESS THROUGH
     FRANCHISING. Phoenix, Arizona: Franchise Group
     Publishers, 1979.

     Counsels present and potential franchisors on busi-
     ness and legal aspects of the industry. Covers sub-
     jects of test marketing, planning a franchise system,
     system implementation, legal obligations, recruiting
     franchisees, writing the operations manual, and legal

trends. Appendixes consist of the text of the Federal
Trade Commission Rule 436 (disclosure regulation), a
glossary of terms, and a bibliography.

19. Holland, Philip. THE ENTREPRENEUR'S GUIDE: HOW TO
     START AND SUCCEED IN YOUR OWN BUSINESS. New York:
     Putnam's, 1984.

     Chapter 17, "Shall I Franchise?" reviews history of
     the industry, pros and cons, case histories, and
     elements of the successful franchise.

20. International Franchise Association. ANSWERS TO THE
     TWENTY-ONE MOST COMMONLY ASKED QUESTIONS ABOUT
     FRANCHISING. Washington, D.C.: The Association, n.d.

     Brochure that offers answers to questions most fre-
     quently asked by prospective franchisees.

21. International Franchise Association. GLOSSARY OF FRAN-
     CHISING TERMS. Washington, D.C.: The Association,
     n.d.

     Defines over 160 terms used in the franchising
     industry. Offers definitions of terms including
     "Franchise Advisory Board," "Subfranchising," "Ter-
     ritory," and "FTC Rule." Explains terms commonly
     found in franchise contracts.

22. Jones, Thomas Burton. A FRANCHISING GUIDE FOR BLACKS.
     New York: Pilot Books, 1973.

     Guide to various aspects of franchising including
     advantages and disadvantages, financing, and oppor-
     tunities available.

23. Keup, Erwin J. HOW TO SELECT A FRANCHISE. Newport
     Beach, California: Consigliare Publications, 1982.

     Written for the individual who wishes to be his/her
     own boss by purchasing a franchise or existing busi-
     ness. The first portion of the book concerns buying a
     franchise; the second discusses buying a small busi-

ness. Analyzes: reasons for buying a franchise,
factors in evaluating the franchise offering circular,
financing arrangements, legal obligations, and the
franchise contract. Refers readers to the FRANCHISE
OPPORTUNITIES HANDBOOK for further details. Appendixes list: "Evaluation of Franchisor Form," "Checklist of Questions to Ask Existing Franchisees,"
"Checklist of Information to Secure about Franchisor,"
and "State Statutes Pertaining to Franchising."

24.   Kinch, John E. with John P. Hayes. FRANCHISING: THE
      INSIDE STORY: HOW TO START YOUR OWN BUSINESS AND
      SUCCEED! Wilmington, Delaware: TriMark Publishing
      Co., 1986.

      Overview of franchising by the President of TriMark,
      one of the nation's largest co-op direct mail adver-
      tising firms. Counsels prospective franchisees/fran-
      chisors on how to evaluate a franchise opportunity,
      what the advantages/disadvantages are, and managing
      the business. Profiles the franchised businesses:
      7-Eleven, Computerland, Midas Mufflers, Pizza Hut, and
      TriMark. Provides glossary of franchise terms. Ap-
      pendixes consist of: A. Are you an entrepreneur? (a
      self-evaluative guide); B. Questions to ask a Fran-
      chisor; C. Acts or Practices which Violate the Fran-
      chise Rule; D. Contents of Disclosure Documents; E.
      States with Franchise Registration Laws; F. Questions
      to ask Franchisees; G. Site Selection Checklist; H.
      Small Business Administration Regional Offices; I.
      Suggested Franchise Reading List; J. Federal Trade
      Commission Offices; and K. Some Franchise Oppor-
      tunities.

25.   Koach, Joseph L. HOW TO ORGANIZE A FRANCHISEE ADVISORY
      COUNCIL. Washington, D.C.: International Franchise
      Association, 1982.

      "How-to" manual for those who wish to start a coun-
      cil and for those who already have a council. Con-
      tains sample by-laws, systems of organization, and a
      sample agenda. Provides result of a survey of
      franchise councils conducted by the International
      Franchise Association.

26.   Koach, Joseph L. HOW TO SELECT SERVICES FOR FRAN-
      CHISORS: AN INTERNATIONAL FRANCHISE ASSOCIATION

GUIDE INCLUDING DIRECTORY OF PROFESSIONAL SERVICES AND LAW LIST. Washington, D.C. International Franchise Association, 1980.

Examines strategies for choosing the right franchise consultant in fields of law, finance, marketing, personnel, manufacturing, office and program management, career counseling, patents, accounting systems, etc. Part of book is "Checklist for Choosing," by Raymond O. Burch, Past-President of the IFA; the checklist rates factors in deciding which consultant to choose. The "Directory of Consultants" lists names, addresses, telephone numbers, contacts, and descriptions of consulting services.

27.   Kursh, Harry. THE FRANCHISE BOOM: HOW YOU CAN PROFIT IN IT. New revised edition. Englewood Cliffs, N.J.: Prentice-Hall, 1968.

Appraises opportunities in franchising with profiles of successful franchises such as Mister Donut of America, Inc. and Rexall. Describes second-generation developments in franchising as "an outgrowth of the precedents and patterns of success established by franchising pioneers." (p. vi) Discusses history of franchising, investment requirements, locating franchising opportunities, understanding the contract, opportunities for women and minorities in franchising, history of the International Franchise Association, and choosing a consultant. Appendixes consist of A. Master List of Franchise Companies According to Category of Product or Service; B. Alphabetical List of Franchise Companies including Addresses and Types of Businesses Franchised; C. List of Small Business Administration Field Offices; D. List of United States Department of Commerce Field Offices; E. List of Small Business Administration Publications Available Free on Request; F. List of Small Business Administration Publications available on Sale through the Government Printing Office; G. Specimen of Typical Questions Required of Franchisees for "Qualification" and "Financial Information." H. Selected Specimens of Franchise Contracts. Features fifty page bibliography of pre-1968 franchising resources.

28.   Lester, Mary. A WOMAN'S GUIDE TO STARTING A SMALL BUSINESS. Babylon, N.Y.: Pilot Books, 1981.

Offers advice to women on owning a small business,
including franchises. Provides a list of bibliographical references and small business organizations.

* Lewis, Edwin H. and Robert S. Hancock. THE FRANCHISE
  SYSTEM OF DISTRIBUTION. Cited below as item 194.

29. Lewis, Mack O. HOW TO FRANCHISE YOUR BUSINESS.
    Babylon, N.Y.: Pilot Books, 1981, c1974.

    Explains procedures to follow in franchising a
    business. Describes steps to take in selecting the
    site, marketing, selling franchises, locating fran-
    chisees, establishing a training program, writing
    the dealer's manual, and preparing the contract.

30. Meaney, James A. EVALUATING AND BUYING A FRANCHISE.
    Babylon, N.Y.: Pilot Books, 1987.

    Counsels future franchisees about the steps to take
    in the purchase of a franchise. Stresses importance
    of gathering data before buying a franchise. Dis-
    cusses: reasons for purchasing a franchise, analyzing
    a disclosure statement, negotiating the contract,
    studying financial and sales information, and contin-
    uing relationships with the franchisor. Describes
    present state and federal franchise laws.

31. Mendelsohn, Martin. THE GUIDE TO FRANCHISING. 1st ed.
    Oxford and New York: Pergamon Press, 1970.

    Reference guide to basic principles of franchising.
    Defines franchising, describes advantages and
    disadvantages, and discusses franchisor-franchisee
    relationship. Highlights role of franchising in the
    United Kingdom. Features case histories of fran-
    chises: Budget Rent-a-Car, Five Minute Car Wash,
    Pleasure Foods Ltd., Wimpy's, and Dyno-Rod. Stresses
    need for a franchise trade association in the United
    Kingdom.

32. Mendelsohn, Martin. THE GUIDE TO FRANCHISING. 2nd ed.
    Oxford and New York: Pergamon Press, 1979.

Updated edition with developments of franchising in
the United Kingdom since 1970. Describes role of the
British Franchise Association which was organized
since the first edition. Analyzes: advantages and
disadvantages, setting up a franchise, franchisor-
franchisee relationship, selecting a franchise, and
entering the United Kingdom market from abroad.
Offers case histories of Wimpy's, Dyno-Rod, Service-
master, Budget Rent-a-Car, Holiday Inns, Kentucky
Fried Chicken, Pronta Print Ltd, and Ziebart Mobile
Transport Service.

33. Mendelsohn, Martin. THE GUIDE TO FRANCHISING. 3rd ed.
    Oxford and New York: Pergamon Press, 1982.

    Third edition of reference guide describes topics
    listed above and case histories of Holiday Inns,
    Kentucky Fried Chicken, and Budget Rent-a-Car.
    Franchising statistics are updated since last edition.

34. Mendelsohn, Martin. THE GUIDE TO FRANCHISING. 4th ed.
    Oxford and New York: Pergamon Press, 1985.

    Updates previous edition's chapters on setting up a
    franchise, the franchise contract, and current indus-
    try developments. New chapter written discusses
    role of the British Franchise Association. Describes
    new developments in companies: Holiday Inns, Kentucky
    Fried Chicken, and Budget Rent-a-Car.

35. Mendelsohn, Martin. HOW TO EVALUATE A FRANCHISE: A
    GUIDE FOR THOSE WHO ARE PLANNING TO SET UP ON THEIR
    OWN IN A FRANCHISE BUSINESS. London: James House,
    1980.

    Booklet for the prospective franchisee and his/her
    professional advisor. Defines franchising and other
    concepts such as pyramid selling. Describes reasons
    for buying a franchise, advantages and disadvantages,
    investigating the business, and understanding the
    contract. Appendix includes the British Franchise
    Association's Code of Ethics.

36. Mendelsohn, Martin and David Acheson. HOW TO FRANCHISE
    YOUR BUSINESS: A GUIDE FOR THOSE WHO ARE PLANNING TO

EXPAND THEIR BUSINESS THROUGH FRANCHISING. A World
Franchise Publication. London: James House, 1981.

Based on a series of articles from the journal
FRANCHISE WORLD, with four chapters added by the
authors. Covers advantages and disadvantages, pyramid
selling, the pilot operation, developing and marketing
the franchise package, developing the operations
manual, and selecting the franchisees. Appendix
includes Code of Ethics of the British Franchise
Association.

37. Metz, Robert. FRANCHISING: HOW TO SELECT A BUSINESS OF
     YOUR OWN. New York: Hawthorn Books, 1969.

     Provides future franchisees with guidelines on
     selecting a franchise, making a profit, training,
     advertising, financing the venture, and choosing a
     location. Companies profiled are Shell, Dunkin'
     Donuts, Dairy Queen, Burger King, International House
     of Pancakes, and McDonald's. Appendixes include a
     sample contract and the International Franchise
     Associaton's Code of Ethics.

38. Midland Bank. BUSINESS SERVICES FRANCHISING. London,
     198-.

     Six-page pamphlet introduces concept of business
     services franchising and discusses benefits to
     franchisees and franchisors, investigation techniques,
     the franchise contract, and financial services at
     Midland Bank.

39. Mockler, Robert J. and Harrison Easop. GUIDELINES FOR
     MORE EFFECTIVE PLANNING AND MANAGEMENT OF FRANCHISE
     SYSTEMS. Research Paper No. 42. Atlanta, Georgia:
     Georgia State College, School of Business Adminis-
     tration, Bureau of Business and Economic Research,
     1968.

     Studies factors that contribute to successful
     management of franchise systems. Examines franchise
     management from the viewpoint of the company offering
     the franchise. Research based on review of the
     literature and on interviews conducted with managers

of successful franchise systems. Covers history of
franchising, advantages and disadvantages, products
and services best suited to franchising, legal issues,
guidelines for successful franchise selection and
financing, measures for establishing franchisor
services and controls, and maintaining franchisor-
franchisee relationships.

40. Modica, Alfred. FRANCHISING: GET YOUR OWN BUSINESS AND
     BE YOUR OWN BOSS FOR UNDER $5,000. New York: Quick
     Fox, 1981.

     Written for individuals who wish to start their own
     businesses. Discusses advantages and disadvantages of
     the industry, the franchise agreement, finding and
     evaluating franchise opportunities, financing, fran-
     chising and the law, and projections of opportunities
     for the eighties. Appendixes consist of A. Defini-
     tions; B. The Franchise Agreement; C. State and Feder-
     al Laws and Rules Affecting Franchising; D. FTC Rule
     vs. State Laws; E. State Officials Responsible for
     Franchise Regulation; and F. Federal Trade Commission
     Assistance. Includes bibliographical references.

41. Munna, Raymond J. FRANCHISE SELECTION: SEPARATING FACT
     FROM FICTION: A GUIDE FOR ENTREPRENEURS, INVESTORS,
     ATTORNEYS, ACCOUNTANTS AND MANAGEMENT/MARKETING
     ADVISORS: HANDBOOK FOR FRANCHISEES. Kenner,
     Louisiana: A Granite Publishers, 1987.

     Helps prospective franchisees understand the
     differences between what franchisors promise and what
     many do not deliver for their fees. Guides readers in
     locating the franchises with best profit potential,
     choosing professional advisors, guarding against
     possible fraud, and investigating a business. Also
     discusses history of franchising and advantages/dis-
     advantages. Features bibliography of books, journals,
     and newspapers. Appendixes consist of: A. Small
     Business Association Offices; B. Small Business
     Administration; C. SBA Bibliography No. 18; D. SBA
     Management Aids, no. 4.019; E. SBA Small Business
     Bibliography, No. 9; F. National Directories
     for Use in Marketing; G. SBA Management Aids, No.
     2.021; and H. Vital Information.

42. Murley, Robert J. FULL CIRCLE MARKETING: AN IN DEPTH
     ANALYSIS OF THE FRANCHISE PHENOMENON. n.p., 1971.

     Offers advice to prospective franchisees who need to
     decide which business to buy. Author is a consultant
     and franchise owner. Covers: how to investigate a
     franchise, legal considerations, the pilot operation,
     selling the franchise package, preparing the sales
     brochure, and marketing programs. Provides questions
     for franchisees to ask about a business and a glossary
     of commonly used terms. Illustrates franchising
     concepts with study of the Mr. Swiss franchise.

43. National Westminster Bank. NATWEST FRANCHISING.
     London, November 1984.

     Furnishes checklist for choosing a franchise and a
     description of services for franchisees offered by
     National Westminster Bank.

44. Nedell, Harold. THE FRANCHISE GAME (RULES AND
     PLAYERS). Houston, Texas: Olempco, 1980.

     Written by founder of Meineke Discount Muffler
     Shops, Inc. for present and potential franchisors and
     franchisees. Describes "the emotional, physical and
     mental trauma experienced by new franchisees and
     provides insight from the points of view of fran-
     chisors as well as franchisees." (p. iv) Studies:
     process of franchise investigation, franchise
     legislation and consumer protection, the franchise
     agreement, history of franchising, and industry
     projections. Includes bibliographical references.

45. Pannell Kerr Forster. SELECTING AND MANAGING A
     PROFITABLE FRANCHISE BUSINESS. New York, 198-

     Four page pamphlet outlines key points of fran-
     chising. Offers answers to questions: "Why buy a
     franchised business?" "What types of franchises are
     available?" "How do I get started?" "What's the
     difference between success and failure?" "What is
     franchising?" and "What does the franchisor provide?"
     Describes the role of the firm Pannell Kerr Forster
     and lists addresses of offices.

46. PILOT'S QUESTION AND ANSWER GUIDE TO SUCCESSFUL
    FRANCHISING. Babylon, N.Y.: Pilot Books, 1988.

    Furnishes, for potential franchise buyers, the
    "right questions" to ask and what the "right answers"
    should be. Underscores importance of full investiga-
    tion before the franchise is purchased. Urges read-
    ers to seek advice of experts in the field, especially
    attorneys and accountants.

47. Raab, Steven S. with Gregory Matusky. THE BLUEPRINT
    FOR FRANCHISING A BUSINESS. New York: Wiley, 1987.

    Written for owners and managers of businesses,
    attorneys, accountants, consultants, marketers, and
    other professionals who wish to be involved in turning
    small or regional businesses into franchise networks.
    Discusses role of franchising in today's economy, five
    factors for franchise success, franchisor-franchisee
    relationship, selling a franchise, managing the
    franchise system, and legal obligations.

48. Raab, Steven S. HOW TO BUY A FRANCHISE THAT'S RIGHT
    FOR YOU. Wiley Sound Business Cassettebooks. New
    York: Wiley, 1987.

    Consists of two cassettes whose running time is
    approximately two hours. Presented as an interview
    with the author by Howard J. Blumenthal. Interspersed
    in program are interviews with franchise owners.
    Analyzes what one needs to know about buying a
    franchise. Covers: history of franchising, sources
    with franchising information, fees, site selection,
    legal matters, case studies, and industry projections.

49. Rosenberg, Robert with Madelon Bedell. PROFITS FROM
    FRANCHISING. New York: McGraw-Hill, 1969.

    Analyzes the franchise industry and strategies for
    purchasing and managing a franchise. Discusses: the
    history of franchising, finding the right franchise,
    financing considerations, the franchise agreement, the
    franchisor-franchisee relationship, and industry
    trends and predictions. Furnishes case histories of
    Dunkin' Donuts, Howard Johnson, McDonald's, American

Dairy Queen, and Midas International. Appendixes
contain: A. Master Index to Franchising Organizations
and B. Sample Contract: Dunkin' Donuts.

50. Scher, Bruce. FRANCHISING: HOW TO SUCCESSFULLY SELECT
     A MONEY MAKING BUSINESS OF YOUR OWN. New York: Bay
     Publishing Co., 1978.

     Guide to investing in a franchise from point of view
     of the prospective franchisee. Covers: investigative
     techniques, costs of franchises, obtaining financing,
     understanding the contract, buying insurance, legal
     considerations, and trends and projections in the
     industry. Presents statistics from the Department of
     Commerce. Appendixes consist of a glossary of terms
     and a bibliography.

51. Scherer, Daniel J. FINANCIAL SECURITY AND INDEPENDENCE
     THROUGH A SMALL BUSINESS FRANCHISE. Babylon, N.Y.:
     Pilot Books, 1986.

     Counsels readers on selecting a franchise with
     limited investment and minimum risk. Shows where to
     find opportunities, how to raise capital, how to
     protect the investment, and pitfalls to avoid.
     Presents the FTC Full Disclosure Regulation and a
     sample franchise agreement.

52. Seltz, David D. THE COMPLETE HANDBOOK OF FRANCHISING.
     Reading, Massachusetts: Addison-Wesley, 1982.

     Assists in the development of business expansion
     programs through presentation of franchising guide-
     lines and information. Describes for potential fran-
     chisors: planning strategies, determining feasibili-
     ty, financing, franchisee recruitment, advertising
     and promotions, franchisee training, the operations
     manual, and legal considerations. Explores franchise
     trends and advantages/disadvantages.

53. Seltz, David D. HOW TO GET STARTED IN YOUR OWN FRAN-
     CHISED BUSINESS: SHORTCUT TO PROFIT AND INDEPEN-
     ENCE. New York: Farnsworth Publishing Co., 1967.

"How to" guide for potential franchisees interested
in selecting the most appropriate franchise.
Discusses: how to judge a franchise, where to look for
advice on making the best selection, the franchise
agreement, site selection, financing, and marketing
techniques.

54. Seltz, David D. A TREASURY OF BUSINESS OPPORTUNI-
     TIES...FEATURING OVER 400 WAYS TO MAKE A FORTUNE
     WITHOUT LEAVING YOUR HOUSE. Rockville Centre, N.Y.:
     Farnsworth Publishing Co., Inc., 1976.

     Chapter 7, "400 Franchised Business Opportunities,"
     was compiled from information taken from the FRANCHISE
     OPPORTUNITIES HANDBOOK. Lists names, addresses, and
     investment costs. Discusses franchising as a viable
     investment opportunity.

55. Serif, Med. BUSINESS BUILDING IDEAS FOR FRANCHISES AND
     SMALL BUSINESSES. New York: Pilot Books, 1985.

     Provides practical promotion ideas and methods for
     the franchised operation. Details promotion strate-
     gies such as television and radio advertising, com-
     munity drives, news releases, and the open house.

56. Siegel, William Laird. FRANCHISING. Wiley Small
     Business Series. New York: Wiley, 1983.

     Explores various aspects of choosing the most suit-
     able franchise and what happens after it is pur-
     chased. Stresses importance of taking the time to
     find the right franchise. Treats matters of: deciding
     whether or not to purchase the franchise, selecting a
     site, hiring employees, managing employees, promoting
     the franchise, and seeking legal advice. Features
     checklist for evaluating the franchise.

57. Small, Anne. A WOMAN'S GUIDE TO HER OWN FRANCHISED
     BUSINESS. Babylon, N.Y.: Pilot Books, 1986.

     Designed for women of all ages who are single,
     married, widowed, or divorced. Reviews methods of
     finding the right franchise, lists franchising
     opportunities, and provides a sample contract.

58. Small, Samuel. STARTING A BUSINESS AFTER 50. Babylon,
     N.Y.: Pilot Books, 1977.

     Shows how those over age 50 can establish a small
     business, a franchised business, or a home-based
     business. Lists over 175 franchise opportunities.
     Demonstrates how to capitalize on lifetime experience
     and contacts.

59. Smart, Albert. THE HOW TO'S OF RETAIL FRANCHISING.
     Retailing for profit series; v. 6. New York: Chain
     Store Publishing Corp., 1982.

     Examines the various aspects of franchising.
     Covers: the history of franchising, advantages/dis-
     advantages, legal aspects, the franchise agreement,
     Federal Trade Commission rulings, and the franchisor-
     franchisee relationship. Lists sources of opportuni-
     ties, publications, and exhibitions.

60. Smith, Brian and Thomas L. West. BUYING A FRANCHISE.
     Lexington, Massachusetts: The Stephen Greene Press,
     1986.

     "How-to" guide studies the franchise market and
     offers advice on legal and ethical considerations in
     purchasing the franchise. Also covers self-assessment
     procedures to test entrepreneurial skills, selecting
     and analyzing opportunities, financing the venture,
     and managing the new franchise in its earliest
     operational stages.

61. Stewart, William Robert. MODERN FRANCHISING HANDBOOK.
     Des Plaines, Illinois: Modern Franchising Magazine,
     1969.

     Relates "inside stories" of franchisees. Lists and
     describes current (ca. 1969) franchise opportunities
     for the potential investor.

62. Stigelman, C. R. FRANCHISE INDEX/PROFILE: A FRANCHISE
     EVALUATION PROCESS. Small Business Management
     Series, No. 35. Washington, D.C.: Small Business
     Administration; For Sale by the Superintendent of
     Documents, U.S. Government Printing Office, 1986.

Guidebook for those interested in buying a franchise. Presents information through series of questions to be asked of franchisors. Chapter 2, "The
Franchise Index" lists both questions and what the
answers to them should be or how to determine the
appropriate answers. Chapter 3, "Franchise Profile"
repeats these questions and leaves blanks to be filled
in by the prospective franchisee. Questions are designed to gather information about such topics as
the reputation of the franchise, its products and
services, its competitors, financial and legal considerations, and franchisee training programs. Appendixes consist of: A. Federal Trade Commission and
Disclosure Documents Required; B. International
Franchise Association (describes its role and includes
their Code of Ethics); and C. Small Business Administration (describes its role and lists locations of
field offices).

63. THE SUCCESSFUL FRANCHISE: A WORKING STRATEGY.
     Aldershot, Hants, England: Gower, 1985.

     Examines methods for selecting a profitable fran-
     chise. Chronicles case studies of franchisees who
     have had both positive and negative experiences in
     buying a franchise. Covers: profiles of the ideal
     franchisee, investigating the franchisor, selecting
     professional advisors, understanding the contract, and
     financing the venture. Emphasizes franchising indus-
     try in the United Kingdom. Includes bibliographical
     references.

64. Tarbutton, Lloyd T. FRANCHISING: THE HOW-TO BOOK.
     Englewood Cliffs, N.J.: Prentice-Hall, 1986.

     Documents for present and future franchisors ways of
     franchising a business. Offers information on: the
     history of franchising, qualities of a successful
     franchise, preparing the franchise agreement, se-
     lecting franchisees, franchisor-franchisee relation-
     ship, managing the franchise system, the role of
     the International Franchise Association, the FTC
     Disclosure Rule. Features addresses of government
     agencies and a glossary.

65. United States. Small Business Administration. Office
     of Business Development. EVALUATING FRANCHISE

OPPORTUNITIES. SBA Management Aids; No. 7.007. Fort
Worth, Texas: Small Business Administration, 1985.

Four-page booklet designed to assist potential
franchisees in evaluating the franchise business, the
franchisor, and the franchise package. A personal
assessment checklist which examines potential franchisees' skills is provided. Defines terms, lists
sources of information, and pinpoints benefits of
franchising.

66. United States. Small Business Administration. Office
     of Management Assistance. Education Division.
     FRANCHISING: INSTRUCTOR'S MANUAL. Small Business
     Management Development Program. Second Series. Topic
     18. Washington, D.C.: Small Business Administration;
     for sale by the Superintendent of Documents, U.S.
     Government Printing Office, 1968.

     Provides material for lecture on franchising to be
     conducted in a small business management course,
     conference, clinic, or workshop. Furnishes lesson
     plan, lecture, visual aids, case studies, selected
     bibliography, and handout material. Section on the
     lesson plan outlines the instructional objectives.
     The lecture or presentation section is an essay on
     franchising with definitions, types of franchises,
     history, advantages and disadvantages, locating
     franchise opportunities, evaluating the franchise
     opportunity, legal counseling, financial assistance,
     and management assistance. Visual aids section
     furnishes illustrations to accompany the lecture.
     Among handout material provided are a series of Small
     Business Administration's SMALL MARKETERS AIDS,
     a series of reports on franchising and small busi-
     ness. Other sections consist of two case studies
     and a selected bibliography.

67. Vaughn, Charles L. FRANCHISING: ITS NATURE, SCOPE,
     ADVANTAGES, AND DEVELOPMENT. Lexington, Massachu-
     setts: Lexington Books, 1974.

     Studies franchising in its history, advantages and
     disadvantages, and management. Offers to present and
     future franchisors a "how to" guide to setting up
     franchises, recruiting franchisees, financing, and

understanding legal aspects. Appendixes consist of:
A. A Franchise Contract; B. The Franchise Agreement;
C. Sample Franchise Contract--Revised Chicken Delight
Agreement.

68. Vaughn, Charles L. FRANCHISING: ITS NATURE, SCOPE,
     ADVANTAGES, AND DEVELOPMENT. 2nd rev. ed. Lexington,
     Massachusetts: Lexington Books, 1979.

     Updated edition with revised statistics on fran-
     chising and section on the Federal Trade Commission's
     Franchise Rule. Offers case studies on Holiday Inns,
     Howard Johnson, and Kentucky Fried Chicken.

69. WWWWW Information Services, Inc. BUYERISM: HOW TO BUY
     A FRANCHISE OR SMALL BUSINESS. Rochester, N.Y.:
     WWWWW Information Services, Inc., 1970.

     Designed to improve "buying skills" of those looking
     for a franchise or small business. Describes: what to
     look for in purchasing a franchise, how to go about
     buying a franchise or small business, overall op-
     portunities in franchising, and where to find informa-
     tion. Includes industry forecasts and lists of
     current (ca. 1970) opportunities.

70. Webster, Bryce. THE INSIDER'S GUIDE TO FRANCHISING.
     New York: Amacom (American Management Association),
     1986.

     Counsels future franchisees in methods of investi-
     gating and buying a franchise. Covers: definitions of
     terms, history of franchising, advantages and dis-
     advantages, questions to ask franchisors, research
     sources on franchising, women and franchising,
     franchisor-franchisee relationship, the franchise
     contract, and setting up a franchise. Rates the best
     United States franchises by category. Each company
     entry lists name, address, product/service, number of
     franchises, fees, minimum capital required, and if
     financing is available. Also furnishes: list of
     state franchise regulatory agencies, franchise and
     business organizations, franchise education programs,
     Federal government agencies, and a bibliography.

CHAPTER II
DIRECTORIES OF FRANCHISING OPPORTUNITIES

Locating the appropriate franchise involves consulting directories of business ventures. Directories of franchised businesses generally list names, addresses, telephone numbers, capital required to purchase the business, and availability of financial assistance. Some listings such as those found in the ENTREPRENEUR and BLACK ENTERPRISE journals rate franchises by such factors as industry category and amount of investment required to purchase the business. Most of the directories are indexed or grouped by subject category. Those interested in purchasing a fast food restaurant may check and compare businesses available in that category. By writing to the franchisor, individuals obtain an information package that usually includes a document called a disclosure statement. This document is also referred to as a prospectus or offering circular. The disclosure statement consists of data such as: business experience of executives in the business, descriptions of any bankruptcies and/or lawsuits affecting officers in the company, statistics on numbers of franchises, information about franchise fees, and a report on training programs for franchisees.

Books and journal articles listed in this chapter have as their primary contents directories of franchises. It should be noted that many of the "How-to and Introductory Guides" listed in Chapter I also include listings of franchise opportunities.

71. "Annual Franchise 500." ENTREPRENEUR, 1980-

Annual issue, published in January, is a guide to the leading 500 franchises in the United States and Canada. Factors in ENTREPRENEUR'S ranking process include the number of years a company has been in

25

business and franchising, the number of franchised
units and company-owned operating units, start-up
costs, and growth rate. These factors are weighed
according to a formula by the editorial staff and the
resulting number is the Weighed Rating. The larger
the Weighed Rating number, the higher the rating.
Each franchised company is then given an Industrial
Ranking based on its Weighed Rating. The franchised
company with the highest Weighed Rating is given the
number one Industrial Ranking. Each "Franchise 500"
company entry includes: name of franchise, address,
product or service category, whether or not experience
is required, the year the business began and when it
started franchising, whether it is seeking U.S. and/or
international franchises, the number of franchises and
how many are company owned, range of capital needed,
franchise fee, royalty required, advertising royalty,
whether or not financing is provided, the Weighed
Rating, and Industrial Rank. Rated franchises are
listed under various industry categories including
Restaurants, Automotive, Beauty & Health, Publishing,
Real Estate, Fast Foods, Retail, etc. "Ready Reference Listings" contain the ratings: "The Top 100
Franchises," "The 40 Fastest-Growing Franchises," "The
Top 25 New Franchises," "The Top 25 Low-Investment
Franchises," "The Top 20 Canadian Franchises," and
"Top in Each Subcategory (Industry)." An Alphabetical
Index to the listings is featured. "The Annual Fran-
chise 400" issue also presents articles on franchising
that describe trends and projections, case histories,
and methods of financing. The "Franchise Show Sched-
ule" refers to a calendar of trade shows.

72.   "The BLACK ENTERPRISE Franchise 50." BLACK ENTERPRISE,
      Annual issue published in September.

      Annual feature rates franchisors based on the
      number of their black-owned franchise units. In
      addition to statistics on number of black-owned units,
      the "Franchise 50" also provides data on the fran-
      chise's location, industry category, total units,
      and start-up costs. Focuses on the business-format
      franchise, an arrangement where the franchisee gets
      the product, service and trademark and receives
      training, marketing strategy techniques, operating
      manuals, and guidance in quality control. Information

based on BLACK ENTERPRISE editors' survey of franchisors, franchisees, trade associations, company
officials, and industry analysts. The "Franchise 50"
issue also features articles and case studies on black
franchisees.

73.   Bond, Robert E. THE SOURCE BOOK OF FRANCHISE
      OPPORTUNITIES. Homewood, Illinois: Dow Jones-Irwin,
      1985.

      Directory of 1400 franchised companies in 126
      business categories. Data based on responses to
      questionnaires sent to companies. Each entry in-
      cludes name, address, and cash investment required.

74.   British Franchise Association. FULL MEMBERS LIST.
      Henley-on-Thames, Oxon, England: The Association,
      January 1986.

      List of franchised businesses that are part of the
      British Franchise Association. Each entry consists of
      name, address, telephone number, and type of product.

75.   DIRECTORY OF CHAIN RESTAURANT OPERATORS. Chain Store
      Guides. New York: Business Guides, Annual.

      Directory of United States chain restaurants,
      including franchised operations. Lists the top 100
      leading restaurant companies both company-owned and
      franchised. Provides food service industry sales
      statistics. Restaurants listed in directory are
      arranged by state. Within each state, restaurants are
      listed alphabetically. Each entry includes head-
      quarters or division office address, number of units,
      whether restaurant is franchised or company-owned
      type of menu featured, and a listing of key person-
      nel. Provides indexes according to type of menu
      (e.g. American, pizza), type of food service (e.g.
      fast food, cafeteria), and names of restaurants and
      their parent companies. Features calendar of industry
      trade shows.

76.   DIRECTORY OF DRUG STORE AND HBA CHAINS INCLUDING DRUG
      WHOLESALERS. Chain Store Guides. New York: Business
      Guides, Annual.

Directory of drug stores and HBA (health and beauty
aids) chains including listings of franchised units.
Features statistics on the industry and lists the top
100 drug store chains. Drug stores are listed by
state; within each state the listing is alphabetical.
Each entry consists of name of unit, owner, location,
and total units. With a calendar of major trade
shows.

77. DIRECTORY OF FRANCHISING ORGANIZATIONS. Babylon, New
    York: Pilot Books, Annual.

Guide to franchises in the industries: "Accounting
and Tax Services," "Advertising Services," "Art
Galleries," "Candy Shops," "Business Services,"
"Automobile Products and Services," "Donut Shops,"
"Food--Drive-in," "Carry-Out Restaurants," "Retail
Stores," etc. Each entry consists of name, address,
concise description of business, and approximate
investment. Also features a franchise evaluation
checklist and the Federal Trade Commission's Full
Disclosure Regulation.

78. Entrepreneur Group, Inc. THE FRANCHISE YEARBOOK. Los
    Angeles, California: Entrepreneur Group, Inc., 1987-

Annual directory provides listings of 1500 companies
currently offering franchises in the United States and
Canada. Also contains articles on franchising
"success stories," industry trends, and "how-to"
guides.

79. Foster, Dennis L. THE RATING GUIDE TO FRANCHISES. New
    York: Facts on File, 1988.

Offers evaluations of leading franchisors in the
United States and Canada. Divides franchises into
industry categories: Apparel and Soft Goods
Franchises; Automotive Franchises; Business Services;
Construction, Decoration, and Maintenance; Educational
Services; Electronics, Video, and Appliances; Food
Service Franchises; Lodging Franchises; Personal
Services; Real Estate Franchises; Recreation and
Amusement; Retail and Convenience Stores; and Travel
Franchises. Within each industrial category are the

franchisor listings. Each franchise profile consists of ratings according to: industry experience, franchising experience, financial strength, training and services, fees and royalties, and satisfied franchisees. Each criterion is given a rating of between one and four stars, with four the highest rating. Each profile contains name, address, and telephone number of franchise; a description of the business; experience required of franchisees; franchisor's services; initial investment; projected earnings; fees and royalties; advertising; and contract highlights. Companies are indexed by name and category.

80. FRANCHISE ANNUAL. Lewiston, N.Y.: Info Press, 1976-

Annual directory of franchise opportunities in the United States and Canada with selected overseas listings. Categories of industries represented include: Entertainment, Travel, Pet Products, Real Estate, etc. Entries contain name, address, telephone number, description of franchise, number of units, year of establishment, investment required, royalty fees, and whether or not financing is available. Indexed by franchise name and industry category. In addition to the directory, other sections discuss the concept of franchising, trends and projections, the Federal Trade Commission rule, state regulations, and the franchise contract. Information in the Annual supplemented by data in the INFO FRANCHISE NEWSLETTER (see Appendix II).

81. Franchise Development Services Ltd. UNITED KINGDOM FRANCHISE DIRECTORY. 3rd ed. Norwich, Norfolk, England: Franchise Development Services Ltd., 1986.

Arranged franchises in the United Kingdom by industry category. Directory information for each company consists of: name, address, contact person, telephone number, number of outlets, description of operation, date of establishment, investment required, support services, financial assistance available, and projections for number of franchises planned. Indexed by franchisor companies and franchised outlets.

82.   "The Franchise Fast-Track: The Country's 50 Fastest-
       Growing New Franchises." VENTURE, Annual issue.

       Annual rating of business-format franchisors or
       those that offer a complete business system provide
       continuing support, and collect royalties. All
       companies listed were required to supply VENTURE
       magazine with a Federal Trade Commission registered
       disclosure document. Companies included were those
       founded in 1982 or later and the franchisor must have
       opened its first unit in January 1986 or later. The
       50 franchisors were ranked by number of units open and
       in operation. In addition to number of units, other
       statistics provided are: year founded, parent company,
       number of company-owned units, date that first fran-
       chised unit opened, franchise fee, other start-up
       costs, royalty fee, advertising fee, term of agree-
       ment, sub-franchising or area development available,
       franchisor revenues, franchisor net income, and notes
       on the franchise. "The Franchise Fast-Track" issue
       also includes articles on case histories and advice on
       how to buy a franchise.

83.   FRANCHISE GUIDE: AN ENCYCLOPEDIA OF FRANCHISE
       OPPORTUNITES. Edited by Robert M. Goldenson.
       Princeton, N.J.: Resource Publications, a Gulf &
       Western Co., 1969.

       Directory to over 400 franchise opportunities.
       Full-page company profiles describe features of the
       franchise including name, address, telephone number,
       history of the parent company, the nature of the
       product or service offered, investment required,
       potential return on investment, and components of the
       franchise program encompassing site selection, market
       analysis, training, financing, advertising, and
       promotion. Lists and examines selected franchising
       consulting organizations and their role in franchise
       development. Section on "Selected Readings on "Fran-
       chising Today," consists of the essays: "The Fran-
       chise Revolution," by Robert M. Goldenson; "19 Ways
       a Franchise Can Help You, 9 Ways it Can Hinder You,"
       by David D. Seltz, from his book, HOW TO GET STARTED
       IN YOUR OWN FRANCHISED BUSINESS, Farnsworth Pub. Co.,
       1967; "Facts about Franchising," by the National
       Better Business Bureau; "Are You Ready for Fran-
       chising," by A.L. Tunick, SMALL MARKETERS AIDS,

No. 115, Small Business Administration, 1965; "Some
Socio-Economic Footnotes on Franchising," by David B.
Slater, BOSTON UNIVERSITY BUSINESS REVIEW, Volume 11,
Number 1, Summer 1964; "Understanding Franchise
Contracts," by Harry Kursh, from THE FRANCHISE BOOM,
Prentice-Hall, Englewood Cliffs, N.J., 1968; "The
Continuing Relationship," by J.A.H. Curry, from
PARTNERS FOR PROFIT, American Management Association,
1966; "Franchising Failures Few and Far Between," by
J.F. Atkinson, from FRANCHISING: THE ODDS-ON FAVORITE,
International Franchise Association, 1968; "Judging
Your Qualifications as a Potential Franchisor," by
David D. Seltz, from Seminar on Franchising Today for
Profit and Growth, Chicago, 1969. Franchises arranged
by industry and product categories.

84.   THE FRANCHISE HANDBOOK: A GUIDE TO COMPANIES OFFERING
      FRANCHISES. Milwaukee, Wisconsin: DMR Publications,
      Inc., 1981.

      Directory of franchising companies by industry
category.   Each entry consists of name, address, name
of president or officer, description of operation,
number of franchisees, year business started, equity
capital needed, financial assistance available,
training provided, and managerial assistance
available.   Introduction contains definitions of
franchising, how to investigate a franchise, the
International Franchise Association Code of Ethics,
and checklist for evaluating a franchise.   Indexes
franchise entries by company name and by industry
category.

85.   FRANCHISE OPPORTUNITIES. 16th ed. New York: Sterling
      Publishing Co., 1985.

      Arranges listings of franchised companies by
industry category.   Each entry contains name, address,
name of president, description of business, number of
franchisees, year established, equity capital needed,
financial assistance available, training provided, and
managerial assistance available.   Asterisk after
company name denotes that company is member of the
International Franchise Association.   Introduction
features guide to evaluating franchises.   Indexed by
category and by name of company.

86. FRANCHISING INDUSTRY SOURCEBOOK, May 1975-April 1976.
    Edison, N.J.: Lasky-Lanouette, 1977.

    Profiles 230 companies in franchising and allied
    industries, with emphasis on chain store, restaurant,
    and other facility operations. Companies listed had
    filed reports with the Securities and Exchange Com-
    mission. Each entry contains name, state of incor-
    poration, main office, financial data, descrip-
    tion of business, and index terms describing busi-
    ness.

87. Friedlander, Mark, Jr. and Gene Gurney. HANDBOOK OF
    SUCCESSFUL FRANCHISING. New York: Van Nostrand
    Reinhold, 1981.

    Reference guide to various types of franchises in
    industries which include Automotive Products and
    Services, Drug Store Services, Employment Services,
    Foods, Real Estate, etc. Each franchise entry
    consists of name, address, description of operation,
    number of franchisees, year established, equity
    capital needed, financial assistance available, and
    name of president. Additionally discusses current
    state and federal regulations and the components of a
    franchise agreement. Appendixes list directories of
    government and non-government agencies' assistance
    programs in addition to a bibliography of information
    sources.

88. Friedlander, Mark, Jr. and Gene Gurney. HANDBOOK OF
    SUCCESSFUL FRANCHISING. New York: Van Nostrand
    Reinhold, 1985.

    Updated reference guide to franchising.

89. Gruber, Kathleen M., comp. THE TRAVELER'S DIRECTORY OF
    FAST-FOOD RESTAURANTS, EASTERN EDITION. New York:
    Pilot Books, 1979.

    Lists over 3800 eating places in cities of Con-
    necticut, District of Columbia, Maine, Maryland,
    Massachusetts, New Hampshire, New Jersey, New York,
    Pennsylvania, Rhode Island, and Vermont. Locates
    franchised restaurants and provides addresses in each

city. Covers listings for Arby's, Burger King,
Dunkin' Donuts, Wendy's, McDonald's, Howard Johnson's,
etc.

90. International Franchise Association. DIRECTORY OF
     MEMBERSHIP. Washington, D.C.: The Association, 1960-

     Directory of IFA member companies arranged by
franchise industry. Indexed by industry and by IFA
member company name. Each entry consists of name,
address, telephone number, type of IFA membership
(i.e. full, associate, subsidiary), description of
business, number of franchised outlets, year established, investment required, qualifications (of
franchisees), and contact person. Lists IFA officers,
board members, committee chairmen, educational affiliates, foreign affiliates, and staff. Describes
IFA history and membership requirements and presents
guidelines in selecting a franchise. Includes the
IFA Code of Ethics.

91. Jones, Constance and The Philip Lief Group. THE 220
     BEST FRANCHISES TO BUY: THE SOURCEBOOK FOR EVALU-
     ATING THE BEST FRANCHISE OPPORTUNITIES. New York:
     Bantam Books, 1987.

     Directory of 220 franchises which range from
established industry leaders to new companies, many of
which are targeting new markets. Each entry consists
of name, address, telephone number, description and
purpose, initial license fee required, royalties,
advertising royalties, minimum cash required, capital
required, financing, length of contract, year
established, year of first franchise, total number of
units, number of company-operated units, and total
number of units planned. Listings for companies are
arranged within their product categories including the
Automotive Industry, the Employment Industry, the Food
Industry, the Travel Industry, and the Real Estate
Industry. Franchises are also indexed alphabetically
by company name. Tables rank franchises according to
total number of units in operation, minimum capital
required, and royalties charged. Offers advice on
choosing and buying a franchise.

92. Norback, Peter G. and Craig T. Norback. THE DOW JONES-
     IRWIN GUIDE TO FRANCHISES. Homewood, Illinois: Dow
     Jones-Irwin, 1978.

     Lists approximately 500 franchises with data for
     each on: name, address, telephone number, contact
     person, type of business, number of franchised units,
     when founded, required capital, financial assistance,
     training, and managerial assistance provided. Fea-
     tures information on the International Franchise
     Association, the Federal Trade Commission, Department
     of Commerce, and the Small Business Administration.

93. Norback, Peter G. and Craig T. Norback. THE DOW JONES-
     IRWIN GUIDE TO FRANCHISES. 2nd ed. Homewood,
     Illinois: Dow Jones-Irwin, 1982.

     Updated edition of franchising reference guide.

94. United States. Department of Commerce. FRANCHISE
     OPPORTUNITIES HANDBOOK. Washington, D.C.: U.S.
     Department of Commerce. International Trade
     Administration and Minority Business Development
     Agency; for sale by the Superintendent of Documents,
     U.S. Government Printing Office, 1965-

     Former title: FRANCHISE COMPANY DATA FOR EQUAL
     OPPORTUNITY IN BUSINESS (1965-1970). Annual directory
     of equal opportunity franchisors or those who do not
     discriminate on the basis of race, color, or national
     origin in selection of their franchisees. Each entry
     includes name, address, description of the franchise,
     number of franchisees, capital requirements, availa-
     bility of financial assistance, and training and
     managerial assistance. Entries are indexed by fran-
     chise product category and by name of franchisor.
     The HANDBOOK also contains a checklist of questions
     for franchise evaluation, the International Franchise
     Association's Code of Ethics, definitions of fran-
     chising terms, and an annotated bibliography of re-
     cent books, pamphlets, and periodicals. Provides
     directory of government and non-government agencies
     which offer assistance. These agencies are the Small
     Business Administration; U.S. Department of Commerce
     International Trade Administration; Internal Revenue

Service Department of the Treasury; Better Business Bureaus; the Minority Business Development Agency; and the International Franchise Association.

*   Webster, Bryce. THE INSIDER'S GUIDE TO FRANCHISING. Cited above as item 70.

95.   Williamson, Garry, ed. FRANCHISE OPPORTUNITIES HANDBOOK. 1984/85. Sydney, Australia: Robert Harris and Associates, 1983.

Lists franchises in Australia by their industrial grouping. Each entry contains name, address, telephone number, and description of business. Other sections feature information on government regulations, legal considerations, the franchise agreement, evaluation of franchise opportunities, and marketing techniques.

CHAPTER III
BIBLIOGRAPHIES AND SOURCE BOOKS

Bibliographies on franchising literature appear in
various formats, including books and pamphlets, periodical
articles, and as sections of books and articles. Most books
on franchising feature a bibliography or bibliographical
footnotes. This chapter lists bibliographies appearing in
book, pamphlet, and periodical form. The bibliographical
material is the entire content of the book material listed and
not just a section. The periodical special issue included
contains a list of sources as well as narrative material. It
should be noted that some of the guides listed below also list
organizations which offer assistance to franchisors and
franchisees.

96. FRANCHISE LAW BIBLIOGRAPHY. Chicago, Illinois: Section
    of Antitrust Law, American Bar Association, 1984.

       Annotated bibliography of treatises, articles, and
       symposia dealing with franchising law. Covers
       materials published from 1966 to mid-1982. Divided
       into two sections: A. Books, Reporting Services,
       Symposia, Miscellaneous Publications; B. Articles
       Appearing in Law Reviews and other Periodicals. Top-
       ics covered include labor, tax, antitrust, and tort
       law. Designed primarily for franchise attorneys and
       lawyers investigating franchise-related matter for the
       first time. Subject and author index included.
       Entries arranged by number.

97. Goodman, Steven E. GUIDE TO 150 SOURCES OF FRANCHISING
    INFORMATION. Dunellen, N.J.: Franchise Information
    Institute, A Division of Education and Training
    Associates, 1970.

Thirty-nine page guide to franchising books,
papers, magazines, consultants, advisory services,
seminars, etc. Divided into sections: A. General
Information about Franchising; B. How to Start Your
Own Franchise; C. Listings of Companies that Offer
Franchises; D. Research Studies on Franchising; E.
Reports of Franchising Conferences; F. Franchise
Associations; G. University Centers for Technical
Assistance; H. Small Business Development Centers; I.
Minority Business Enterprises Organizations; J.
Recruitment of Franchise Executives; K. Franchise
Consultants and Advisory Services. It is important to
note that some of the addresses of organizations have
changed since this book was published.

*   Huls, Mary Ellen. MCARCHITECTURE: A BIBLIOGRAPHY ON
         FAST FOOD RESTAURANT DESIGN. Cited below as item
         235.

98.   Kryszak, Wayne D. THE SMALL BUSINESS INDEX. Methuen,
         N.J.: Scarecrow, 1978.

         Index to books, directories, articles, associations,
         and periodicals on various aspects of small business.
         Includes section on "Franchising" as well as specific
         franchised industries such as "Ice Cream" and "Fried
         Chicken Stand."

99.   Lewis, Edwin H. FRANCHISING: A SELECTIVE BIBLIOGRAPHY.
         University of Minnesota, Graduate School of Business
         Administration; No. 2, January 1966. Minneapolis,
         Minnesota: University of Minnesota, Graduate School
         of Business Administration, 1966.

         An eight page annotated bibliography of books, pam-
         phlets, periodicals, and public documents, articles of
         a general nature, economic and legal aspects of fran-
         chising, and trade associations.

100.   Smith, Solomon. BIBLIOGRAPHY: FRANCHISING--SELECTED
         RECENT WRITINGS. Yale Law Library. Selected New
         Acquisitions. Part II. Volume 15, Number 11, July
         1972. New Haven, Connecticut: Yale University
         Library Publications Office, 1972.

Seven page bibliography of articles and books on
franchising stressing legal issues. Mostly a listing
of articles on antitrust, the contract, and
regulation.

101. Tega, Vasile. FRANCHISING, 1960-1971: AN INTERNATIONAL
      SELECTIVE ANNOTATED BIBLIOGRAPHY/BIBLIOGRAPHIE
      INTERNATIONALE SELECTIVE ET ANNOTEE. Montreal: Ecole
      des Hautes Etudes Commerciales Bibliothèque, 1972.

      Text in English and French. Annotated listings of
      sources that include books, directories, periodical
      articles, and franchise associations. Literature
      described is available at the Library of Ecole des
      Hautes Etudes Commerciales de Montréal. Covers
      subject of franchising in U.S., Canada, and Western
      European countries. Indexed by subject and author.
      Other sections of source are an English/French
      franchising glossary and an introduction to the
      concept of franchising.

102. "VENTURE'S 1986 Guide to Franchising," VENTURE 8 (July
      1986): 69-92.

      Special issue lists and describes information
      sources to consult on franchising. Provides: anno-
      tated guide to major information sources, courses
      on franchising, list of franchising attorneys, the
      "Big Eight" (accounting firms) Franchise Specialists,
      International Franchise Association officers, and
      State Franchise Regulators. Also features articles on
      current trends in franchising and case studies.

CHAPTER IV
GUIDES TO FINANCING OF FRANCHISES

Locating money to borrow for the purchase of a franchise is often one of the major tasks of prospective franchisees. Guides to locating funds and directories of financing sources are listed in this chapter. References to
franchise financing appear also in the how-to and introductory
guides. Books listed below have financing as their primary
content.

103. Foster, Dennis L. FRANCHISING FOR FREE: OWNING YOUR
OWN BUSINESS WITHOUT INVESTING YOUR OWN CASH. New
York: Wiley, 1988.

Advises prospective franchisees on financing as well
as business planning techniques. Describes methods of
obtaining funds from a Small Business Investment
Company (SBIC), a Minority Enterprise Small Business
Investment Company (MESBIC), a venture capital group
or independent investor, the Small Business Administration, and the franchisor. Divided into three
sections: the first covers preparation of a Business
Financial Plan for a franchise start-up; the second
offers advice on locating sources of financial assistance; and the third discusses the role of the
financing franchisor. Section three also contains
names and addresses of franchisors who offer financial
assistance. Appendix consists of financial plan
worksheets that are designed to organize information
found in a Business Financial Plan. Includes
bibliography.

104. PRATT'S GUIDE TO VENTURE CAPITAL SOURCES. Edited by
Stanley E. Pratt and Jane K. Morris. 11th ed.

Wellesley Hills, Mass.: Venture Economics, Inc.,
1987.

Provides directory of venture capital sources and a
series of essays on venture financing. Essays are:
"Overview and Introduction to the Venture Capital
Industry," by Stanley E. Pratt; "Characteristics of a
Successful Entrepreneurial Management Team," by
Alexander L. M. Dingee, Jr., Brian Haslett and Leonard
E. Smollen; "Guidelines for Dealing with Venture
Capitalists," by Stanley E. Pratt; "Preparing a Busi-
ness Plan," by Brian Haslett and Leonard E. Smollen;
"Market Information Sources for the Entrepreneur,"
by James R. Fries; "Investment of Interest to Ven-
ture Capitalists," by Elwood D. Howse, Jr.; "How to
Choose and Approach a Venture Capitalist," by G.
Jackson Tankersley, Jr.; "Meeting with the Venture
Capitalist," by Wayne B. Kingsley; "Venture Capital:
More Than Money?" by Dr. J. A. Timmons; "Structuring
the Financing," by Stanley C. Golder; " The Pricing of
a Venture Capital Investment," by Jane Kolosoki
Morris; "Preliminary Legal Considerations in Forming a
New Enterprise," by Michael P. Ridley, Esq.; "The
Legal Process of Venture Capital Investment," by
Richard J. Testa, Esq.; "Venture Capital in Practice:
A Case History," by Timothy M. Pennington; "The Key
to Successful Leveraged Buyouts: Analysis of Manage-
ment," by Gregory P. Barber; "The Organized Venture
Capital Community," by Stanley E. Pratt; "Informal
Investors--When and Where to Look," by William E.
Wetzel, Jr.; "How to Organize and Finance the Start-
up Role of the Seed Capital Fund," by John B. Mum-
ford and Frederick J. Dotzler; "SBA Programs for
Financing a Small Business," by David J. Gladstone;
"The MESBIC Connection: Venture Capital for the
Forgotten Entrepreneur," by William M. McMurtry, Jr.;
"Dealing with the Corporate Venture Capitalist," by
Kenneth W. Rind; "The Art of Venturing," by Frederick
R. Adler; "Relationship Between Venture Capitalist and
the Entrepreneur," by Brook H. Byers; "An Entrepre-
neur's Guide to Financing the High Technology
Company," by Thomas H. Bruggere; "Creating Successful
Venture-Backed Companies," by Thomas J. Davis, Jr.
and Charles P. Stetson, Jr.; "Public Financing for
Smaller Companies," by Peter W. Wallace; and
"Strategic Communications and Public Relations for
Emerging High Technology Companies," by Lee James.

Directory section is a listing of venture capital
companies in the United States and Canada. Entries,
arranged by state, list names, addresses, telephone
numbers, officers, project preferences, geographical
preferences, industry preferences, year founded,
investments, capital under management, and method of
compensation. Indexed by: Names of Companies, Names
of Officers, and Industry Preferences.

105. VENTURE'S GUIDE TO INTERNATIONAL VENTURE CAPITAL, by
the Editors of VENTURE, THE MAGAZINE FOR ENTREPRE-
NEURS. New York: Simon and Schuster, 1985.

Contains series of articles on venture capital and a
directory listing of domestic and international
sources of capital. Articles are: "What Venture
Capitalists Want," by Lee Kravitz; "Money for the
Asking," by Jon Levine; "How to Write a Business Plan
that Works," by Michelle Bekey; "What Investors Hate
Most About Business Plans," by Russell Sabin; and
"Holding on to Equity," by G. Thomas Gibson. U.S
Directory is divided into sections: Venture Firms $10
Million and Up (minimum of $10 million in paid-in
capital or made a minimum of $4 million in investments
in 1983); Venture Firms Under $10 Million; Small Busi-
ness and Investment Companies $3 Million and Up; Small
Business and Investment Companies Under $3 Million;
Minority Enterprise Small Business Investment Companies $1.5 Million and Up; and Minority Enterprise
Small Business Investment Companies Under $1.5 Mil-
lion. International Directory Section lists companies in Canada, the United Kingdom, Belgium, Denmark, France, the Netherlands, West Germany, Ireland,
Italy, Luxembourg, Israel, Japan, Malaysia, and
Singapore. Entries in domestic and international
sections list names, addresses, telephone numbers,
officers, project preferences, investment history,
year founded, type of firm, and total paid in capital.
Additional section features venture capital associations in the United States, Canada, and Europe.
Entries indexed by name of firm, domestic locations,
industry preferences, and geographical preferences.

CHAPTER V
LEGAL INFORMATION SOURCES

The growing expansion of franchising as a form of business has encouraged individuals to invest money in their own franchised companies. Unfortunately, there have been cases of loss of these investments due to the failure of franchisors to deliver what they promised. To protect rights of franchisees, "franchise disclosure laws" were adopted in many states. Disclosure laws make it mandatory for franchisors to distribute to franchisees information on the business including: business background of officers, past criminal convictions and civil judgments involving these officers, required fees, financing arrangements, terms of the contract, balance sheets, and number of franchised units currently in operation. Since 1979, the Federal Trade Commission requires disclosure of all pertinent information concerning the business to all prospective franchisees. These disclosure regulations are the subject of many of the books and serials in this chapter. Also covered are antitrust, trademark, and contract laws. Landmark court cases are cited in many of the publications. Also covered are relevant accounting rulings and regulations. Legal sources encompass franchising in the United States and in other parts of the world. To locate periodical articles and citations of court cases, databases through LEXIS and WESTLAW should be searched. The print and database formats of H.W. Wilson's INDEX TO LEGAL PERIODICALS may also be scanned.

106. Adams, John and K. V. Prichard Jones. FRANCHISING: PRACTICE AND PRECEDENCE IN BUSINESS FORMAT FRANCHISING. London: Butterworths, 1981.

Guide to the legal problems involved in business format franchising focuses on the situation in the

United Kingdom. Examines major court decisions and
legislation such as the Fair Trading Act (1973),
Competition Act (1980), and Restrictive Trade
Practices Act (1976). Discusses role of the British
Franchise Association and includes their Code of
Ethics.

107.   American Bar Association. Forum Committee on Fran-
        chising. FIRST ANNUAL FORUM. Chicago, Ill.: American
        Bar Association, 1978.

        Series of papers by specialists in field of
        franchise law. Contents: "What is Franchising?" by M.
        Rollinson; "Competing Relationship in Franchising," by
        H. Brown; "Antitrust Developments Affecting Fran-
        chising," by R. A. Solomon; "Overview of State Fran-
        chising Laws," by C. Erickson; "State Regulation
        of Franchising," by R. M. Langer; "Role of Trademarks
        and other Forms of Intellectual Property," by J.
        Gibson and A. Robin; "Establishment of a Franchise
        System," by J. L. Hay; "Negotiation of Franchise
        Agreements," by J. L. Garel; "Workshop on Termina-
        tions," by T. H. Fine; and "Representing a Fran-
        chisor," by B. E. McCranie, Jr.

108.   American Bar Association. Forum Committee on
        Franchising. SECOND ANNUAL FORUM. Chicago, Ill.:
        American Bar Association, 1979.

        Contents of papers: "Alternatives to Franchising--
        Achieving the Financial and Motivational Advantages of
        Franchising Without Becoming a Franchisor," by M.
        Rollinson; "Corporate Names, Trade Names, Trademarks,
        Service Marks--Clearance and Registration," by R. A.
        Wallen; "Structuring the Franchise Relationship," by
        L. G. Rudnick; "Preparation of Offering Circulars and
        the Registration Process," by A. R. Pierno; "Account-
        ing Practices and Taxation," by W. C. Frank; "Fran-
        chise Trade Associations," by M. H. Rodman; "Valua-
        tion of a Franchise," by E.J. Lawinger; Workshop on
        Transferability," by B. K. Cohn; "Approved Supplier
        Programs," by B. Feagin; "Developments in State Law
        Affecting Franchising," by T. H. Fine; "Developing,
        Using, and Protecting Trade Secrets in the Franchising
        Context," by R. M. Milgrim; "Caveat Franchisor: Why
        You May Be Held 'Accountable' for the Torts of Your

"Franchisee," by K. B. Germain; "Private Remedies,"
by H. Brown; "Federal Trade Commission: Disclosure
Requirements and Prohibitions Concerning Franchising;"
"Interfaces of the FTC Trade Regulation Rule and
State Franchise Laws," by L. A. Mackey; and "Relation-
ship of State Franchise Statutes to the Federal Trade
Regulation Rule from the Standpoint of Franchisors,"
by R. Jonas.

109.   American Bar Association. Forum Committee on
        Franchising. THIRD ANNUAL FORUM. Chicago, Ill.:
        American Bar Association, 1980.

        Contents: "The Rule of Reason Revisited in a
        Franchise Context," by P. F. Zeidman; "Antitrust
        Developments--State," by S. L. Foley; "Franchise
        Litigation and Trends," by H. L. Ward; "Franchise
        Regulation in Transition," by H. H. Makens; "Federal
        Franchise Legislation: Is Competition Preempted?" by
        T. M. Wilson, III; "Franchising in Canada," by A.
        Karp; "Franchising in England and Europe," by M.
        Mendelsohn; "Franchising in the Andean Common Market,"
        by H. S. Brown; "Franchising Impediments: Which Laws
        to Obey?" by H. Brown; "Structuring the Franchise
        Relationship: Product Franchises," by J. P. Melican,
        Jr. and M. Rollinson; "Franchise Sales and Service
        Agreement," by J. P. Melican, Jr. and M. Rollinson;
        and "Selecting, Policing and Changing Trademarks and
        Service Marks," by L. Pirkey and A. Robin.

110.   American Bar Association. Forum Committee on
        Franchising. FOURTH ANNUAL FORUM. Chicago, Ill.:
        American Bar Association, 1981.

        Contents: "Federal Antitrust Developments and
        Trends," by L. N. Abrams; "Antitrust Developments and
        Trends--State," by R. A. Solomon; "Common Law
        Developments in Franchising," by P. W. Tone;
        "Variations on the Theme of Franchising," by P. F.
        Zeidman; "State and Federal Regulation Developments
        and Trends," by A. C. Selden; "Franchisor and
        Franchisee Bankruptcy Under the Bankruptcy Reform Act
        of 1978," by G. F. Munitz and L. Gesas; "Dealing with
        Franchisee Associations," by D. A. Mackay; "Financing
        Techniques for Franchising," by R. A. Nykiel and H. S.
        Brown; "Financing in Canada--The Legal Considera-

tions," by F. Zaid; "Survey of State Little FTC Acts
and Consumer Protection Statutes," by L. S. Stadfeld;
"Unfairness Doctrine in Franchising," by H. Brown;
and "Termination and Nonrenewal of Franchises," by
T. H. Fine.

111.   American Bar Association. Forum Committee on
        Franchising. FIFTH ANNUAL FORUM. Chicago, Ill.:
        American Bar Association, 1982.

        Contents: "Franchise Sales Regulation: A
        Revisionist's Approach," by R. M. Barkoff; "Federal
        Antitrust Developments in Franchising," by J. J.
        McGrath, Jr.; "Workshop Materials: Litigation Basics
        and Advanced Litigation," by J. J. Keyes; "Relation-
        ship and Litigation Trends," by R. N. Asbill;
        "Breakaway Franchisees," by B. E. Fox; "Curtailing the
        Use of Franchise Marks by a Former Franchisee," by L.
        R. Hefter; "Terminations and Transfers," by A. O.
        Riteris; "The Newly Franchising Enterprise: An Outline
        of Major Legal Considerations," by S. S. Raab;
        "Petroleum Marketing Practices Act: The Federal Law
        Controlling the Right of a Franchisor to Terminate or
        Nonrenew a Franchise Agreement," by R. G. Abrams; and
        "Living with Franchisees and Trying to Live Without
        Them," by W. W. Curcio.

*   American Bar Association. Section on Antitrust Law.
        Franchising Committee. SURVEY OF FOREIGN LAWS AND
        REGULATIONS AFFECTING INTERNATIONAL FRANCHISING.
        Cited below as item 206.

112.   American Institute of Certified Public Accountants.
        Committee on Franchise Accounting and Auditing.
        ACCOUNTING FOR FRANCHISE FEE REVENUE. New York:
        AICPA, 1973.

        Describes AICPA regulations on methods of accounting
        for franchise fees. Covers the franchise agreement,
        revenues and costs, and disclosure statements.

113.   ANNUAL FRANCHISE LAW SEMINAR (FIRST). Kansas City,
        Mo.: University of Missouri-Kansas City Law Center
        and Kansas City Bar Association, 1979.

Series of papers by experts in the field. Contents:
"The Purchase of a Franchised Business--The Role of
the Purchaser's Attorney," by M. J. Klein; "Introduction to Antitrust Terminology and Antitrust Applica-
tion to Franchising," by R. C. Bern; "Restraints on
the Franchisee: Restrictions on Sources of Supplies,
Services and Business Premises," by R. F. Adams and
J. M. Kilroy, Jr.; "Franchising and the Federal Trade
Rule," by D. E. Schierer; "Interbrand Competition--
Customer and Territorial Restrictions," by J. C.
Monica; "Intrabrand Competition--Pricing Restrictions," by J. R. Wyrsch; "Resolution of Problems on
the Winding-up of a Franchised Business--Refusal to
Renew and Terminations," by L. H. Rowland; and
"Assignment, Releases and Covenants not to Compete,"
by D. W. Butts.

114.   ANNUAL FRANCHISE LAW SEMINAR (SECOND). Kansas City,
       Mo.: University of Missouri-Kansas City Law Center
       and Kansas City Bar Association, 1980.

       Contents: "The Valuation of a Franchised Business,"
       by B. L. Balkin and J. N. Vader; "What is a
       'Franchisor' for the Purpose of the FTC Franchise
       Disclosure Rule?" by W. T. Smith; "Problems in
       Preparation and Use of Disclosure Statements," by E.
       M. Dolson; "Alternative Routes Available for the
       Resolution of Disputes between Franchisee and
       Franchisor," by M. J. Klein; "Franchising and
       Distribution Under the Rule of Reason," by L. H.
       Rowland; and "Representing the Selling Franchisee, the
       Prospective Purchasing Franchisee and the Franchisor
       in the Purchase and Sale of an Existing Franchised
       Business," by C. W. Kramer, R. B. Keim and R. L.
       Coleman.

115.   ANNUAL FRANCHISE LAW SEMINAR (THIRD). Kansas City,
       Mo.: University of Missouri-Kansas City Law Center
       and Kansas City Bar Association, 1981.

       Contents: "Remedies Available to Resolve Franchising
       Disputes," by M. J. Klein and D. D. Palmer; "Dual
       Distribution by Franchisors--the Risks of Company-
       Owned Outlets," by M. M. Eaton; "The Federal Trade
       Commission and Its Impact on Franchising," by E. W.
       Kintner; "An Overview of Proposed Changes to the UFOC
       and Enforcement of Those Changes by State Administra-
       tors," by J. L. Hiersteiner; "Advising the Prospective

Franchisee: Is a Franchise Agreement a 'Negotiable'
Instrument," by R. M. Barkoff; "Come Judgment Day,
Will the Franchisor be held Accountable for the Acts
of its Franchisee?" by J. C. Monica and A. E. Goos;
"Franchise Terminations, Cancellations and Non-
Renewals--Injunctive Relief," by J. R. Wyrsch; and
"Franchise Terminations, Cancellations and Non-
Renewals--Proof of the Quantum of Damages," by G. M.
Bock.

116. ANNUAL FRANCHISE LAW SEMINAR (FOURTH). Kansas City,
      Mo.: University of Missouri-Kansas City Law Center
      and Kansas City Bar Association, 1982.

      Contents: "Selected Issues Under State Registration
      and Disclosure," by J. R. Conohan; "Vertical
      Restraints in Franchising: As the Lights Change
      (Franchisor Aspect)," by R. J. Favretto; "Vertical
      Restraints and Franchising: As the Lights Change--
      Franchisee View," by R. C. Bern; "Franchisee
      Organizations--Their Creation, Operation and Effect on
      Franchise Relations," by M. P. Gordon; "Franchisee
      Organizations--Their Creation, Operation and Effect on
      Franchise Relations...A Franchisor's Perspective," by
      S. B. Early; "Trademarks: The Responsibilities of
      Franchisors and Franchisees," by M. A. Litman; "Are
      There Any Swords for Franchisees in the Trademark
      Laws?" by D. D. Palmer; "Using the Lanham Act to
      Defend against a Vicarious Liability Claim--Should
      Agency be Imputed Where the Exercise of Control is
      Mandated by Federal Statute," by J. C. Monica and A.
      E. Goos; "Termination of Franchise and Franchisor's
      Immediate Remedies," by L. S. Hellman; "Termination of
      Franchise and Franchisee's Immediate Remedies," by J.
      R. Wyrsch; and "The Franchise Relationship: Problem
      Areas for the 80's," by L. G. Rudnick.

117. Axelrad, Norman D., Lewis G. Rudnick, Dennis E.
      Wieczorek, and Pamela J. Mills. FRANCHISING: A
      PLANNING AND SALES COMPLIANCE GUIDE. New York:
      Commerce Clearing House, 1987.

      Published in cooperation with the International
      Franchise Association. Discusses business, legal, and
      accounting considerations as well as management and
      marketing strategies in the franchise program. Pro-

LEGAL INFORMATION SOURCES   51

        vides an overview of laws affecting franchising and
        outlines disclosure requirements, regulation of fran-
        chisee recruitment advertising, and administration
        of a franchise legal compliance program.

118. Bock, Betty. ANTITRUST ISSUES IN RESTRICTING SALES
      TERRITORIES AND OUTLETS (THE SCHWINN DECISION). The
      Conference Board. Studies in Business Economics, No.
      98. New York: National Industrial Conference Board,
      1967.

        Analyzes implications of court case, United States
        v. Arnold Schwinn & Co. (1967). According to the
        author: "Schwinn raises far-reaching questions
        concerning the rights of a manufacturer, or other
        supplier, to prevent distributors or dealers handling
        his products from selling in each other's territories,
        or to 'reserved' accounts." (p. 1) Appendix contains
        statistical stables on "Ownership of Distribution
        Establishments by Manufacturers."

119. Braun, Ernest A. POLICY ISSUES OF FRANCHISING. n.p.,
      n.d.

        Reprint of article from SOUTHWESTERN UNIVERSITY LAW
        REVIEW, Vol. 14, No. 2, 1984. Chronicles history of
        developments in franchise law. Covers franchisor-
        franchisee relationship, antitrust law, trademarks,
        etc. Cites key decisions. Bibliographical refer-
        ences.

120. Brown, Harold. FRANCHISING COURSE MANUAL. Washington,
      D.C., Federal Publications, 1977.

        Covers various aspects of franchise law including
        state and federal legislation, court decisions, and
        the franchise agreement. Provides sample agreement, a
        Uniform Franchise Registration Application, and a
        bibliography of books and articles by the author.

121. Brown, Harold. FRANCHISING: REALITIES AND REMEDIES.
      2nd ed. New York: Law Journal Press, 1978.

        Analyzes legal elements of the franchisor-franchisee
        relationship, stressing means of protecting franchisee

rights. Studies state and federal legislation
involving full disclosure rulings and antitrust laws.
Appendixes contain sample franchise agreement, a
Uniform Franchise Registration Application, and text
of the Franchising Termination Practices Reform Act.
With bibliographical references and table of cases.

122.   Brown, Harold. FRANCHISING: REALITIES AND REMEDIES.
       Rev. ed. New York: Law Journal Seminars-Press, 1981-

       Published in loose-leaf format for the addition of
       updated supplements. Designed to aid franchisors,
       franchisees, and franchise attorneys. Examines
       franchisor-franchisee relationship, the franchising
       manual, full disclosure regulations, antitrust laws,
       etc. Appendixes consist of: a sample franchise
       agreement, a Uniform Franchise Registration
       Application, and the Federal Trade Commission Rule on
       Basic Disclosure to Prospective Franchisees.

123.   Brown, Harold. FRANCHISING: TRAP FOR THE TRUSTING.
       Boston, Mass.: Little, Brown, 1969.

       Discusses legal problems involved in the franchisor-
       franchisee relationship and outlines present and
       proposed legal remedies for the franchisee. Examines
       current and pending legislation on the state and
       federal levels. Appendixes consist of a sample
       contract, court case listings, and federal statutes.
       Foreword is by Senator Philip Hart, Chairman of the
       Subcommittee on Antitrust and Monopoly.

124.   California Certified Public Accountants Foundation for
       Education and Research. 1980 FRANCHISING CONFERENCE.
       Palo Alto California, The Foundation, 1980.

       Series of outlines from program on accounting and
       taxation regulations. Contents: "State Tax Aspects of
       Franchising," by A. Caffey; "The Regulatory Environ-
       ment in Franchising Today," by J. L. Baker; "A Fran-
       chise Agreement: How to Study It," by M. D. Fern;
       "Financial Control for the Franchisee," by R. L.
       Eichel; "The How, Where and Why of a Franchise," by M.
       A. McConnell; "What's New in Franchising Real Estate,"

by J. P. Moravek; and "Federal Tax Aspects of
Franchising Today," by D. L. Miller.

125. Causey, Fred B. WHOLESALE DISTRIBUTORS' HANDBOOK ON
FRANCHISE PROTECTION UNDER THE PETROLEUM MARKETING
PRACTICES ACT. Atlanta, Georgia: National Associa-
tion of Texaco Wholesalers, 1981.

Includes Title I of the "Petroleum Marketing
Practices Act." Analyzes related court decisions.

126. Commerce Clearing House. BUSINESS FRANCHISE GUIDE.
Chicago, Ill.: Commerce Clearing House, 1980-

Consists of two loose-leaf volumes with updates.
Documents the Federal Trade Commission Full Disclosure
Rule, federal and state legislation, court cases,
registration laws, and the Uniform Circular and
guidelines. Also covers Canadian rulings. Topical
index included.

127. Commerce Clearing House. NASAA REPORTS: NORTH AMERICAN
SECURITIES ADMINISTRATORS ASSOCIATION, INC. Chicago,
Ill.: Commerce Clearing House, 19--

One loose-leaf volume with updates. Includes
"Uniform Franchise Registration Application," adopted
on September 2, 1975, amended on October 21, 1979.

* Dias, Robert N. and Stanley L. Gurnick. FRANCHISING:
THE INVESTOR'S COMPLETE HANDBOOK. Cited above as
item 10.

128. Fels, Jerome. FRANCHISING AND THE LAW: AN OVERVIEW FOR
CORPORATE COUNSEL AND MANAGEMENT. Washington, D.C.:
International Franchise Association, 1976.

Reprinted, with revisions and addition of
supplementary information from "Organizing and
Advising Illinois Business," with permission of the
Illinois Institute for Continuing Legal Education.
Reviews legal problems in franchising including
antitrust and trade regulation law. Analyzes landmark

cases: White Motor Company vs. United States and
United States vs. Arnold Schwinn Co. Also contains
IFA Code of Ethics and IFA Ethical Advertising
Code.

129. Fern, Martin D. ESTABLISHING AND OPERATING UNDER A
      FRANCHISE CONTRACT. Business Law Monographs; BLM 18.
      New York: Matthew Bender, 1986-

      One looseleaf volume with updates. Designed to
      assist franchise attorneys as well as franchisors and
      franchisees. Covers: analysis of the franchise
      agreement, franchising's advantages and disadvantages,
      role of attorneys, and regulation of offers and sales
      of franchises. Provides texts of the Federal Trade
      Commission's "Trade Regulation Rule: Disclosure
      Requirements Concerning Franchising and Business
      Opportunity Ventures Trade Regulation Rule"; Uniform
      Franchise Offering Circular (Uniform Franchise
      Registration Application and Guidelines); and
      California Franchise Investment Law and Regula-
      tions. Subject index provided.

130. Financial Accounting Standards Board. STATEMENT OF
      FINANCIAL ACCOUNTING STANDARDS NO. 45: ACCOUNTING
      FOR FRANCHISE FEE REVENUE, March 1981. Stamford,
      Ct.: FASB, 1981.

      Extracts the specialized accounting principles from
      the AICPA guide, ACCOUNTING FOR FRANCHISE FEE REVENUE
      (Item 112 above) and establishes accounting and
      reporting standards for franchisors. Also establishes
      standards for continuing franchise fees, continuing
      product sales, agency sales, repossessed franchises,
      franchising costs, etc. Glossary section defines such
      terms as "area franchise," "franchisor," "franchisee,"
      "franchise agreement," etc.

131. FLORIDA FRANCHISE LAW AND PRACTICE. Tallahassee,
      Florida: Florida Bar Continuing Legal Education,
      1984.

      Series of essays about Florida laws with texts of
      Florida Statutes and sections of U.S. Code, Internal
      Revenue Code, etc. With citations of cases.

*   FRANCHISE LAW BIBLIOGRAPHY. Cited above as item 96.

132.   FRANCHISING. Chairperson, David P. Roberts; Faculty,
       Paul A. Bastine, et al. Sponsored by the Intel-
       lectual and Industrial Property Section and the
       Continuing Legal Education Committee, Washington
       State Bar Association. Seattle: Washington State Bar
       Association, 1979.

       Series of papers from the Washington State Bar
       Association's Continuing Legal Education Program on
       Franchising, March 23, 1979. Supporting documents
       also provided are: A. Information--Uniform Franchise
       Registration Application and Offering Circular; B.
       Sample Application for Registration; and C. Applica-
       tion for a Franchise Broker or Selling Agent Certifi-
       cate (Washington). Contents of papers: "The Scope
       of Franchising," by T. McTigue; "Trade and Service
       Mark of Franchise," by D. Roberts; "General Business
       Considerations of the Franchisor," by J. Starin;
       "General Business Considerations of the Franchisee,"
       by P. Bastine; and "Government Regulation of Fran-
       chises," by L. Kuhn. Among topics covered are: anti-
       trust and trademark laws, franchise contracts, and
       the Federal Trade Commission Rule. With citations of
       court decisions.

133.   FRANCHISING DEVELOPMENTS: SIXTEENTH ANNUAL SUMMER
       PROGRAM FOR CALIFORNIA LAWYERS, by Wesley J.
       Liebeler, and others. Berkeley: University of
       California Schools of Law and Extension, 1970.

       Contains outline and case citations from program
       held from August 21 - August 28, 1970. Contents:
       "Antitrust Developments in Franchising," by W. J.
       Liebeler; "California Franchise Investment Law," by R.
       I. Gilbert; and "Tax Aspects of Franchising," by J. K.
       McNulty.

134.   THE FRANCHISING PHENOMENON. Edited by James E. Rice.
       Creative Business Library, vol. 6. Ann Arbor,
       Michigan: Institute of Continuing Legal Education,
       1969.

       Series of papers presented at an Institute of
       Continuing Legal Education Program. Contents: "The

Franchising Phenomenon: An Overview," by J. L. Fels;
"Unfair Trade Practices and Trademark Problems," by J.
Gilson; "Franchise Terminations: Some Problems, Pit-
falls and Proposals," by E. Gellhorn; "Problems of
Principal and Agent: Franchisor Exposure to Uninsur-
able Risks for Acts and Omissions of Others," by
J. L. Fels; "Antitrust Problems," by E. E. Pollock;
"Securities Problems in Franchising," by R. L.
Krauss; "Tax Problems," by J. N. Simon; "A Federal
Trade Commissioner Looks at Franchising," by M. G.
Jones; "Raising the Required Cash and Credits," by L.
L. Allen; "Financing for the Franchisee," by B.
Goodwin; and "Documentation and Negotiation," by H.
Kemker. Appendixes consist of: A. Outline of Unfair
Trade Practices; B. Outline of Franchise Termina-
tions; C. Outline of Tax Problems; D. Documentation:
A Checklist of Basic Provisions of a Franchise
Agreement; E. Senate Bill 2321; F. Opinion of the
California Attorney General; and G. Franchising
and the Schwinn Case. With tables of cases, statutory
and regulatory materials, and publications.

135.   Gillespie, Samuel Mabry. "An Analysis of Antitrust
       Policy Toward Franchising," Ph.D. dissertation.
       University of Illinois, 1970.

       Tests hypothesis that recent (ca. 1970) federal
       court legislation and statements made by federal
       enforcement agencies discourages growth of franchising
       in the United States. Analyzes key court decisions:
       U.S. v. Arnold Schwinn & Co. (1967); White Motor Co.
       v. U.S. (1963); and U.S. v. Sealy, Inc. (1967).
       Studies court interpretations of the contractual
       arrangments: interbrand or interproduct restrictions
       (those which isolate franchisees from other potential
       suppliers) and intrabrand or interproduct competition
       (those which may isolate franchisees from competition
       among themselves). Concludes, through study of recent
       decisions, that the federal courts have taken a
       position that does not encourage growth of fran-
       chising. Includes bibliography of public documents,
       books, articles and periodicals, legal cases cited,
       federal statutes, and unpublished material.

136.   Glickman, Gladys. FRANCHISING. New York: Matthew
       Bender, 1969-

Two volume loose-leaf service on franchise law.
Covers: Federal Trade Commission regulations, state
laws, taxation, antitrust, trademarks, the franchise
agreement, etc.

137. Grissom, Donald H. PETROLEUM MARKETING PRACTICES ACT
      MANUAL. Austin, Texas: Texas Oil Marketers
      Association, 1981.

      Analyzes the Petroleum Marketing Practices Act and
      explains its provisions. The Appendix includes a
      sample contract.

138. Hammond, Alexander. FRANCHISEE RIGHTS: A SELF-DEFENSE
      MANUAL FOR DEALERS, DISTRIBUTORS, WHOLESALERS AND
      OTHER FRANCHISEES. Greenvale, N.Y.: Panel Publish-
      ers, 1979.

      Counsels franchisees on their legal rights and
      provides guidelines for dealing with franchisor
      coercion and termination of contract. Advises con-
      sultation with a lawyer and keeping a file of let-
      ters, bulletins, reports, price and product lists,
      etc. Also discusses role of trade associations, state
      and federal regulations, and the franchise agreement.
      Appendix contains the Franchisee Protection Bill,
      introduced by Congressman Mikva (H.R. 2305, 96th
      Congress, First Session).

*   Hewitt, Charles M. AUTOMOBILE FRANCHISE AGREEMENTS.
      Cited below as item 226.

139. Hjelmfelt, David C. UNDERSTANDING FRANCHISE CONTRACTS.
      Babylon, N.Y.: Pilot Books, 1984.

      Examines various aspects of franchise contracts.
      Also Analyzes the Federal Trade Commission Disclosure
      Regulation and includes a sample franchise contract
      and disclosure statement.

140. Illinois Institute for Continuing Legal Education.
      SEMINAR ON FRANCHISING. Springfield, Illinois:
      Illinois Institute for Continuing Legal Education,
      Illinois Bar Center, 1969.

Papers on legal aspects of franchising. Contents:
"Advantages and Disadvantages of Franchising as a
Distribution Medium," by N. D. Axelrod; "Analysis and
Solutions to Franchising, Advertising, and Selling
Franchises," by J. H. McDermott and F. M. Covey;
"Analysis and Solutions to Common Trademark, Trade
Secret and Copyright Problems," by J. Gilson;
"Analysis and Solutions to Typical Anti-Trust Problems
Raised in Franchise Situations," by E. Pollock; and
"Analysis and Solutions to Contract Problems," by J.
Fels. Bibliographical references.

141.   International Franchise Association. A DECADE OF
       FRANCHISE REGULATION. Washington, D.C.: The
       Association, 198-

       Chronicles development of franchise laws (ca. 1970s
       and 1980s).

142.   International Franchise Association. FTC FRANCHISING
       RULE: THE IFA COMPLIANCE KIT. Washington, D.C.: The
       Association, 1979.

       Contains the FTC rule and UFOC application. Ana-
       lyzes the FTC Rule, outlines compliance steps, and
       provides FTC advisory opinions issued through July 14,
       1980.

143.   International Franchise Association. FRANCHISE LAWS,
       REGULATIONS, AND RULINGS. Editor: Carl E. Zwisler
       III; Assistant Editor: Marc A. Aprea; Managing
       Editor: Kathleen L. Day. Compiled by the Inter-
       national Franchise Association. Washington, D.C.:
       The Association, 1975-

       Composed of four loose-leaf volumes with provision
       for updates. Contains seven types of legal materials:
       1. Statutes; 2. Regulations; 3. Judicial Opinions; 4.
       Uniform Franchise Offering Circular (UFOC) and guide-
       lines for its implementation; 5. Charts and Tables,
       comparing portions of various laws and other state
       requirements; 6. FTC Trade Regulation Rule on Fran-
       chising; and 7. Court Interpretations. Supplements
       issued monthly or when change in franchise law has
       occurred.

144. International Franchise Association. FIFTH ANNUAL
      LEGAL AND GOVERNMENT AFFAIRS SYMPOSIUM. Washington,
      D.C.: The Association, 1972.

      Contains papers presented at symposium. Contents:
      "The Federal Trade Commission and Franchising," by R.
      Pitofsky; "Franchising and Restraint of Trade," by D.
      Hanscom; "The Proposed Trade Regulation Rule on Fran-
      chising," by R. Burch; "The Labor Law Aspects of
      Franchising," by E. Platt; "The Labor Law Aspects of
      Franchising," by R. McGuire; "Franchising and Minority
      Business Enterprises," by J. Jenkins; "Distinguishing
      Franchising from Pyramid Schemes," by H. Rudnick;
      Franchising and the Securities Laws," by A. Rusch;
      "Franchising and Small Business," by B. Gennetti;
      "Multi-level Sales Plans," by D. Kingsley; "Antitrust
      Class Action Litigation," by P. Zeidman; "State
      Franchise Requirements," by L. Rudnick; "Franchise
      Regulation in California," by J. Kelly; and "Franchise
      Regulation in Virginia," by R. Parker.

145. International Franchise Association. FRANCHISING AND
      ANTITRUST: ANTICIPATING CHANGE IN FRANCHISING.
      Washington, D.C.: The Association, 1977.

      Transcript of proceedings of the International
      Franchise Association's Tenth Annual Legal and
      Government Affairs Symposium. Contents: "Location
      Clauses and Territorial Restrictions," by M. L. Popof-
      sky; "Product Mix," by M. L. Denger; "Substandard
      Sales," by J. F. Graybeal; "Pricing," by W. D. Mc-
      Sweeney; "Franchise Tie-Ins and the Antitrust Laws,"
      by G. D. Reycraft; "Quality of Product and Image of
      the Franchise," by J. T. Rosch; "Franchisor-Franchisee
      Competition: Dual Distribution," by E. M. Zimmerman;
      and "Contracting With and Termination of Distributors
      and Franchisees," by J. T. Halverson.

146. International Franchise Association. FRANCHISING AND
      ANTITRUST: CULTIVATING THE FRANCHISE RELATIONSHIP.
      Washington, D.C.: The Association, 1979.

      Transcript of proceedings of the International
      Franchise Association's Twelfth Annual Legal and
      Government Affairs Symposium. Presented in the form
      of a play whose subject is a case study concerning
      legal ramifications of the relationship between

franchisees and a prospective supplier. Also presents
a panel discussion on product liability, trademarks,
purchasing programs, and multi-unit franchising.

147.   International Franchise Association. FRANCHISING AND
        ANTITRUST: "FRANCHISING'S TRYING ISSUES."
        Washington, D.C.: The Association, 1978.

        Transcript of proceedings of the International
        Franchise Association's Eleventh Annual Legal and
        Government Affairs Symposium. Presented in the form
        of a play in five acts, written by Lewis Rudnick and
        Philip Zeidman. Play is a case study of a franchisor
        of solar heating systems. Legal topics of play
        include tying arrangements, price fixing, and ter-
        ritorial restrictions. Also provides transcript of
        panel discussion on FTC Trade Regulation Rule and the
        Uniform Franchise Offering Circular.

148.   International Franchise Association. FRANCHISING AND
        ANTITRUST: MANAGEMENT AND LAW. Washington, D.C.: The
        Association, 1980.

        Transcript of proceedings of the International
        Franchise Association's Thirteenth Annual Legal and
        Government Affairs Symposium. Presents a case study
        of an auto parts manufacturer with 200 franchised
        dealers and legal problems encountered by the manu-
        facturer. Legal aspects covered include dual dis-
        tribution and territorial exclusivity. Also pro-
        vides transcript of panel discussion on such topics
        as franchise termination and nonrenewal and vertical
        and horizontal advertising restrictions.

149.   International Franchise Association. FRANCHISING AND
        ANTITRUST: OPERATING IN THE FRANCHISE RELATIONSHIP.
        Washington, D.C.: The Association, 1976.

        Transcript of proceedings of the International
        Franchise Association's Ninth Annual Legal and
        Government Affairs Symposium. Contents: "Franchisor
        Sales to the Franchisee: Tying and Exclusive Dealer
        Arrangements and Full Line Forcing," by O. M. Johnson;
        "Where the Franchisee Operates: Limitations on Loca-
        tion, Sales Territories and Classes of Customers,"

by R. S. Sherman; "Cooperative Buying, Advertising and
Promotions," by I. Scher; "Special Problems of Dual
Distribution and Mergers Under Section 7, Clayton
Act," by J. T. Halverson; "Special Problems of
Multiple Franchising: Franchisee Operating More Than
One Franchise in the Same Business, Different Busi-
nesses; Franchisor Goes Into Different System or
Concept," by W. T. Lifland; "Common Law Rules and
Techniques of Terminating; Contract Rights, Covenants
not to Compete; Documentation, Records, Authority,
Role of Counsel," by P. K. Bleakley; "Ending the Fran-
chise Relationship, Termination and Failure to
Renew, Rights of the Parties: Statutory Limitations--
Federal: Antitrust Laws, Administrative Rulings,
Proposed Legislation," by P. F. Zeidman; and "Ending
the Franchise Relationship, Termination and Failure to
Renew, Rights of the Parties: Statutory Limitations--
State: State Legislation, Administrative Rulings," by
L. G. Rudnick.

150. International Franchise Association. FRANCHISING AND
      ANTITRUST: THE ANTITRUST PROBLEMS AND SOLUTIONS OF
      DISTRIBUTION THROUGH FRANCHISED OUTLETS AND/OR
      COMPANY OWNED OUTLETS. Washington, D.C.: The
      Association, 1973.

      Transcript of proceedings of the International
Franchise Association's Sixth Annual Legal and
Government Affairs Symposium. Contents: "Selecting
Franchised Outlets and Supplying their Requirements--
Problems," by W. D. Dixon; "Selecting Franchised
Outlets and Supplying their Requirements--Solutions,"
by L. G. Rudnick; "Selecting Company Outlets and
Supplying Their Requirements--Problems," by W. B.
Comegys; "Selecting Company Outlets and Supplying
their Requirements--Solutions," by S. Timberg;
"Establishing Prices and Controlling Resales in
Franchised Outlets--Problems," by A. S. Ward;
"Establishing Prices and Controlling Resales in
Franchised Outlets--Solutions," by E. W. Kintner;
"Establishing Prices and Controlling Resales in
Company Outlets--Problems," by B. B. Grossman;
"Establishing Prices and Controlling Resales in
Company Outlets--Solutions," by E. E. Pollock; "The
Substance of Franchising," by R. L. Grover;
"Subsidizing Losses and Closing out Failures in
Franchised Outlets--Problems," by D. A. Randall;
"Subsidizing Losses and Closing out Failures in

Franchised Outlets--Solutions," by P. F. Zeidman;
"Subsidizing Losses and Closing out Failures in
Company Outlets--Problems," by J. S. Cohen; and
"Subsidizing Losses and Closing Out Failures in
Company Outlets--Solutions," by E. M. Zimmerman.

151.   International Franchise Association. FRANCHISING AND
       ANTITRUST: THE PRACTICAL APPLICATION OF ANTITRUST
       LAWS TO FRANCHISED DISTRIBUTION. Washington, D.C.:
       The Association, 1974.

       Transcript of proceedings of the International
       Franchise Association's Seventh Annual Legal and
       Government Affairs Symposium. Contents: "The Fran-
       chisor-Franchisee Relationship: Location Clauses
       and 'Spacing' Franchisees," by S. D. Robinson; "The
       Franchisor-Franchisee Relationship: Influencing Fran-
       chisee Prices," by R. J. Hoerner; "The Franchisor-
       Franchisee Relationship: Franchisee Covenants not to
       Compete," by W. T. Lifland; "The Franchisor-Franchisee
       Relationship: Perils and Rewards of Consulting with
       Franchisees," by P. F. Zeidman; "The Franchisor-
       Franchisee Relationship: Franchisor Acquisitions of
       Franchised Units," by M. Corash; "Maintaining Quality-
       Uniformity Standards and the Franchisor's Image:
       Administering a QSC Program," by D. P. Horwitz;
       "Maintaining Quality-Uniformity Standards and the
       Franchisor's Image: Requiring Purchases from the
       Franchisor," by H. Kemker; "Maintaining Quality-
       Uniformity Standards and the Franchisor's Image:
       Requiring Purchases from Designated Third Parties," by
       M. Flinn; "Maintaining Quality-Uniformity Standards
       and the Franchisor's Image: Controlling Menus and
       Product Lists," by L. G. Rudnick; "Maintaining
       Quality-Uniformity Standards and the Franchisor's
       Image: Terminations and Non-Renewals," by H. Adler;
       "Franchising Class Actions," by P. K. Bleakley;
       "Settling Franchising Class Actions," by H. L.
       Gershon; "Advice from the Prosecutors," by J. T.
       Halverson; and "Advice from the Prosecutors," by K.
       I. Clearwaters.

152.   International Franchise Association. FRANCHISING AND
       GOVERNMENT SYMPOSIUM. Washington, D.C.: The
       Association, 1971.

Transcript of proceedings of the International Fran-
chise Association's Fourth Annual Legal and
Government Affairs Symposium. Contents:
"Availability and Cost of Financing," by J. Eachon;
"Entering the Franchise Operation," by R. Martin;
"Selling the Franchise Opportunity," by G. A.
Pelletier; "Selling to the Franchisee," by S. Keane;
"Financing the Franchisee," by S. A. West; "The Fran-
chisee's Sale of the Product/Service," by M. Flinn;
"Current Trends in the Design and Location of Com-
mercial Facilities," by J. P. Carlahian; "Expanding
the Franchise: Some Fundamental Considerations, To
Another City," by R. L. Plavnick; "Expanding the
Franchise: Some Fundamental Considerations, To Anoth-
er State," by C. J. Matthews; "Expanding the Fran-
chise: Some Fundamental Considerations, To Another
Country," by R. P. Parker; "Changing the Nature of
the Franchise System," by R. B. Style; "How a
Franchisor Can Protect the System after Termination of
the Franchise," by J. L. Fels; "Sale, Merger or
Failure of the System: Rights of the Franchisor,
Franchisee and Third Parties," by M. M. Gaynor;
"Securities Law," by M. Beach; "Tax Law," by A.
Schwartz; "Antitrust Law," by A. Joseph; "Planning an
Antitrust Compliance Program," by P. F. Zeidman; and
"Preparing for and Defending a Class Action Suit," by
H. L. Gershon.

153.   International Franchise Association. THE GOVERNMENT
       AND FINANCING. Washington, D.C.: The Association,
       1970.

       Transcript of proceedings of the International
       Franchise Association's Third Annual Legal and
       Government Affairs Symposium. Contents: "Protecting
       the Trademark," by T. Arnold; "Limitations on the
       Franchisee," by B. Keck; "Selling to the Franchisee,"
       by E. Pollock; "Negative Covenants on Competition," by
       N. Axelrad; "Assignments and other Transfers," by J.
       Fels; "Terminating the Franchise," by T. Dieterich;
       "Preparation of Registration Statements by Franchising
       Companies," by H. Hodges; "Disclosure in Registration
       Statements of Financing Companies," by M. Beach; "The
       Franchise Agreement and the Definition of a 'Securi-
       ty,'" by W. Weckstein; "Tax Treatment for Franchising
       Companies," by D. Bedell; "Accounting Principles
       for Franchising Companies," by C. Saunders; "Tax
       Aspects of International Franchising," by O. Gottscho;

"Introduction of American Franchise Operations
Abroad," by M. Lifflander; "Legal Problems of Inter-
national Franchising," by P. Drew; "Franchising and
Small Business," by A. Chase; "Preserving the Deci-
sion-Making Freedom of Independent Entrepreneurs," by
B. Grossman; "State Franchise Litigation," by H.
Kemker; "Salvaging Delight from our Chicken," by H.
Gershon; "Recent FTC Developments," by P. Zeidman;
"Responsibilities of the Ethical Franchisor," by R.
Grover; "The Ills of Franchising," by H. Rudnick;
"State Law Developments," by L. Rudnick; "Massachu-
chusetts Franchise Legislation," by J. Alpert; "Fran-
chise Regulation in California," by E. Posnick; and
"Federal Franchise Regulation," by H. Williams, Jr.

154. International Franchise Associatin. GROWING WITH
      ANTITRUST: PRACTICAL ADVICE ON ADAPTING SUCCESSFULLY
      TO ANTITRUST LIMITATIONS ON FRANCHISING AND LICENSED
      DISTRIBUTION. Washington, D.C.: The Association,
      1975.

Transcript of proceedings of the International Fran-
chise Association's Eighth Annual Legal and Government
Affairs Symposium. Contents: "A Review of Franchising
Antitrust Decisions in Private and Government Suits
During the Past Year," by F. Auwarter; "Significant
New Franchising Complaints, Developments in Pending
Matters and Emerging Areas of Concern," by P. F. Zeid-
man; "Experience Under State Franchise Termination
Laws: Decisions and Interpretations," by L. G. Rud-
nick; "What's in Store at the Federal Trade Commis-
sion," by J. T. Halverson; "Proposed Franchising Trade
Regulation Rule: Possible Application of New Statutory
Powers to Franchising," by J. T. Rosch; "Riding with
the Schwinn Case: A Review of the Schwinn Decision and
Consent Order; Practices Forbidden and Permitted the
Effect on Schwinn," by A. H. Silberman; "When Per Se
is Not Per Se," by M. Malina; "Alternatives to Territorial and Customer Restrictions," by J. C. Slaton,
Jr.; "Application of Schwinn Per Se Rules to Sale,"
by L. L. Smith; "Permissibility of Location Clauses
and Geographic Exclusivity," by V. Grimm; "The Trademark Franchise as a Tying Product: The Restrictive
Decisions," by H. M. Applebaum; "The Trademark Franchise as a Tying Product: The Liberal Decisions," by
J. Gilson; "Redd v. Shell and the Franchisor's Risk
of Loss of Trademark Rights," by A. Robin; "Trade Se-

cret Protection, Designating Sources of Supply, Speci-
fications, Ingredients and Quality," by D. Levitt;
and "Prohibiting Unauthorized Products and Services
and Requiring Sale of Authorized Products and
Services," by L. L. Williams.

155. Kaul, Donald A. PROTECTING YOUR FRANCHISING TRADEMARKS
AND TRADE SECRETS. Washington, D.C.: The
Association, 1983.

Guide to methods of protecting franchisors' trademarks and trade secrets. Cites pertinent cases and
regulations.

156. Keating, William J. FRANCHISING ADVISER. Colorado
Springs, Colorado: Shepard's McGraw-Hill, 1987.

Examines legal aspects of franchising among which
are trademark licensing, franchise agreements, trade
secret licensing, disclosure, and antitrust law.
Covers the Federal Trade Commission Rule and the
Uniform Franchise Offering Circular (UFOC), state
franchise regulations, and court decisions. Additionally reviews franchising developments outside the
United States, in countries which include Canada,
Great Britain, France, Italy, Spain, West Germany,
Japan, and Mexico. Appendixes contain: A. Form Fran-
chise Agreement; B. Federal Trade Commission Fran-
chise Rule, 16 CFR; C. Antitrust Statutes; D. Federal
Trade Commission Act, 15 USC, paragraph 45; E. Auto-
mobile Dealers' Day in Court Act, 15 USC, paragraphs
1221-1225; F. Petroleum Marketing Practices Act, 15,
USC, paragraphs 2801-2806; G. Franchise Offering Cir-
cular for Prospective Franchisees Required by the
State of Wisconsin; H. Copyright Application Form TX
(Literary Works); I. Copyright Application Form VA
(Artistic Works); J. Regulations for Copyright Regulation of Computer Programs; K. Proposed Revision of
Uniform Franchise Offering Circular (UFOC) Guidelines
Regarding Earnings Claims and Termination of Franchises; L. Federal Trademark Application Form; and
M. Addresses of State Agencies Responsible for Franchise Registration. With bibliography and tables of
cases, rulings and procedures, statutes, and regulations.

157. Laufer, David. UPDATE ON FRANCHISE LAW DEVELOPMENTS:
      PROGRAM MATERIAL, August 1985. Berkeley, California:
      California Continuing Education of the Bar, 1985.

      Booklet prepared for use with course on UPDATE ON
      FRANCHISE LAW PRACTICE. Outline covers: "Analysis of
      the California Franchise Relations Act of 1981, as
      Amended"; "Constructive Termination of a Franchise";
      "Arbitration of Franchise Disputes"; "Assignment of
      Franchises"; and "The Use of Expert Testimony in
      Franchise Litigation." Includes Tables of Cases and of
      Statutes, Regulations, and Rules.

158. LEGAL ASPECTS OF SELLING AND BUYING: ANSWERS TO
      QUESTIONS ON ANTITRUST, FRANCHISING AND CURRENT
      DEVELOPMENTS IN DISTRIBUTION LAW. Editor: Philip P.
      Zeidman and Contributors: Harvey M. Applebaum, et
      al. Colorado Springs, Colorado: Shepard's/McGraw-
      Hill, 1983-

      Analyzes franchise law and cites cases, regulations,
      and statutes. Updated by supplements.

159. Mendelsohn, Martin and Arthur Nicholson. THE LAW AND
      PRACTICE OF FRANCHISING. n.p.: Franchise Publica-
      tions, 1982.

      Studies franchise law in the United Kingdom and
      discusses trademarks, trade names, the franchise
      contract, and good will.

160. PARTNERS IN DESIGN: ADVISING SMALL BUSINESS OWNERS AND
      ENTREPRENEURS. St. Paul, Minnesota: Advanced Legal
      Education, Hamline University School of Law, 1986.

      Series of outlines of seminars presented as educa-
      tional service for practicing attorneys. Includes
      outline for "Evaluating and Structuring a Franchise
      Program," by Lavon Emerson-Henry and G. Thomas Mac-
      Intosh, Jr. Reviews role of the lawyer in advising
      a client concerning implementation of a franchising
      program and the planning and structuring of such a
      program. Covers: definitions of terms, advantages
      and disadvantages, financial considerations, mar-
      keting, and legal considerations. Cites court
      decisions.

161.   Practicing Law Institute. BUSINESS AND LEGAL PROBLEMS
       OF THE FRANCHISE. Jim McCord, Ira A. Cohen, Editors.
       Commercial Law and Practice. Transcript Series, no.
       1. New York: Practicing Law Institute, 1968.

       Transcript of program on September 27-28, 1968 in
       New York City. Contents: "Franchising: Legal Problems
       and the Business Framework of Reference--An Overview,"
       by J. L. Fels; "What to Look for in Franchise Agree-
       ments: House Counsel and the Franchisor," by P. L.
       Herzog; "Agency Problems," by J. L. Fels; "New Fi-
       nancing Possibilities," by S. E. Wisdom; "The Fran-
       chise as a Security," by B. Goodwin; "Tax Aspects
       of Franchising," by T. N. Lawler; "Franchising from
       the Standpoint of the Federal Trade Commission," by M.
       G. Jones; "Permissible Limits of Control over Fran-
       chisees," by T. A. Dieterich; "Trademark and Unfair
       Competition Considerations in Franchised Business
       Operations," by T. Arnold; "Franchise Termination,"
       by T. A. Dieterich; and "Investment and Expansion
       into the Canadian Market/Case in Point: Franchise
       Companies," by N. P. Goldman.

162.   Practicing Law Institute. FINANCING CORPORATE GROWTH.
       Philip F. Zeidman and Anthony Chase, Co-Chairmen.
       Commercial Law and Practice. Course Handbook Series,
       No. 98. New York: Practicing Law Institute, 1973.

       Prepared for distribution at the Financing Corporate
       Growth Seminar in October-November 1973. Series of
       outlines are: "Financing Small and Medium Size Busi-
       ness--a Comparison of Criteria used by Banks and
       Commercial Finance Companies," by M. A. Simon; "Gov-
       ernment Sources," by A. Chase; "Equipment Leasing,"
       by R. J. Larkin, Jr.; "The ABCs of Leasing," by S. L.
       Shapiro; "Private Placement Covenants," by C. S.
       McMillan, J. M. Schell, and R. J. Tarr, Jr.; "Fran-
       chising as a Device for the Organization, Financing,
       Control, and Growth of the Small Business," by J. C.
       Evans, Jr.; "Franchising as a Financing Method," by
       by P. L. Herzog; and "Franchising: Legal Problems
       and the Business Framework of Reference: An Overview,"
       by J. L. Fels. Includes copies of forms: "A Master
       Lease Agreement," "Avis Truck Lease and Service Agree-
       ment," and "Computer Equipment Lease with Fair Market
       Value Purchase Option."

163. Practicing Law Institute. FRANCHISE LITIGATION AND
      LEGISLATION. George A. Pelletier and Harold Brown,
      Chairmen. Commercial Law and Practice. Course
      Handbook Series, No. 58. New York: Practicing Law
      Institute, 1971.

      Prepared for distribution at a workshop and forum on
      Franchise Litigation. Presented in form of outlines
      of lectures and texts of laws. Contents: "The Sale
      of Franchises--Abuses and Remedial Steps," by G. A.
      Pelletier; "Multi-Level Marketing," by B. Goodwin;
      "New Theories to Protect Franchisees Under the Anti-
      trust Laws," by H. Brown; "The FTC," by L. G. Meyer;
      "Texas Antitrust Law," by C. Mayer; "An Antitrust
      Compliance Program for Franchise Companies," by P. F.
      Zeidman; "Defending Against Antitrust Actions," by H.
      L. Gershon; "The Franchising Relationship and Equi-
      table Relief," by H. Brown; "Failure of Franchisor to
      Perform," by D. Berger and H. B. Newberg; "Class
      Actions and Multidistrict Litigation," by D. Berger
      and H. B. Newberg; "Franchise Legislation," by G. A.
      Pelletier and R. Strauser; "Federal Franchise Legisla-
      tion," by C. E. Bangert; "State Legislation," by L.
      G. Rudnick; "The California Franchise Investment Law,"
      by A. R. Pierno; and "Selected Bibliography of Legal
      Materials Relating to Franchising."

164. Practicing Law Institute. FRANCHISING IN NEW YORK.
      David J. Kaufmann, Chairman. New York Law Course
      Handbook, No. 58. New York: Practicing Law Insti-
      tute, 1984.

      Prepared for distribution at the Franchising in New
      York Program, March 15, 1984, New York City. Con-
      tents: "The New York Franchise Sales Act," by D. J.
      Kaufman; "Franchise Disclosure Compliance," by A. A.
      Caffey; "Differences Between New York and other Fran-
      chise Sales Regulations and the Implications Thereof
      for Franchisors Offering Franchises in and from New
      York," by C. E. Zwisler III; and the "FTC Franchise
      Rule," by J. M. Tifford.

165. Practicing Law Institute. FRANCHISING--SECOND GENERA-
      TION PROBLEMS. New York: Practicing Law Institute,
      1969.

Series of outlines of papers presented at a 1969
seminar. Contents: "The Franchise Contract," by H.
Kemker; "Financing Problems of Franchising," by C. R.
Lanman; "Real Estate Financing," by P. D. Fine; "Regu-
lation of Franchisors and Franchisees in Non-Antitrust
Fields," by B. Goodwin; "Litigation Techniques in Rep-
resenting Franchisees," by A. Hammond; and "Antitrust
Considerations in Franchising," by T. A. Dieterich.
With a bibliography of publications on legal aspects
of franchising.

166. Practicing Law Institute. THE FRANCHISING SOURCEBOOK.
Jim McCord, Editor. Commercial Law and Practice.
Sourcebook Series, No. 2. New York: Practicing Law
Institute, 1970.

Series of outlines of papers presented at a 1970
seminar. Covers business and legal considerations of
franchising. Contents: "Franchising; Legal Problems
and the Business Framework of Reference--An Overview,"
by J. L. Fels; "Franchising from the Standpoint of the
Federal Trade Commissioner," by M. G. Jones; "Some
Observations and Reservations about Franchising," by
J. M. Nicholson; "What to Look for in Franchise Agree-
ments: House Counsel and the Franchisor," by P. L.
Herzog; "A Franchise Contract," by J. Van Cise; "New
Financing Possibilities," by S. E. Wisdom; "Financing
Franchise Expansion," by P. D. Fine; "Organizational
Relationships within Franchising," by D. C. Basil and
C. W. Cook; "Managerial Behavior and Management
Styles in Franchising," by D. C. Basil and C. W. Cook;
"Legislative Proposals to Curb Franchisor Abuse";
"The Franchise as a Security and 10b-5 Considera-
tions," by B. Goodwin; "Agency and Related Problems,"
by J. L. Fels; "Disputes and Termination," by T. A.
Dieterich; "Litigation Techniques in Representing
Franchisees," by A. Hammond; "Measure of Damages from
Breach of Distributorship Agreements"; "Termination
Problems and Conduct of Litigation in the Automobile
Industry," by A. Hammond; "Protecting Intellectual
Property and Good Will in Franchised Business Opera-
tions," by T. Arnold; "Permissible Limits of Control
over Franchises," by T. A. Dieterich; "Applicability
of the Price and Promotional Provisions of Robinson-
Patman and the Antitrust Implications of Dual Distri-
bution in the Franchising Context"; and "Designing
Distribution Systems: Antitrust Problems in Franchising and Marketing," by L. H. Rowland.

167.   Practicing Law Institute. FRANCHISING--TODAY'S LEGAL
        AND BUSINESS PROBLEMS. Lillian Ratner, Staff Editor.
        Commercial Law and Practice. Course Handbook Series;
        no. 33. New York: Practicing Law Institute, 1970.

        Prepared for distribution at a two day seminar in
        April 1970. Contents: "Reviewing the Franchise
        Contract," by G. A. Pelletier; "Franchise Financing:
        Sources and Techniques," by P. F. Zeidman; "Antitrust
        Aspects of Franchising," by H. F. Roth; "Regulation of
        Franchising in Non-Antitrust Fields, Particularly in
        Application of the Securities Laws," by B. Goodwin;
        "Termination and Litigation Techniques," by A.
        Hammond; and "Future Legislative Prospects," by H.
        Brown. Includes bibliography and a sample restaurant
        franchise agreement.

168.   Practicing Law Institute. MARKETING AND FRANCHISING.
        Ira Millstein, Joshua F. Greenberg, and Lyle L.
        Jones, Chairmen. Corporate Law and Practice. Course
        Handbook Series; no. 164. New York: Practicing Law
        Institute, 1974.

        Prepared for distribution at the Marketing and
        Franchising Program, December 1974-January 1975.
        Provides series of notes, outlines, and bibliography
        to accompany lectures at program. Contents: "Tying
        and Exclusive Dealing Arrangements," by P. C. Warnke;
        "Control of Franchisees' Purchases," by E. E. Pollock;
        "Franchising: Carvel; Chicken Delight; Chock Full
        O'Nuts," by M. L. Popofsky; "Schwinn and its Progeny,"
        by R. Pitofsky; "Schwinn and its Progeny II," by P. G.
        Bower; "Distribution Arrangements in Foreign Com-
        merce," by J. E. Hartz, Jr.; "Dual Distribution,"
        by N. H. Seidler; "Dual Distribution II," by D. T.
        Hibner, Jr.; "Refusals to Deal," by A. M. Voogd;
        "Buyer-Seller Relationships and the FTC's Role," by J.
        T. Halverson; "Remedies and Defenses," by J. J.
        Shestack; "Remedies: Pari Delicto; Kelly v. Kosuga;
        Class Actions," by P. B. Wells; and "View from the
        Antitrust Division," by A. E. Desmond.

169.   Practicing Law Institute. NEW DEVELOPMENTS IN
        FRANCHISING. Commercial Law and Practice. Course
        Handbook Series; No. 66. New York: Practicing Law
        Institute, 1971.

Prepared for distribution at a seminar on New
Developments in Franchising, presented December 1971-
January 1972. Consists of series of essays, case
listings, and bibliographical footnotes. Contents:
"Current Developments in Legislation, Litigation and
Regulation Affecting Franchising: An Overview," by P.
F. Zeidman; "Selecting and Recruiting Franchisees and
Assigning Territories," by J. L. Fels; "Tying Arrange-
ments," by T. A. Dieterich; "Trademark and Unfair
Competition Considerations in Franchised Business
Operations: 1971 Update," by T. Arnold, B. Durkee
and P. Van Slyke; "Termination and Litigation Techniques," by A. Hammond; "International Franchising,"
by B. Goodwin; and "Franchise Financing Techniques,"
by T. C. Ford.

170. Practicing Law Institute. THE NEW YORK FRANCHISE SALES
      ACT. David J. Kaufmann and Philip F. Zeidman, co-
      chairmen. Corporate Law and Practice. Course Hand-
      book Series; No. 361. New York: Practicing Law
      Institute, 1981.

      Prepared for distribution at the New York Franchise
      Sales Act Program on February 3, 1981, New York City.
      The New York Franchise Sales Act took effect on
      January 1, 1981 and requires full disclosure before
      sale of a franchise. Contents: "An Approach to
      Analysis: Statutory and Administrative Regulation to
      Franchising," by P. F. Zeidman; "The New York
      Franchise Sales Act, The Uniform Franchise Offering
      Circular, Federal Trade Commission's Franchising Rule
      and Other State Franchise Laws," by C. E. Zwisler; and
      "The Federal Trade Commission Trade Regulation Rule on
      Franchises and Business Opportunity Ventures," by J.
      M. Tifford. Appendix reprints copy of the New York
      Franchise Sales Act.

171. Practicing Law Institute. REPRESENTING THE FRANCHISOR
      AND FRANCHISEE. New York: Practicing Law Institute,
      1979.

      Contents: "Representing the Franchisor in
      Negotiating Franchise Agreements," by P. F. Zeidman;
      "The Franchise Agreement from the Standpoint of the
      Franchisor," by R. Jonas; "Franchise Agreements from
      the Standpoint of Franchisees," by A. Hammond; "Self

Defense Plan for Franchisees." by A. Hammond; "Anti-
trust Considerations in Franchising," by T. A.
Dieterich; "Terminations of Franchisees, Dealers and
Distributors," by T. H. Fine; "Proof of Fact and
Amount of Damages in Franchise and Distributorship
Relationships," by L. A. Freeman; "Litigation Tech-
niques, Discovery and Injunctions," by M. L. Popofsky;
"Class Actions Involving Franchising," by A. S. Jos-
lyn; "The Statutory and Common Law Regulation of
Franchisors," by R. Jonas; and "Termination and Non-
Renewal," by H. L. Montague.

172.   Practicing Law Institute. WORKSHOP ON REPRESENTING
       FRANCHISORS. New York: Practicing Law Institute,
       1968.

       Papers presented at workshop in 1968.   Contents:
       "The Franchise Agreement," by H. Brown; "Franchise
       Controls," by T. A. Dieterich; "Tax Aspects of
       Franchising," by T. N. Lawler and S. K. Easton; and
       "Security Problems in Franchise Sales," by B. Goodwin.

173.   Practicing Law Institute. WORKSHOP ON REPRESENTING
       FRANCHISORS II. New York: Practicing Law Institute,
       1968.

       Papers presented at workshop in 1968.   Contents:
       "Franchise, also a Security," by D. Augustine; "The
       Franchise Agreement--Trap for the Trusting," by H.
       Brown; "Inventory Distribution in Franchise Transac-
       tions: Code, Bankruptcy and Antitrust Considerations,"
       by R. Duesenberg; "Franchising vs. Corporate Owner-
       ship of Retail Outlets," by R. A. Memel; "Problems
       in the Selection and Termination of Franchisees,"
       by I. M. Millstein; "Supplying Goods, Services and
       Facilities to the Franchisee and Controlling the
       Resale Thereof," by H. F. Roth; International Fran-
       chising," by M. L. Lifflander; "Termination of Fran-
       chise Agreements," by S. Marks; "What Steps can a
       Franchise Owner Take to Protect what he Creates," by
       M. Owen; and "Financing the Franchise," by S. E. Tal-
       lent.

174.   THE REALITIES OF FRANCHISING: A GUIDE FOR THE
       PRACTICING ATTORNEY, by Harold Brown, John J.

Curtin, Peter A. Donovan, Phil David Fine, and John R. Hally. Publication Consultant: Roy Miller. Boston, Mass.: Faneuil Press, 1970.

Portion of book is an edited transcript of a course in Franchising presented by the Massachusetts Continuing Legal Education, Inc. Aims to familiarize readers with various legal concepts that are a part of franchising. Examines how franchises start and legal aspects of the franchisor-franchisee relationship. Analyzes court decisions and pending legislation. Covers the franchise agreement, antitrust laws, labor relations, financing, and mediation in disputes. Includes bibliographical references. Contents: "Franchising--The Franchisor's Viewpoint," by P. D. Fine; "Franchising--the Franchisee's Viewpoint; Remedies; Application of Antitrust and Trade Regulation Statutes," by J. J. Curtin, Jr., P. Donovan, and J. R. Hally; "Sources of Financing," by P. D. Fine; "Procedures for Handling Disputes," by H. Brown; "An Illustrative Franchise Agreement;" "An Illustrative Complaint;" "Citations and Authorities," by J. J. Curtin, Jr., P. A. Donovan, and J. R. Hally; and "The Automobile Dealers Act; the Hart Bill," by J. J. Curtin, Jr. Appendixes consist of reprints of articles that have appeared in the journal, THE BUSINESS LAWYER. These articles are: "The Franchise Agreement as a 'Security,'" by B. Goodwin; "The Franchise Agreement: Not a 'Security,'" by M. M. Coleman; "Termination of Dealer Franchises," by C. M. Hewitt; "Franchising in the Ghetto," by W. M. Sayre; and "Financing the Franchise Program," by P. D. Fine.

175. Rosenfield, Coleman R. THE LAW OF FRANCHISING. Rochester, N.Y.: Lawyers Co-operative Publishing Co., 1970.

Examines how the franchising system operates and all relevant case and statutory law associated with the system. Covers: history of franchising, definitions of key terms, reasons for franchising, trademark law, financing, tax considerations, the franchise contract, and antitrust law. Appendixes consist of: A. Basic Franchise Agreement; B. Federal Fairness in Franchising Act; C. Massachusetts Franchise Fair Dealing Act; D. Dealer Franchise Agreement; F. Opinion

of California Attorney General; and G. Franchising
Questionnaire. With bibliographical references and
case citations.

176. Thompson, Donald N. FRANCHISE OPERATIONS AND
     ANTITRUST. Lexington, Mass.: D. C. Heath, 1971.

     Provides comprehensive coverage of franchising and
     antitrust laws and regulations. Evaluates major
     controls contained in franchise agreements. Examines
     cases and theories of tying arrangements, exclusive
     franchising, and exclusive dealing. Includes bib-
     liography.

177. Udell, Gerald G. THE FRANCHISE AGREEMENT HANDBOOK: AN
     ANALYSIS OF THE CONTRACTUAL ELEMENTS OF FRANCHISING.
     Purdue University, Agricultural Experiment Station:
     Research Bulletin, No. 889. West Lafayette, Indiana:
     Purdue University, Agricultural Experiment Station,
     1973.

     Examines components of the franchise agreement,
     which "defines and governs the relationship between
     members of the system." (p. 18) Research based on
     survey of the literature; personal interviews with
     franchisors, franchisees, consultants, and lawyers;
     and questionnaires sent to franchise experts, fran-
     chisors, and franchisees. Analyzes contract pro-
     visions of uniformity, occupancy, obligations of
     the franchisor, employee conduct and training,
     insurance, conditions of purchase, advertising,
     termination, etc.

178. United States. Congress. Senate. Select Committee on
     Small Business. REVIEW OF FTC FRANCHISE DISCLOSURE
     RULE: HEARING BEFORE THE SELECT COMMITTEE ON SMALL
     BUSINESS OF THE UNITED STATES SENATE, NINETY SIXTH
     CONGRESS, FIRST SESSION ON REVIEW OF FTC FRANCHISE
     DISCLOSURE RULE, JULY 17, 1979. Washington, D.C.:
     U.S. Government Printing Office, 1979.

     Reviews potential impact of the FTC Disclosure Rule
     and the scope of the definition of 'franchise' as used
     in the rule. The FTC Rule requires franchisors to
     furnish prospective franchisees with twenty detailed

items of information about the franchisor, the
business, and forms of the franchise agreement.

179. United States. Federal Trade Commission. FRANCHISING
     AND BUSINESS OPPORTUNITIES: RULES AND GUIDES.
     Washington, D.C.: The Commission; for sale by the
     Superintendent of Documents, U.S. Government
     Printing Office, 1980.

     Describes provisions of the Federal Trade Commission
     Rule entitled: "Disclosure Requirements and Prohibi-
     tions concerning Franchising and Business Opportunity
     Ventures." Reviews each disclosure required in the
     basic disclosure document.

180. Van Cise, Jerrold G. A FRANCHISE CONTRACT. Washington,
     D.C.: International Franchise Association, 1975.

     Analyzes nature of the contract and its provisions
     on fees, equipment, training, sales, etc.

181. Zeidman, Philip. FRANCHISING. Washington, D.C.:
     Federal Publications, 1982.

     Course manual discusses advantages and disadvantages
     of franchising, state and federal regulations, the
     Federal Trade Commission Disclosure Rule, the
     franchise contract, etc.

CHAPTER VI
FRANCHISING IN THE UNITED STATES

     The earliest forms of franchises had their origins in the
United States in the nineteenth century. A pioneer in
franchises was I. M. Singer who, during the 1850s, sold
businessmen the rights to sell his sewing machines in various
areas of the United States. At the turn of the century, the
Coca-Cola Company and Rexall Drug Stores became franchised
businesses by selling the rights to use their names and
products to entrepreneurs throughout America. Howard Johnson
established his franchised chain of restaurants in the 1920s.
After World War II, the franchise phenomenon flourished and
chains were developed and expanded. The franchising industry
continues to grow today and covers such industries as health
clubs, pet shops, and temporary help services.
     Information sources listed in this chapter trace the
history of franchising in the United States, describe its
current status, and offer projections as to its future.
Sources listed are monographs and serial publications such as
the United States government's FRANCHISING IN THE ECONOMY.
Case histories of companies and legal guides are the subjects
of other chapters. Sources listed below provide an overview
of franchising in America.

182. Atkinson, J. F. FRANCHISING: THE ODDS-ON FAVORITE.
     Washington, D.C.: International Franchise Associa-
     tion, 1968.

     Written by the author for his Master's Degree from
     the Graduate School of Business, Northwestern Uni-
     versity, Chicago. Compares, quantitatively, the
     potential for success of franchises with that of the
     independent small business. Describes the history of
     franchising in the United States and offers case his-

tories of Rexall. McDonald's. Dunkin' Donuts. Aamco
Transmission Centers. Holiday Inns. Dairy Queen, and
Kentucky Fried Chicken. Concludes that "odds are
indisputably in favor of a franchised business as
compared to an independent. unfranchised venture."
(p. 28)

183. CONTRACTUAL MARKETING SYSTEMS. Edited by Donald N.
      Thompson, with an introduction by E. T. Grether.
      Lexington, Mass.: Heath Lexington Books, 1971.

      Transcripts of papers presented at a conference
      sponsored by the American Marketing Association and
      held at the C. W. Post Campus of Long Island Uni-
      versity in August 1970. Among essays are those on
      theories and trends in franchising as a contractual
      marketing system. Contents: "Contractual Marketing
      Systems: An Overview," by Donald N. Thompson; "The
      Economic Base of Franchising," by Louis P. Bucklin;
      "The Feasibility of Minority-Group Capitalism through
      Franchising," by Patrick McGuire; "Franchising and
      the Inner City," by Roger Dickinson; "Potential Con-
      flict Management Mechanisms in Distribution Channels:
      An Interorganizational Analysis," by Louis S. Stern;
      "The Development of Conflict in Contractual Marketing
      Systems: A Case Study," by Larry J. Rosenberg; "Con-
      flict and its Resolution in a Franchise System," by
      Jerry S. Cohen; "The Internationalization of Contrac-
      tual Marketing Systems," by Stanley C. Hollander;
      "Contractual Interdependence in Marketing Processes
      of Developing Latin American Communities," by Charles
      C. Slater; "Contractual Marketing Systems in Canada:
      The Anticombines Response," by Joel Bell; "The Evolu-
      tion of Various Forms of Contractual Marketing Systems
      in Japan," by Masanori Tamura; "The Development of
      Contractual Marketing Systems in the Textile Industry
      in Japan," by T. Ishihara; and "Contractual Marketing
      in the Government Industry Procurement Administra-
      tion," by S. Hassen. Includes bibliographical
      references.

184. Curry, J.A.H., et al. PARTNERS FOR PROFIT: A STUDY OF
      FRANCHISING. New York: American Management Associa-
      tion, 1966.

      Originally prepared as a research report submitted
      in partial fulfillment of the requirements for a

course in manufacturing at the Harvard University
Graduate School of Business Administration. Isolates
and studies factors that make the franchise relationship function. Analyzes franchisor-franchisee relationship, role of the U.S. government, management
training, leading court decisions, history of franchising, role of the International Franchise Association, and legal aspects. Research based on literature studies and questionnaires sent to franchisors
and franchisees.

185.   Doyel, Tommy Terry. "The Economic Outlook for Small
       Business Franchising." Ph.D. Dissertation. Univer-
       sity of California, 1971.

       Examines the economic nature of franchise systems
       and assesses the long-term outlook for these systems.
       Covers history, types of franchises, advantages and
       disadvantages, and management. Concludes that the
       long-term outlook is favorable. Research based on
       literature review and data from a large restaurant
       organization which operates part of its restaurants as
       franchised units and the rest as wholly-owned shops.
       Includes bibliography and statistical tables.

186.   Emmons, Robert J. THE AMERICAN FRANCHISE REVOLUTION: A
       NEW MANAGEMENT THRUST. Newport Beach, California:
       Burton House, 1970.

       Focuses on management issues and techniques in
       franchising. Stresses need to achieve balance between
       goals of franchisee and objectives of franchisor.
       Reviews history of franchising in America and legal
       considerations. Features transcript of interview with
       Dr. Leonard Korot, psychological consultant to fran-
       chise companies. The Appendix contains "Two-Plus-
       You," a case study of minority business development.
       Includes bibliography.

187.   FRANCHISING: RECENT TRENDS. Based on special issue on
       Franchising, edited by Alfred R. Oxenfeldt and
       recent articles compiled and edited by Sallie Sewell
       and Eleanor Rak. JOURNAL OF RETAILING, Volume 44,
       Number 4. Winter 1968-69. New York: New York
       University. Institute of Retail Management, 1974.

Series of articles focus on various aspects of
franchising including history, trends, legal issues,
etc. Contents: "Franchising in Perspective," by
Alfred R. Oxenfeldt and Donald N. Thompson; "Sources
of Revenue to the Franchisor and Their Strategic
Implications," by Milton Woll; "Does Franchising
Create a Secure Outlet for the Small Aspiring Entre-
preneur?" by Louis M. Bernstein; "Franchise Opera-
tions and Antitrust Law," by Donald N. Thompson;
"Are Franchisors Realistic and Successful in Their
Selection of Franchisees," by Harold Wattel; "Will
Successful Franchise Systems Ultimately become Wholly-
Owned Chains?" by Alfred R. Oxenfeldt and Anthony O.
Kelly; "An Analysis of Decision Criteria in Fran-
chisor/Franchisee Selection Processes," by Ronald L.
Tatham, Robert Douglass, and Ronald F. Bush; "The
Fast Food Franchise: Psychographic and Demographic
Segmentation Analysis," by Douglas J. Tigert, Richard
Lathrope, and Michael Bleeg; "Negroes in Franchising,"
by J. Carroll Swart and Robert R. Carter; "The Trend
Toward Company-Operated Units in Franchise Chains," by
Shelby D. Hunt; and "The Literature on Franchising: a
Selected, Classified Bibliography," by Donald N.
Thompson.

188.   FRANCHISING TODAY, 1966-67. Edited by Charles L.
        Vaughn and David B. Slater. New York: Matthew
        Bender, 1967.

        Papers presented at the Boston College Center for
the Study of Franchise Distribution's Second Annual
Management Conference on Franchising. Covers topics
of the franchise "package," finance, marketing,
management, legal problems, and training. Contents:
"Pro--Why, How, Advantages," by S. A. Preston; "Pro--
Why, How, Advantages," by R. E. Bennett; "Con--Why
Company-Owned Units," by L. E. Singer; "Con--Why
Company-Owned Units," by W. Ware; "Pro and Con," by E.
Henderson III; "The Elements of the Franchise Package-
-Its Demand, Acceptance, and Services," by D. D.
Seltz; "Distribution of the Franchise Through
Individual Units, Territorial Franchises, and Master
Franchises with Sub-Franchising Rights," by D. W.
Smart; "International Licensing," by R. A. Weaver,
Jr.; "Consumer Profiles, Potentials, and Buying
Habits," by J. Toigo; "Factors Affecting the Selection
of Market Areas and Sites," by E. Goldberg; "Consumer
Motivation," by W. R. Hoelscher; "Consumer and

Financial Public Relations," by W. Ruder; "Who is
Eating Out?" by G. F. Dillman; "Franchising and
Antitrust," by M. G. Jones; "Sources of Funds--Public
or Private," by A. Lapin, Jr.; "Real Estate Fi-
nancing," by P. D. Fine; "Equipment Financing," by
R. D. Wooton; "Leasing," by L. Sherry; "Sources of
Franchise Leads," by E. J. Keating; "The Profile of a
Franchisee," by M. J. Evans; "Role of the Franchise
Consultant," by T. Magida; "Consumer and Product
Marketing," by R. O. Kearns; "Consumer and Product
Marketing," by S. Costello; "Protecting the Consumer,"
by A. G. Seidman; "Reporting Methods and Frequency,"
by F. S. Christian; "Reporting Methods and Frequency,"
by C. E. Skala; "How to Organize the Company from a
Control Point of View," by G. K. Thompson; "Organiza-
tion Structure," by W. A. Toomey, Jr.; "New Develop-
ments in EDP," by C. M. Jones; "Executive Recruitment," by R. P. Rita; "Executive Recruitment," by
M. I. Radlauer; "The Role of the Supplier in Administrative Controls," by M. Schechter; "Franchising
Yesterday," by E. Henderson, Sr.; "Franchising Today,"
by H. J. Sonneborn; "Franchising Tomorrow," by R. A.
Hammond, III; "The Training Program and Franchisor's
Backup," by L. E. Board; "New Training Methods," by
J. H. Stevens; "Role of the Supervisor (Selection),"
by R. M. Geer; "Role of the Supervisor (Training),"
by J. R. Titlow; "Franchisor-Franchisee Relations--
Ethics," by W. R. Stewart; "Franchisor-Franchisee
Relations--Motivation," by N. J. Fiorentino; "Recom-
mendations to the Franchise Industry," by T. Carvel;
"Guiding Principles of Antitrust Law," by J. G. Van
Cise; "Are Your Controls Necessary?" by P. F. Zeid-
man; "Enforcement of the Franchise Agreement," by
M. L. Lifflander; "Interstate Problems," by W. D.
Wekstein; "New Services Needed," by R. Sherwood;
and "New Services Needed," by H. Kursh.

189. FRANCHISING TODAY, 1967-1968. Edited by Charles L.
Vaughn and David B. Slater. Lynbrook, N.Y.:
Farnsworth Publishing Co., 1968.

Papers presented at the Boston College Center for
the Study of Franchise Distribution's Third Annual
Management Conference on Franchising. Reports business and legal aspects of franchising. Contents:
"Profits from Creativity," by M. Schechter; "Creative

Marketing," by W. H. Maahs; "Three Keys to Creative
Marketing," by J. Santo; "Creative Image Making," by
J. Selame; "Creative Advertising and Public Rela-
tions," by R. Morgan; "Creative Public Relations,"
by R. M. Bernstein; "Creative Public Relations in
Franchising," by J. M. Kiss; "From $158,000 to
$5,000,000 in Five Years from Franchising," by R.
Roth; "Creative Organizations Structuring," by E. F.
Huse; "Creative Organization Planning," by R. D.
White; "Executive Leadership in Acquisitions," by R.
A. Weaver, Jr.; "Criteria for Evaluating Acquisi-
tions," by D. D. McConkey; "Evaluation and Pricing
of Acquisitions," by R. Campobello; "Being Acquired,"
by R. H. Frost; "When You Become an Acquisition," by
J. McLamore; "Raising Capital: Its Advantages, Prob-
lems and Pitfalls," by A. Lapin; "Going Public: 'Our
House is Made of Glass,'" by J. C. Massey; "Today's
Problems and the Specifics of Management," by R.
Parks; "Today's Control: Tomorrow's Growth," by W. D.
Eberle; "The Climate for Small Business," by F. B.
Morse; "Franchising and the Supreme Court," by J. G.
Van Cise; "Antitrust and Franchising," by J. Shuman;
"An Ounce of Prevention: Legal Aspects of the Selec-
tion of the Franchise," by P. F. Zeidman; "Free
Markets and Franchise Arrangements," by R. E. Wilson;
"Legal Problems in Supply to Franchisees," by H. L.
Rudnick; "Legal Problems: Sales by Franchisees," by W.
Rowley; "The Evolution of a Franchise Division," by E.
Henderson; "Location Analysis and Selection," by S. J.
Loscocco; "Analyzing Franchise Locations," by F. B.
Raffel; "Recruiting Prospective Franchisees," by W. R.
Stewart; "Franchise Motivation and Communications," by
R. Sherwood; "Franchisor-Franchisee Relations: Train-
ing, Motivation, Communications," by J. W. Kosseff;
"Communications and Retaining the Franchisee," by V.
F. Martin; "Motivation through Dealer Programs and
Financial Reward," by S. L. Black; "Franchising in
the Commerce Department," by W. G. Kaye; "Business and
Defense Service Administration Franchise Programs for
Equal Opportunity in Business," by R. J. Bond; "United
States Programs Pertinent to Franchising: Franchise
Industry Training (Project FIT) 1966," by J. D.
O'Brien; "Setting up Franchise Operations in Canada,"
by N. P. Goldman; "Types of Franchises and Legal
Considerations," by M. L. Lifflander; "Training
Franchisees," by R. Burch; and "Recruiting and
Selecting Franchisees," by C. L. Vaughn.

190. FRANCHISING TODAY, 1969. Edited by Charles L. Vaughn
and David B. Slater. Lynbrook, N.Y.: Farnsworth
Publishing Co., 1968.

Papers presented at the Fourth International
Management Conference on Franchising. Sponsored by
the Boston College Center for the Study of Franchise
Distribution. Contents: "Current Management Problems
in Franchising," by A. Lapin, Jr.: "Franchise Con-
sulting: Uses and Abuses in Today's Boom," by R. J.
Murley; "Evaluation of Media in Franchise and Product
Sales," by A. Z. Rosoff; "Franchise Statistics: Their
Uses and Abuses," by R. Bond; "Dealer (Franchisee)
Relations," by J. L. Ash; "Franchisor-Franchisee
Relations," by D. W. Motte; "Sources of Funds and the
Tight Money Market," by P. Fine; "Executing a Real
Estate Program in Today's Competitive Market," by D.
Case; "Computerized Site Selection," By F. R. Cella;
"Utilization of Real Estate Brokers-Competitive Mar-
ket," by W. B. Rubey; "Current Trends in Mergers
and Acquisitions," by R. Sheridan; "The Product Life
Cycle--Growth, Saturation and Decay," by J. P. Shen-
field; "Life Cycle of a Limited Products (Services)
Franchise Unit: New Products, Expanded Services," by
by L. Gurnick; "The Life Cycle of a Limited Product
Franchise: Long Range Planning," by D. McConkey;
"Modern Franchising," by R. Kroc; "Current Legal
Problems in Franchising as seen by Congress," by C.
E. Bangert; "Current Legal Problems in Franchising as
seen by the Legal Public," by J. R. Hoffman; "Current
Legal Problems in Franchising as seen by the Enforcement Agencies," by R. E. Wilson; "Current Legal Prob-
lems in Franchising as seen by the Franchise Indus-
try," by R. L. Grover; "Current Legal Problems in
Franchising as seen by the Small Business Administra-
tion," by P. F. Zeidman; "The Boston College Center's
Special Committee on Unfair and Deceptive Practices
in Franchising: The Chairman's Final Report," by J.
G. Van Cise; "The Trend in Company-Owned vs. Fran-
chised Units at Howard Johnson's--Underlying Causes,"
by B. M. Sack; "Starting and Developing a Franchisor
Operation," by E. L. Silverberg; "Developing the
Franchisor Operation," by J. Y. Brown; "Developing the
Franchise Package," by B. H. Fargo; "An Established
Company Takes the Franchise Route," by F. Wyman, Jr.;
"Supplying Franchise Companies," by L. L. Perlman;
"What Makes a Supplier Valuable." by W. N. Grace;
"Developing and Implementing the Customer's Image," by

G. Flaherty: "Common Problems in Franchising
Distributorships," by D. B. Staynor; "The Impact of
New Government Regulations on Foreign Operations," by
R. A. Weaver, Jr.: and "Growth and Future of Fran-
chising," by C. L. Vaughn.

191. FRANCHISING TODAY. 1970. Edited by Charles L. Vaughn.
     Lynbrook. N.Y.: Farnsworth Publishing Co., 1970.

     Transcript of proceedings of the Boston College
     Center for the Study of Franchise Distribution's Fifth
     International Management Conference on Franchising.
     Emphasizes legal and management aspects of fran-
     chising. Contents: "Special Problems in Structuring
     and Developing the Management Organization of the
     Franchisor Firm." by J. F. Pomroy; "Sound Management
     Structuring, Financing and Expansion in Today's Growth
     Minded Franchisor Firms." by R. Sheridan; "Starting
     the Franchisor Firm," by B. S. Browning; "The Second
     Generation Franchise Executive," by R. J. Emmons;
     "Structuring and Developing the Management Organiza-
     tion of the Franchisor Firm," by J. L. Hopwood;
     "Special Problems in Structuring and Developing the
     Management Organization of the Franchisor Firm--Legal
     Problems," by M. Davis; "Going Public 1969," by W. M.
     Lendman: "Why and How Snelling and Snelling Went
     Public," by R. O. Snelling, Sr.; "A Road to Instant
     Wealth--Disparities Between Market Reality and
     Corporate Reality," by M. J. Whitman; "Legal Problems
     in Going Public," by W. D. Wekstein; "Mergers and
     Acquisitions in Today's Conglomerate Society," by R.
     W. Schramm: "Mergers and Acquisitions in Today's
     Conglomerate Society--Tax Comments," by A. Tobin: "The
     Story of Holiday Inns," by W. E. Johnson; "The Story
     of Minnie Pearl," by J. J. Hooker; "Three Recurrent
     and Acute Major Problems in Franchising," by K. Coo-
     mer: "Recruiting, Selecting and Training Franchisees
     in a Highly Competitive Rapidly Expanding Market
     Place," by G. F. Dillman; "Recruiting, Selecting and
     Training Franchisees as Franchisor Firms Multiply," by
     J. R. Titlow: "How to Succeed in Franchisee Recruit-
     ment Advertising," by L. T. Patterson; "The Psycholo-
     gist and Franchisee-Manager Selection," by R. L. Berk;
     "Recruiting, Selecting and Training Franchisees as
     Franchisor Firms Multiply--Legal Comments," by I.
     Scher: "Developing the Real Estate Program with Sky-
     Rocketing Costs," by S. J. Loscocco; "Developing the

Real Estate Program." by J. Gorman; "Developing the
Real Estate Program--Legal Comment." by L. J. Sperber;
"Franchisor-Franchisee Relations to Prevent a Hostile
Environment," by D. W. Motte; "Franchisor-Franchisee
Relationships," by W. T. Morgan; "Franchisee Rela-
tions." by T. F. Perlman; "Communications through
Design," by J. Selame; "A Franchise Contract." by J.
G. Van Cise; "Equitable Protection for Franchisees."
by H. Brown; "Franchising in the Economy," by B.
Goodwin; "Franchising: Power for Economic Equality."
by A. Lapin, Jr.; "Franchising: Power for Economic
Equality--Commentary," by W. D. Nelson; "The Small
Business Administration's Project OWN: Progress,
Problems and Potential," by D. A. Furtado; "Minority
Group Participation in Business Ownership," by F.
Christian; "The American Franchisor's Challenge--
International Opportunities." by M. L. Lifflander;
"International Franchising," by S. Shepett; "Franchise
Facts of Life in the 70's." by E. L. Winter; and
"Franchising and Franchise Systems: The Marketing,
Management, and Economic Literature: Part III." by D.
N. Thompson.

192.   Frost & Sullivan. THE FRANCHISING MARKET. New York:
       Frost & Sullivan, Inc., September 1976.

       Investigates and describes retail franchising and
its nature, history, present structure, and future
trends.   Part I analyzes the nature of franchising and
the benefits it offers to franchisors, franchisees,
and consumers.   Discusses the franchise agreement and
sources of revenue.   Lists products and services
available through franchises.   Part II examines the
current (ca. 1976) structure of franchising in the
United States and presents statistics on the number of
outlets for all companies involved in franchising and
retail sales of franchised establishments.   Identifies
major franchisors by types of business.   Part III
traces the origin of franchising and its patterns of
growth over the past two decades.   Part IV concerns
retail franchising in the fast foods and soft drink
bottling areas.   Part V describes economic effects of
retail franchising in the United States.   Part VI
reviews the legal problems of franchising including
state and federal rulings and leading court decisions.
Part VII discusses managerial aspects of franchising
which include franchisor-franchisee relationships,

evaluation of franchise opportunities, and site and
location analysis. Part VIII covers international
franchising, stgressing the status of United States
franchising in the United Kingdom. Part IX describes
forces for change that have the potential of
influencing the shape and size of franchising over the
next decade. Part X offers forecasts of numbers of
franchised outlets and sales by types of business for
1980 and 1985.

193.   Hackett, Donald W. FRANCHISING: THE STATE OF THE ART.
        Monograph Series--American Marketing Association,
        No. 9. Chicago, Ill.: American Marketing Associa-
        tion, 1977.

        Survey of franchising trends in the United States.
        The first section focuses on the nature of fran-
        chising, its history and its impact as a social
        force. The second section examines franchisor manage-
        ment strategy. The third section reviews major trends
        influencing franchising. Emphasizes three topics:
        the legal environment, ownership trends, and inter-
        national marketing trends. In addition to three
        sections, provides "Franchising: A Selected Bib-
        liography Since 1970."

*   Kursh, Harry. THE FRANCHISE BOOM: HOW YOU CAN PROFIT
        IN IT. Cited above as item 27.

194.   Lewis, Edwin H. and Robert S. Hancock. THE FRANCHISE
        SYSTEM OF DISTRIBUTION. Prepared by the University
        of Minnesota under the Small Business Administration
        Management Research Grant Program. Project Director:
        Robert S. Hancock, Professor of Marketing. Minne-
        apolis, Minnesota: Division of Research, Graduate
        School of Business Administration, University of
        Minnesota, 1963.

        Objectives of study are: to analyze the working
        relationship between franchise companies and their
        franchised dealers; to determine the benefits of the
        franchise system to franchisors and franchisees; to
        examine the major problems of the franchise agreement
        to franchisors and franchisees; and to evaluate the
        franchised distribution system from viewpoints of the

franchise company and franchised dealers and to assess
the system's impact on the United States' marketing
economy. Studies franchised industries: automobile
and equipment rental services, automotive services and
petroleum products, swimming pools, home services,
business services, hearing aids, variety stores, shoe
stores, drug stores, and miscellaneous consumer
services. Reviews major serial and journal publications that list franchise offerings. Research based
on interviews with franchisees operating in Minne-
apolis-St. Paul metropolitan area.

195. McGuire, Edward Patrick. FRANCHISED DISTRIBUTION.
     Conference Board report, no. 523. New York:
     Conference Board, 1971.

     Written primarily to assist managements who are
     using or considering use of franchised distribution.
     Data based on study of operating practices of 223
     franchise companies and over 500 owner-managers of
     franchised outlets. Describes history and present
     structure of franchising, management and organization,
     franchisee recruitment, the franchise contract, site
     selection, and minority franchising.

*   Mockler, Robert J. and Harrison Easop. GUIDELINES FOR
     MORE EFFECTIVE PLANNING AND MANAGEMENT OF FRANCHISE
     SYSTEMS. Cited above as item 39.

196. Norton, Seth W. FRANCHISING AS AN ORGANIZATIONAL FORM:
     AN EMPIRICAL LOOK. Working Paper Number 97. St.
     Louis, Missouri: Center for the Study of American
     Business, Washington University, 1986.

     Identifies market parameters that encourage use of
     franchising as an organizational form and tests the
     parameters empirically. Includes bibliographical
     references.

197. Ozanne, Urban B. and Shelby D. Hunt. THE ECONOMIC
     EFFECTS OF FRANCHISING. Washington, D.C.: U.S.
     Government Printing Office, 1971.

     Report prepared by the University of Wisconsin
     Graduate School of Business for the Small Business

Administration and published by the Senate Select
Committee on Small Business. Presents statistical and
empirical information about franchising, with emphasis
on the fast food, convenience grocery, and laundry/dry
cleaning. Studies franchisor-franchisee relationship
and recommends measures be taken to protect franchisee
rights. Also recommends enactment at the federal
level of full disclosure legislation. Discusses the
franchise contract, minority franchising, advertising,
and roles of government agencies and trade associations. Data from review of the literature and questionnaires sent to franchisors and franchisees. With
extensive bibliography.

198.   Partridge, Scott H., Jr. "The Origins and Development
       of Modern Franchising," MBA Thesis. Harvard Univer-
       sity, 1970.

       Chronicles the history of franchising in the United
       States from its beginnings to 1970. Includes descrip-
       tions of the I. M. Singer Co. and developments in
       industries of retail drug stores, soft drink manu-
       facturing, automobiles, gasoline service stations,
       fast foods, etc. Provides case histories of Rexall,
       Coca-Cola, General Motors, etc.

199.   Raab, John William. "An Empirical Examination of the
       Characteristics and Attributes of Entrepreneurs,
       Franchise Owners, and Managers Engaged in Retail
       Ventures." Ph.D. dissertation. University of South
       Carolina, 1982.

       Profiles entrepreneurs, franchise owners, and
       managers engaged in the retail trades. Studies these
       individuals in terms of characteristics of birth rank,
       family, business ownership background, education,
       previous relevant experience, times fired or laid off,
       need to achieve, and risk propensity. Results of
       study indicate there are differences between charac-
       teristics of "traditional" entrepreneurs and retail
       venture entrepreneurs. Examines relationship between
       characteristics and potential for a business success.
       Data from literature review and questionnaires sent to
       entrepreneurs.

200.   Rubin. Laura Shiskin. "A Theory of Franchising." Ph.D.
       dissertation. University of Pennsylvania. 1973.

       Purpose of study is to develop a model of fran-
       chising. Also represents "a first attempt by an
       economist to deal with the issue of franchising." (p.
       7) The franchising model has the major advantages of
       a vertically integrated system and is characterized by
       having a motivated owner operator, an ability to tap
       imperfect capital markets. and a potential for con-
       flict. Research based on review of the literature and
       court cases in addition to interviews with fran-
       chisees.

201.   Schwartz. David Joseph. THE FRANCHISE SYSTEM FOR
       ESTABLISHING INDEPENDENT RETAIL OUTLETS. Bureau of
       Business and Economic Research. Georgia State
       College of Business Administration Research Paper
       Series, No. 14. Atlanta. Georgia: Bureau of Business
       and Economic Research, School of Business Admin-
       istration, Georgia State College of Business
       Administration, 1959.

       Exploratory discussion of the franchising of inde-
       pendent retailers. Discusses services provided by
       franchisors and the nature of the contract.

202.   Society of Franchising. FIRST ANNUAL CONFERENCE.
       Omaha, Nebraska: The Society, September 28-30, 1986.

       Papers presented at conference cover the latest
       developments in franchising. Contents: "An Evaluation
       of Franchising Trends and their Implications for the
       Retailing Industry," by R. A. Marquardt and G. W.
       Murdock; "The Franchising Economy," by R. T. Justis.
       L. Taylor, and W. Nielsen; "Changing Antitrust Policy
       and Franchise Agreements," by K. A. Strasser; "Legal
       Issues in Dual Distribution Systems," by K. A. Stras-
       ser; "Legal Issues in Dual Distribution Systems," by
       M. J. Sheffet and D. L. Scammon; "The Co-Existence
       of Franchising and Entrepreneurship: A Look at Fran-
       chisee Characteristics," by K. C. Brannen; "The Fran-
       chise Contract from an Economic Agency Perspective,"
       by T. S. Zorn and S. Mann; "Training and Development
       in the Franchisor-Franchisee Relationship," by H.
       LaVan. J. C. Latona, and R. W. Coye; "Behavioral

Relations in Marketing Channels: A Review of Cross-
Channel Comparisons." by J. R. Brown. J. L. Johnson.
and Y. K. Lim: "Exploring the Environmental and Be-
havioral Antecedents of Franchise Trust and Satis-
faction." by F. R. Dwyer. S. Oh, and Rosemary Lagace:
"Applicability of Federal and State Securities Laws to
Offers and Sales of Franchises," by M. T. Arnold:
"Retroactive Application of State Laws Regulating
Franchise Relationships." by M. J. O'Hara; "Financing
Growth: Franchise Compared to Corporate." by S. J.
Wright: "Are the Franchised Businesses less risky
than the Non-Franchised Businesses?" by K. H. Pad-
manabhan; "Franchising: Entrepreneurial Development,"
by R. T. Justis and C. Babcock: "Another Look at
Recognition of Initial Franchise Fees," by W. M.
Higley; "Should Franchisor and Franchisee Elect Iden-
tical Accounting Conventions?" by R. H. Raymond and
J. L. Armitage; "Franchising: Excess Market Value
and Advertising Intensity," by E. O. Lyn; "Franchise
System: The Internal Dynamics of Sales Growth and Dual
Distribution," by M. J. O'Hara and W. L. Thomas;
"Industry Impediments to Franchising--A Study of the
Equipment Rental Industry," by A. Peterson and R. D.
Goddard: and "The Newest Franchise: An Overview of
Bank and Savings & Loan Franchise Systems," by W. J.
Carne.

203.   Sweeney, Christopher J. "Franchising: A Venture
        Decision." M.S. Thesis. Bucknell University, 1974.

        Explores current (ca. 1974) status of franchise
        operations and indicates trend of franchising as a
        venture industry. Covers the post-World War II United
        States franchise growth and franchising's relationship
        to small business. Topics covered are: history of
        franchising from its earliest developments, reasons
        for the growth of franchising, projections for the
        industry, financing considerations. and the franchise
        contract. Statistics presented include: Annual Net
        Profit of Franchised Outlets as Estimated by Fran-
        chisor, Franchising Trends and Projections (1971-
        1974), and the record of Business Mortalities. In-
        cludes bibliography.

204.   United States. Congress. Senate. Committee on Small
        Business. IMPACT OF FRANCHISING ON SMALL BUSINESS.

91st Congress. 2nd Session. Report No. 91-1344.
Washington, D.C.: U.S. Government Printing Office.
1970.

Full title: THE IMPACT OF FRANCHISING ON SMALL
BUSINESS, BASED ON HEARINGS BEFORE THE SUBCOMMITTEE ON
URBAN AND RURAL ECONOMIC DEVELOPMENT. January 20, 21,
22, 27, March 30, and April 24, 1970. Report of all
aspects of the franchising industry in the United
States from panelists representing franchisors, authors, lawyers, legislators, franchisees, and celeb-
rity franchisors. Among panelists are Minnie Pearl.
Joe Namath, Harold Brown, and J. F. Atkinson. Covers
federal and state legislation, minority franchises,
history, and financing of franchises. Bibliographical
references.

205. United States. Department of Commerce. Bureau of
      Industrial Economics. FRANCHISING IN THE ECONOMY.
      Washington, D.C.: U.S. Government Printing Office,
      1969-

      Originally issued by the United States Industry and
      Trade Administration. Contains results of annual
      survey sent to all known business format franchisors.
      First section presents overview of statistics and
      trends covering sales, number of outlets, number of
      terminations of franchise agreements, number of
      business failures, changes in ownership, and indus-
      tries (e.g. fast food restaurants) that show signs
      of continued growth. Analyses of these trends and
      projections are included in this section. Statis-
      tical tables of survey results comprise the second
      section. Among data presented are number of firms
      by industry category (i.e. automotive products and
      services, retailing, convenience stores, etc.),
      sales, and investment requirements. The third sec-
      tion reports recent developments in federal and
      state legislation.

*   Vaughn, Charles L. FRANCHISING: ITS NATURE, SCOPE,
      ADVANTAGES, AND DEVELOPMENT. Cited above as item 67.

*   Vaughn. Charles L. FRANCHISING: ITS NATURE, SCOPE,
      ADVANTAGES, AND DEVELOPMENT. 2nd Rev. ed. Cited
      above as item 68.

CHAPTER VII
INTERNATIONAL FRANCHISING

During the past few decades, franchising has expanded not only in the United States but throughout the world. Franchise chains such as McDonald's are now found in European, Canadian, and Asian cities. Publications listed in this chapter trace the development of international franchising and study trends for its future. Topics of books listed range from the management of franchises overseas to marketing strategies. Periodical articles may be located by searching data bases and indexes listed in the appendixes. It should also be noted that many of the introductory and legal guides contain chapters or sections on international franchising. The books listed in this chapter have as their major content an analysis of franchising outside the United States.

206. American Bar Association. Section on Antitrust Law. Franchising Committee. SURVEY OF FOREIGN LAWS AND REGULATIONS AFFECTING INTERNATIONAL FRANCHISING. Chicago, Ill.: American Bar Association, 1982.

Offers guidelines to companies seeking to enter foreign markets through franchising. Reports results of responses to questionnaires sent to foreign franchise attorneys. Covers the countries: Australia, Belgium, Brazil, Canada, Denmark, France, West Germany, Hong Kong, Italy, Japan, Mexico, Netherlands, New Zealand, Philippines, South Africa, Spain, Sweden, Switzerland, Taiwan, and the United Kingdom. Reports for each country: business climates affecting franchising, tax aspects of foreign franchising, investment incentives, customs and import-export controls, real estate, labor, forms of doing business, legislation affecting foreign franchising, antitrust laws, and trademarks.

207. British Columbia. Legislative Assembly. Select
      Standing Committee on Agriculture. FRANCHISING IN
      THE BRITISH COLUMBIA FOOD INDUSTRY. Richmond, B.C.:
      Legislative Assembly, Select Standing Committee on
      Franchising, 1979.

      "Phase III" of study of the food industry in British
      Columbia studies processing, wholesaling, and re-
      tailing. Studies the franchising system, advantages
      and disadvantages of franchising, trends in fran-
      chising, legal considerations, and the development
      of the fast food industry. Covers and compares trends
      in the United States and Canada. Appendixes include
      the Franchise Competitive Practices Act (Proposed by
      Senator Philip Hart of Michigan); Province of Alberta,
      the Franchise Act and Regulations, 1975; Newspaper
      Articles Relating to Franchising (Reprints); and a
      Supplementary Reading List.

*   British Franchise Association. WORKBOOK: ESSENTIAL
      INFORMATION FOR DEVELOPING FRANCHISORS. Cited above
      as item 6.

208. Coltman, Michael McDonald. FRANCHISING IN CANADA: PROS
      AND CONS. Self-Counsel Series. Vancouver: Inter-
      national Self-Counsel Press, 1982.

      Written primarily for prospective franchisees based
      in Canada. Describes history of franchising in U.S.
      and Canada, franchised business opportunities in
      Canada, how to investigate a franchisor, site
      selection, financing, and legal issues. Appendix
      contains a sample franchise contract.

209. Commission of the European Communities. THE
      COOPERATION BETWEEN FIRMS IN THE COMMUNITY--
      FRANCHISING. Studies Series: Series Commerce and
      Distribution, 1978-5. Luxembourg: Office for
      Official Publications of the European Communities,
      1978.

      Analyzes franchising in the various member countries
      of the Commission of the European Communities. CEC
      countries studied are Belgium, the United Kingdom,
      West Germany, the Netherlands, France, Italy, and

Ireland. Reports cooperative efforts between firms in
the retail trade of the various CEC countries. Emphasizes cooperation in form of franchising, outlining
its features, advantages, and disadvantages. Research
based on questionnaires sent to member countries.

210. Felter, Edwin L., ed. INTERNATIONAL FRANCHISING:
      CONDITIONS AND PROSPECTS. Denver, Colorado:
      Continental Reports, Inc., 1970.

      Series of essays in first section emphasize the
      legal aspects of franchising overseas. Contents of
      Part I: "An Overview of the Philosophy and Signifi-
      cance of International Franchising," by Bernard
      Goodwin; "The International Franchise Agreement," by
      Matthew Lifflander; "European Legal Techniques Most
      Adaptable and Practical for International Fran-
      chising," by Giorgio Bernini; "European Antitrust
      Aspects of International Franchising," by LaForest
      Phillips; and "Franchising and Antitrust Law in West
      Germany," by Hans Thummel and Werner Wintterlin. Part
      II is a country by country survey of conditions for
      international franchising for the potential fran-
      chisor, prepared by Edwin L. Felter. Covers trends
      in the United Kingdom, France, Italy, the Netherlands,
      Belgium, West Germany, Scandinavia, Denmark, Finland,
      Japan, Taiwan, Malaysia, Thailand, Australia, South
      Africa, Mexico, Central America, Venezuela, Argentina,
      and Brazil. Each country contains data on: The
      Market (i.e. Geography and Population, Income and
      Purchasing, and Local Preferences; Economic Indicators
      and Conditions (i.e. Development, Capital Availabili-
      ty, Financing, Labor and Construction); Investment
      Implications (i.e. Forms of Doing Business, Tax
      Structure, and International Accords); Trademark
      Protection; Licensing and/or Franchising Laws;
      Existing Franchise Operations; and Feasibility of
      Certain Franchises. With bibliography of books and
      journal articles.

211. FRANCHISING. Retail and Distribution Series. London:
      Euromonitor Publications, 1985.

      Examines the history, current trends and future
      prospects for franchising in the United Kingdom.
      Studies industry categories and the major franchisors

within them. Discusses role of the British Franchise
Association. Presents data (1980-1985) on sales by
British Franchise Association member franchises,
number of franchised units, franchise fees, sources of
financing, etc.

212. FRANCHISING IN CANADA'S FOOD SERVING INDUSTRY/LES
      CONCESSIONS DANS LE SECTEUR CANADIEN DE LA
      RESTAURATION. Ottawa: Information Canada, 1973.

      Text in English and French. Published by authority
      of the Ministry of Industry, Trade, and Commerce.
      Summarizes results of a survey covering the franchise
      food serving industry in Canada for 1971. Objectives
      of survey were to measure the impact of franchising in
      the Canadian food service industry; to study the
      nature of facilities and services offered by fran-
      chised food service establishments; to examine the
      franchisor-franchisee relationship; to determine the
      rate of growth of franchise food service establish-
      ments; and to test questionnaire design and method-
      ology for future studies of the entire food serv-
      ing industry in Canada. Reports results of survey
      from twenty-two companies on topics of fee structure,
      services provided by franchisor, services offered by
      franchisee, employment, wages and salaries, and
      operating expenses. Establishments studied include
      McDonald's, Chicken Delight of Canada, Dairy Queen
      Frozen Products, Kentucky Fried Chicken, etc.

213. FRANCHISING IN CANADA'S FOOD SERVING INDUSTRY/LES
      CONCESSIONS DANS LE SECTEUR CANADIEN DE LA
      RESTAURATION. Ottawa: Information Canada, 1975.

      Text in English and French. Reports results of
      survey covering the Canadian franchise food serving
      industry in 1973. In addition to 1971 report objec-
      tives, the 1973 report also aims to measure sales
      by production lines. Forty-two franchisors were
      mailed questionnaires. Survey results measured cost
      of sales, number of outlets and total cross sales,
      salaries and wages, employment, product lines offered
      to the customer by franchise outlets, fee structure,
      services provided by the franchisor, facilities and
      services offered by the franchisee, and selected
      operating expenses of franchisee outlets.

214.   FRANCHISING IN EUROPE, 1980-1990. London: Euromonitor
        Publications, 1987.

        Evaluates European franchising trends from 1980 to
        1985 and projects developments to 1990. Assesses
        national differences in acceptance of the franchising
        concept. Stresses franchising in the United Kingdom,
        France, Belgium, and the Netherlands.

215.   Grant, Clive. BUSINESS FORMAT FRANCHISING: A SYSTEM
        FOR GROWTH. Special Report, No. 185. London:
        Economist Intelligence Unit, 1985.

        Describes and analyzes business format franchising
        in the United Kingdom, its history, growth, present,
        and possible future. Two chapters cover franchising
        outside the UK and describe the industry in the United
        States, Canada, Japan, Australia, West Germany,
        France, Belgium, and Sweden. Features case histories
        of selected franchises in the UK. Tables present
        statistics on: Franchising in Europe, 1981-82; Expan-
        sion of U.S. Franchises Abroad, 1981-82; Purchase
        Prices of Franchises, 1984, etc. Discusses role of
        the British Franchise Association.

*   Gunz, Sally, T. Regan, and Derek F. Channon.
        FRANCHISING. Cited above as item 17.

216.   Izraeli, Dov. FRANCHISING AND THE TOTAL DISTRIBUTION
        SYSTEM. London: Longman, 1972.

        Research study of the franchising industry as it
        relates to food distribution systems in the United
        Kingdom. Section one describes growth of franchising
        in the United States and the United Kingdom. Section
        two analyzes the Voluntary Group System in U.K. gro-
        cery trade. Section three concerns the organization-
        al model, the Total Distribution System, designed "to
        enable a food distribution organization to cater
        successfully for growth and for effective integra-
        tion and control in a flexible manner." (p. xii)
        The Total Distribution Model was developed by Dr.
        Izraeli. Research based on review of the literature
        and consultation with practitioners in franchise and
        distribution systems. Bibliographical references.

217. Hudgins, Edward A., Jr. "Franchising as a Method for
      the International Expansion of Business." MBA
      Thesis. George Washington University, 1970.

      Studies international franchising and offers answer
      to question as to how foreign markets can be entered
      through the use of the franchising concept. Ap-
      proaches topic from point of view of the franchisor.
      Covers topics of: the history of franchising in the
      United States and overseas; managerial and marketing
      considerations in overseas franchises; legal matters;
      and financial aspects, including taxation. Presents
      case histories and lists selected franchising
      organizations overseas (ca. 1970).

218. Kacker, Madhav P. TRANSATLANTIC TRENDS IN RETAILING:
      TAKEOVERS AND FLOW OF KNOW-HOW. Westport, Connecti-
      cut: Quorum Books, 1985.

      Assesses trends in European retailing with sections
      on franchising operations. Analyzes trends in frame-
      work of the European political and economic environ-
      ment, historical perspective, and retailing develop-
      ments in the U.S. and Europe. Covers case histories
      of leading international franchised operators such as
      McDonald's, Pizza Hut, Burger King, Kentucky Fried
      Chicken, and Taco Bell. Statistical tables record
      data on: Growth of Franchise Establishments of U.S.
      Firms in the United Kingdom, 1976-1982; McDonald's
      International Growth, 1978-1982; International
      Franchising in 1982, etc.

219. Langlais, Jean Pierre. FRANCHISING: FROM THE USA TO
      FRANCE. n.p., 1972.

      Studies the application of the juridical technique
      of franchising in French law. Analyzes character-
      istics and elements of the franchise contract. Com-
      pares American and French franchising traits.

220. MARKETING THROUGH FRANCHISING IN AUSTRALIA: ONE DAY
      SEMINAR, AUGUST 24TH, 1972. Melbourne, Australia:
      Victorian Employers' Federation, 1972.

Papers presented at a seminar which studied
franchising in Australia and its issues of site
selection, advertising, psychology, and franchise
contracts.

221. SBL Conference (6th: 1983: Toronto, Ontario).
      INTERNATIONAL FRANCHISING: AN OVERVIEW: PAPERS
      PRESENTED TO THE INTERNATIONAL FRANCHISE COMMITTEE
      AT THE SBL CONFERENCE, HELD IN TORONTO, OCTOBER
      1983. Organized by the SBL Section on Business Law
      of the International Bar Association. Edited by
      Martin Mendelsohn. Amsterdam, New York, Oxford:
      North-Holland, 1984.

      Contains papers presented at the 1983 SBL (Section
      on Business Law) Conference by lawyers covering more
      than twenty countries. Contributed papers are: "An
      Introduction to Franchising," by L. G. Rudnick; "Fran-
      chising: Trade Mark Practitioners' Perspective," by
      I. Baillie; "Character Merchandising," by N. Fyfe;
      "Regulation of Franchising in the United States:
      Implications for International Franchising," by P. F.
      Zeidman; "Legislation and Regulations Affecting Fran-
      chising in Canada: An Overview," by H. A. Shapiro;
      "Franchising in Latin America," by H. S. Brown; "Focus
      on Franchising in the Asia/Pacific Region: Joint
      Ventures, Regulation of Investment, Tax," by D. R.
      Shannon; "Franchising in Europe--United Kingdom," by
      M. Mendelsohn; "Franchising in Europe--EEC," by S. A.
      Crossick; "Franchsing in Europe--France," by O. Gast;
      and "Franchising in Europe--Germany," by Dr. W.
      Skaupy. Essays stress legal aspects of international
      franchising and analyze leading court decisions and
      legislation. Bibliographical references.

222. Shannon, David. FRANCHISING IN AUSTRALIA: A LEGAL
      GUIDE. Sydney, Australia: Law Book Co. Ltd., 1982.

      Deals with various aspects of franchise law and
      regulation in Australia including patents, trade
      marks, income tax, etc. Cites leading court decisions
      in Australia.

223. White, Jerry and Frank Zaid. CANADIAN FRANCHISE GUIDE.
      Ontario: Richard De Boo Publishers, a division of
      International Thomson, Ltd., 1985 (?).

Loose-leaf service designed for lawyers, accountants, bankers, business owners, advertising agencies,
insurance agents, government officials, product and
service suppliers, and prospective franchisors and
franchisees. Covers all aspects of franchising,
specifically legal considerations, history of Canadian
franchising, tax matters, current and future trends,
selecting franchisees, and marketing the franchise.
With glossary and bibliography.

CHAPTER VIII
CASE HISTORIES OF FRANCHISES

McDonald's, Kentucky Fried Chicken, and Domino's Pizza
are just three of the franchises that have been the subjects
of books and articles. This chapter is an annotated listing
of case histories of francises which have appeared in book
form. There are numerous journal articles detailing histories, management techniques, and marketing ventures of franchises. For these, indexes and online databases may be
searched. Additionally, books on franchising, including introductory texts, often include chapters or sections on case
histories. The case histories listed below are arranged by
industry name, then the name of the company. Books that contain many case histories are listed under "Collective Case
Histories."

I. AUTOMOBILE INDUSTRY

COLLECTIVE CASE HISTORIES

224. Ferron, J. and Jake Kelderman. BETTING ON THE FRAN-
      CHISE: CAR AND TRUCK RETAILING INTO THE 1990S.
      McLean, Virginia: National Automobile Dealers
      Association, 1984.

      Explores the franchised dealership in the selling of
      cars and trucks. Data is compiled by the National
      Automobile Dealers Association. Includes survey of
      dealers and experts on the future of franchising.
      Projects trends in automotive franchises through 1994.

225. Helmers, H. O. A MARKETING RATIONALE FOR THE DISTRI-
      BUTION OF AUTOMOBILES/ Davisson, Charles N. and
      Herbert F. Taggart. FINANCIAL AND OPERATING CHAR-
      ACTERISITCS OF AUTOMOBILE DEALERS AND THE FRAN-
      CHISE SYSTEM: TWO STUDIES IN AUTOMOBILE FRANCHISING.
      Ann Arbor, Michigan: University of Michigan, 1974.

      The two studies place the marketing strategies for
      the automobile industry within the framework of
      behavioral concepts, business strategies, and finan-
      cial and accounting analysis. Helmers' report ana-
      lyzes automobile distribution in the context of
      other manufacturer-distributor relationships. The
      Davisson-Taggart study suggests that the automobile
      dealership franchise system development "on the basis
      of an economic rationale reflecting benefits to be
      provided to the several parties involved, consumers as
      well as corporate members." (p. xiii)

226. Hewitt, Charles M. AUTOMOBILE FRANCHISE AGREEMENTS.
      Indiana University Bureau of Business Research
      Study, no. 39. Homewood, Illinois: Richard D. Irwin,
      1956.

      Analyzes automobile franchise agreements from both a
      legal and economic point of view for the time period
      1900-1956. Explains why franchise agreements in the
      industry came into use and traces their evolution.
      Cites specific court cases.

227. Pashigian, Bedros Peter. THE DISTRIBUTION OF AUTOMO-
      MOBILES, AN ECONOMIC ANALYSIS OF THE FRANCHISE
      SYSTEM. Englewood Cliffs, N.J.: Prentice-Hall, 1961.

      Study that "attempts to measure the economies of
      scale in automotive distribution and to determine the
      importance of distribution as a barrier to entrance in
      the market by new manufacturers." (preface) Examines
      profitability of dealerships, wholesale and retail
      price determination, and performance of automobile
      dealers in replacement parts and service markets.

*   Sloan, Alfred P., Jr. MY YEARS WITH GENERAL MOTORS.
      Cited below as item 261.

II. FOOD AND RESTAURANT INDUSTRY

COLLECTIVE CASE HISTORIES

228. Bernstein, Charles. GREAT RESTAURANT INNOVATORS:
      PROFILES IN SUCCESS. New York: Chain Store Pub-
      lishing Corp., subsidiary of Lebhar-Friedman, 1981.

      A series of biographies of restaurateurs. Section
      I, "Fast-Food Pioneers" concerns the stories of Dave
      Thomas, the founder of Wendy's Hamburger Restaurants
      and Donald N. Smith, president of fast-food franchises
      Burger King, Pizza Hut, and Taco Bell. Section II,
      "Conglomerate Food Service Leaders," concerns Joe Lee,
      President of General Mills Restaurant Group; John
      Teets, Executive Vice-President of Bonanza Interna-
      tional; and Charles Lynch, Manager of Saga Corpora-
      tion which provides campus food service. Section
      III, "The Entrepreneurs" features Stuart Anderson,
      Manager of Black Angus Restaurant Chain; Norman
      Brinker, Manager of Steak & Ale and Bennigan's Res-
      taurant Chains; and Alex Schoenbaum, Director of
      Shoney's Drive-ins and Restaurants and Big Boy Res-
      taurants. Section IV, "The Irrepressible Independ-
      ents" concerns Warner LeRoy, Manager of Maxwell's
      Plum and Tavern on the Green and Arnie Morton, Manager
      of Arnie's. Section V, "The Creative Consultants"
      features restaurant consultants, Joe Baum and George
      Lang.

229. Bertram, Peter. FAST FOOD OPERATIONS. London: Barrie
      and Jenkins Ltd., 1975.

      Analyzes the expansion of the fast-food industry
      with emphasis on the situation in the United Kingdom.
      Topics covered include quality in fast foods, restau-
      rant design, why people choose, and menu planning.

230. Emerson, Robert L. FAST-FOOD: THE ENDLESSS SHAKEOUT.
      New York: Lebhar-Friedman Books, 1979.

      Presents an analysis of the fast-food restaurant
      industry and discusses past, present, and possible
      future trends. Describes reasons why consumers choose

fast-foods, and costs of running a business. Case
histories are presented through interviews with R.
David Thomas, Chairman of Wendy's, Jamie Coulter, a
Pizza Hut franchisee; Edward Schmitt, McDonald's
President; and Donald Smith, President of Burger King.
Also discussed are Hardee's and Kentucky Fried Chicken
restaurant chains.

231.   FIND/SVP. SMALL & MEDIUM-SIZED RESTAURANT CHAINS. New
       York: FIND/SVP, 1987.

       Survey of 100 typical companies with fewer than 100
       units throughout the United States. Provides informa-
       tion on types of menus, price ranges, at what levels
       the organization's buying decisions are made, the
       preferred supply purchasing channels, and specific
       quantities chains want in the supplies. Furnishes
       sales of each chain, number of units, numbers of units
       added in 1986, and number projected in 1987. Appen-
       dixes contain an alphabetical listing of chain res-
       taurants surveyed, a list of surveyed chain restau-
       rants sorted by sales, and a list of surveyed chain
       restaurants sorted by units.

232.   FOOD RETAILING REVIEW: SURVEY OF PERFORMANCE AT U.S.
       FOOD STORES AND EATING & DRINKING PLACES. Fairlawn,
       N.J.: The Food Institute, 1985.

       Trends and projections in the industry with section
       on franchised restaurants. Data from U.S. Government
       publication, FRANCHISING IN THE ECONOMY. Features
       brief sketches and five year financial history of
       seventy-four leading publicly held firms.

233.   Frost & Sullivan, Inc. FAST FOOD AND ASSOCIATED
       EQUIPMENT. New York: Frost & Sullivan, 1980.

       In-depth analysis of the development of fast food
       outlets, current and projected, in the nine countries
       of the European Economic Community and assesses the
       demand for equipment at these outlets. This study
       indicates the potential market for specific equipment
       associated with fast food operations over the period
       1979-1990. The nine EEC countries are: the Nether-

lands, Belgium, Luxembourg, France, West Germany, Denmark, Italy, the United Kingdom, and the Irish Republic.

*   Gruber, Kathleen M., comp. THE TRAVELER'S DIRECTORY OF FAST-FOOD RESTAURANTS. Cited above as item 89.

234.   Housden, Janet. FRANCHISING AND OTHER BUSINESS RELATIONSHIPS IN HOTEL AND CATERING SERVICES. London: Heinemann, 1984.

Describes and analyzes four relationships in arrangements among owners and operators of hotel and catering facilities in Great Britain. These relationships are: the tied house system, catering contracts, hotel management contracts, and franchising. Studies franchising systems in the hotel and catering industries. Traces development of franchising in both the United States and Great Britain and discusses topics of franchisor-franchisee relationship, advantages and disadvantages, and projections of future developments. Research based on review of the literature and survey of practitioners and clients involved in business relationships analyzed. Appendixes include: Franchise Agreements: Typical Provisions; Questionnaire to Franchisors and Breweries; Questionnaire to Franchisees and Tied-Trade Tenants; and The British Franchise Association: Objectives, Activities, and Code of Ethics. Includes selected bibliography.

235.   Huls, Mary Ellen. MCARCHITECTURE: A BIBLIOGRAPHY ON FAST FOOD RESTAURANT DESIGN. Monticello, Illinois: Vance Bibliographies, 1986.

Bibliography of articles on fast food restaurant design and articles on architecture of specific restaurants. Journal articles listed are from the 1970s and 1980s. Specific restaurants that are subjects of listed articles include: Arby's, Kentucky Fried Chicken, Burger King, McDonald's, and Wendy's.

236.   Jacobson, Michael and Sarah Fritschner. THE FAST-FOOD GUIDE: WHAT'S GOOD, WHAT'S BAD, AND HOW TO TELL THE DIFFERENCE. New York: Workman Publishing, 1986.

Nutritional evaluation of the leading fast foods
available to consumers. Ingredients are studied for
fast foods offered by Arby's, Arthur Treacher's, Burg-
ger King, Carl's Jr., Church's Fried Chicken, Dairy
Queen, D'Lites, Domino's Pizza, Hardee's, Jack in the
Box, Kentucky Fried Chicken, Long John Silver's, Mc-
Donald's, Popeyes, Roy Rogers, Taco Bell, and Wendy's.
Compares fast foods on the basis of such variables as
number of calories and content of fat, sugar, calcium,
iron, and sodium.

237.   Lundberg, Donald E. THE HOTEL AND RESTAURANT BUSINESS.
       3rd ed. Boston, Mass.: CBI Publishing Co., 1979.

       Chapter 10, "Fast Food and Franchising" analyzes the
       industry and provides brief biographies of pioneers in
       the industry, notably Howard Johnson and Ray Kroc.

238.   National Restaurant Association. THE TAKE OUT MARKET.
       Consumer Attitude and Behavior Study. Washington,
       D.C.: The Association, February 1986.

       Reports results of a consumer survey conducted by
       the National Restaurant Association in April and May
       1985. Purpose of survey was to determine who pur-
       chases take out meals, when they are bought, why they
       are purchased, what meals are purchased, and where
       they are purchased. Copy of questionnaire is
       included.

239.   Soulam, Richard Edward. "Franchising--A Study of the
       Profitability of Fast-Food Franchises." M.A. Thesis.
       San Diego State College, 1970.

       Investigates the profitability of existing fast-food
       franchised businesses and compares this to claims of
       franchisors. Six franchisors were studied and results
       indicated that "all of the six companies predicted a
       level of net profit which was not obtained by their
       franchisees." (p. 42)

240.   Tchudi, Stephen. THE BURG-O-RAMA MAN. New York:
       Delacorte Press, 1983.

A novel for young adults about the filming of a
commercial by a major fast food franchise. The company must choose five Crawford High School students
to be featured in the advertisements.

241. Vaughn, Charles. THE VAUGHN REPORT ON FRANCHISING OF
      FAST FOOD RESTAURANTS. Lynbrook, N.Y.: Farnsworth
      Publishing CO., 1970.

      Reports results of survey of fast food restaurants.
      Survey, conducted in late 1968, analyzed six cate-
      gories of fast food restaurants: chicken, roast beef,
      pizza, sandwiches, hamburger/hot dogs, and seafood
      establishments. Survey sought information in six
      areas: general characteristics of franchisor firms
      including number of units, sources of revenue, es-
      timates of success, etc.; recruiting, selecting, and
      training policies and practices; financing of fran-
      chisees; real estate; consumer marketing; and fran-
      chisee relations. Study sponsored by Boston College
      Center for the Study of Franchise Distribution.

242. Wyckoff, D. Daryl. THE CHAIN-RESTAURANT INDUSTRY. The
      Lexington Case Book Series in Industry Analysis.
      Lexington, Mass.: Lexington Books, 1978.

      Reports research results, based on interviews, of a
      study of fast-food franchise restaurant chains. Case
      histories provide information on franchisor-franchisee
      agreements, restaurant design, and advertising cam-
      paigns. Companies examined in study are: Victoria
      Station, Inc.; Benihana of Tokyo; Brighton Fish Pier;
      Wendy's Old Fashioned Hamburgers, Waffle House, Inc.;
      McDonald's Corporation; and Dobbs House. Among sta-
      tistical tables are: Fast-Food Sales, 1968-76; Struc-
      ture of Retail Food Industry; and Fast-Food Sales by
      Food Type. Appendix A is a glossary of chain res-
      taurant terminology.

                         BENIHANA OF TOKYO

243. McCallum, Jack. MAKING IT IN AMERICA: THE LIFE AND
      TIMES OF ROCKY AOKI, BENIHANA'S PIONEER. New York:
      Dodd Mead, 1985.

Biography of Benihana of Tokyo's founder who developed chain of restaurants specializing in Japanese
cuisine.

BURGER KING CORPORATION

244. Tenenbaum, Mark Dean. "Franchising: With Special Emphasis on the Burger King Corporation." MBA Thesis.
University of Texas at Austin, 1983.

Study of concept of franchising and how it applies
to the fast-food industry using the Burger King Corporation as a case study. Examines investment decision process through application of the integrated
framework, "Management Integrated Model, Information
Capital, Control System" or "MIMICS," developed by Dr.
Eugene B. Konecci. The Burger King Franchise is one
of the possible sources of investment. Provides, for
Burger King, its history, sample franchise agreement,
and training assistance provided. Also offers brief
descriptions of other fast-food franchises including:
Arby's, Kentucky Fried Chicken, McDonald's
Corporation, and Wendy's International.

CARL KARCHER ENTERPRISES

245. Knight, B. Carolyn. MAKING IT HAPPEN: THE STORY OF
CARL KARCHER ENTERPRISES. Anaheim, California: Carl
Karcher Enterprises, 1981.

Biography of Carl Karcher, the "Hamburger King," who
founded several fast-food chains including Carl's Jr.
Restaurants.

DOMINO'S PIZZA

246. Monaghan, Tom, with Robert Anderson. PIZZA TIGER. New
York: Random House, 1986.

Autobiography of the founder of Domino's Pizza
describes development of the business from a single
store to the world's largest pizza delivery company.

Monaghan also bought the baseball team, the Detroit
Tigers, World Series winners in 1984.

KENTUCKY FRIED CHICKEN

247.   Klemm, Edward G., Jr. CLAUDIA: THE STORY OF COLONEL
       HARLAND SANDERS' WIFE. Los Angeles, California:
       Crescent Publications, 1980.

       Biography of Claudia Sanders, wife of the founder of
       Kentucky Fried Chicken. She worked with Colonel
       Sanders in the preparation of recipes and the promo-
       tion of the business.

248.   Pearce, John. THE COLONEL: THE CAPTIVATING BIOGRAPHY
       OF THE DYNAMIC FOUNDER OF A FAST-FOOD EMPIRE. Garden
       City, N.Y.: Doubleday, 1982.

       Biography of Colonel Harland Sanders, founder of
       Kentucky Fried Chicken and how he developed the fast-
       food chain. Foreword is by John Young Brown, Jr.,
       Governor of Kentucky.

249.   Sanders, Harland. LIFE AS I HAVE KNOWN IT HAS BEEN
       FINGER LICKIN' GOOD. Carol Stream, Illinois:
       Creation House, 1974.

       Autobiography of Colonel Sanders from his earliest
       days to age seventy-nine as the multimillionaire foun-
       der of Kentucky Fried Chicken. Details his early
       work in such occupations as farmhand, insurance sales-
       man, tire salesman, locomotive fireman, and motel
       operator. Tells the story of how he founded Kentucky
       Fried Chicken. In his later years, Colonel Sanders
       became a born-again Christian.

MCDONALD'S CORPORATION

250.   Boas, Max and Steve Chain. BIG MAC. New York: E. P.
       Dutton, 1976.

       The story of Ray Kroc, founder of McDonald's Cor-
       poration. Among innovations developed by Kroc are

the training program at "Hamburger U," advertising
strategies, and the fast-food "Big Mac," "Egg
McMuffin," and "Quarter Pounder."

251. Fishwick, Marshall, ed. THE WORLD OF RONALD MCDONALD.
      Bowling Green, Ohio: Popular Press, 1978.

      Reprint of the JOURNAL OF POPULAR CULTURE, Volume 1,
      issue 2, Summer 1978. Series of articles cover his-
      tory of McDonald's Corporation, advertising campaigns,
      nutritive value of the food, and design of stores.
      Contents: "In the Beginning was the Drive-in: Intro-
      duction," by M. Fishwick; "Enter the Wizard," by J. F.
      Trimmer; "Fast Food Flash," by J. Carroll; "The Land-
      scape of McDonald's," by K. I. Helphand; "McDonald's
      Interior Design," by G. Huddleston; "Rituals at Mc-
      Donald's," by C. P. Kottak; "The Ethnography of Big
      Mac," by D. G. Orr; "New York's Biggest Mac," by B.
      Hunter; "The Man Who Sold the First McDonald's Ham-
      burger," by P. Fitzell; "The Psychology of Fast Food
      Happiness," by G. Hall; "Can Mama Mac Get Them to Eat
      Spinach," by M. E. Spencer; "Hamburger University," by
      S. S. King and M. J. King; "Emperors of Popular Cul-
      ture: McDonald's and Disney," by M. J. King; "The War
      Between the Hamburgers," by K. Grover; "Berger vs.
      Burger: A Personal Encounter," by A. A. Berger; "What
      can we learn from Ronald?" by M. R. Steele; "Mao and
      Mac: A Cultural Perspective," by S. L. King and R. A.
      Sanderson; "Exit the Clown: Some Final Thoughts," by
      M. Fishwick; and "A Burger Bibliography," by E. L.
      Huddleston.

252. Kroc, Ray, with Robert Anderson. GRINDING IT OUT. New
      York: Berkeley Medallion Books, 1977.

      Autobiography of the founder of McDonald's and a
      history of the corporation from its beginnings. Kroc
      traces his experiences from the time he sold paper
      cups for the Lily Cup Corporation to his development
      of McDonald's as one of the most successful corpora-
      tions in America and a role model for franchised
      businesses.

253. Love, John. MCDONALD'S: BEHIND THE ARCHES. Toronto and
      New York: Bantam Books, 1986.

History of McDonald's Corporation based on interviews with key individuals involved in the franchise's
operations. Describes role of founder Ray Kroc, not
only in McDonald's Corporation, but as a pioneer in
the franchising industry. Traces development of
McDonald's Corporation in historical context of the
franchise industry.

254. RONALD REVISITED: THE WORLD OF RONALD MCDONALD.
      Bowling Green, Ohio: Bowling Green University
      Popular Press, 1983.

      Series of articles on the McDonald Corporation.
      Contents: "Introduction," by M. Fishwick; "Hamburger
      Stand Industrialization and the Fast Food Phenomenon,"
      by B. A. Lohuf; "You are What you Speak: Menu Language
      Where America Feeds," by S. G. Riley; "Fast Food
      Flash," by J. Carroll; "The Landscape of McDonald's,"
      by K. I. Helphand; "McDonald's Interior Design," by G.
      Huddleston; "Rituals at McDonald's," by C. P. Kottak;
      "The Ethnography of Big Mac," by D. G. Orr; "New
      York's Biggest Mac," by B. Hunter; "The Psychology of
      Fast Food Happiness," by G. Hall; "Can Mama Mac Get
      Them to Eat Spinach?" by M. E. Spencer; "Hamburger
      University," by S. S. King and M. J. King; "Empires of
      Popular Culture: McDonald's and Disney," by M. J.
      King; "The War Between the Hamburgers," by K. Grover;
      "Berger vs. Burger: A Personal Encounter," by A. A.
      Berger; "What can we learn from Ronald?" by M. R.
      Steele; "Mao and Mac: A Cultural Perspective," by S.
      S. King and R. A. Sanderson; "And You Thought Big Macs
      were Fast Food when They're Made for TV Commercials,
      Such Delicacies can Take Hours to Create," by L. Lee;
      "Cloning Clowns: Some Final Thoughts," by M. Fishwick;
      and "A Burger Bibliography," by E. Huddleston.

255. Simpson, Janice Celia. RAY KROC: BIG MAC MAN.
      Headliners II. St. Paul, Minnesota: EMC Corporation,
      1978.

      A biography, for young people, of Ray Kroc, founder
      of the McDonald's Hamburger chain. With illustrations
      of early McDonald's restaurants.

256. Westman, Paul. RAY KROC: MAYOR OF MCDONALD LAND. Il-
      lustrated by Mary Molina. Taking Part, 3. Minne-
      apolis, Minnesota: Dillon Press, 1980.

      A biography, for young people, of Ray Kroc, an
      innovator in fast-food preparation and founder of
      McDonald's.

WENDY'S INTERNATIONAL

257. Vaughan, Michael C. WENDY'S: A TRADITION OF QUALITY.
      Dublin, Ohio: Wendy's International, Inc., 1984.

      History of Wendy's International chronicles its
      growth from one restaurant in 1969 through openings of
      almost three thousand restaurants in 1984. R. David
      Thomas started the restaurant chain which was named
      after his third eldest daughter. Wendy's original
      menu was the hamburger, chili, and a chocolate-vanilla
      milkshake called the "Frosty." Since 1969 different
      fast-foods were added to the menu, the restaurants
      expanded internationally, and advertising campaigns
      such as "Where's the Beef?" television commercials
      were developed. Illustrated with color photographs of
      company executives, commercials, and designs of some
      of the restaurants.

III. HOTEL AND MOTEL INDUSTRY

COLLECTIVE CASE HISTORIES

*   Housden, Janet. FRANCHISING AND OTHER BUSINESS RELA-
      TIONSHIPS IN HOTEL AND CATERING SERVICES. Cited
      above as item 234.

HOLIDAY INNS

258. Wilson, Kemmons. THE HOLIDAY INN STORY. New York: The
      Newcomen Society in North America, 1968.

      Transcript of address delivered by Kemmons Wilson,
      founder of Holiday Inns of America, Inc., held at a

national meeting of the Newcomen Society on May 22,
1968. Wilson was one of three guests of honor at this
meeting. Wilson describes the history of Holiday Inns
from the establishment of the first hotel in Memphis
to its growth as a major hotel chain. He details
major innovations in the chain and the nature of the
franchisor-franchisee relationship.

IV. PIONEER FRANCHISES

COLLECTIVE CASE HISTORIES

259. Luxenberg, Stan. ROADSIDE EMPIRES: HOW THE CHAINS
      FRANCHISED AMERICA. New York: Viking Press, 1985.

      Describes the rise of franchised companies and why
      they have succeeded. Presents case studies of fran-
      chised companies and their founders. Founders and
      companies presented are: Harland Sanders (Kentucky
      Fried Chicken), R. David Thomas (Wendy's), Ray Kroc
      (McDonald's), Henry and Richard Bloch (H & R Block),
      I. M. Singer (I. M. Singer & Co.), and Karl Stanley
      (Cut & Curl). Examines advertising campaigns and
      pluses and minuses of the franchising system.

COCA-COLA BOTTLING COMPANY

260. Rowland, Sanders with Bob Terrell. PAPA COKE: SIXTY-
      FIVE YEARS SELLING COCA-COLA. Asheville, North
      Carolina: Bright Mountain Books, 1986.

      Autobiography of the General Manager of the Coca-
      Cola Bottling Company whose marketing strategy
      represented one of the first franchising formats.

GENERAL MOTORS CORPORATION

261. Sloan, Alfred P., Jr. MY YEARS WITH GENERAL MOTORS.
      Edited by John McDonald, with Catharine Stevens.
      Garden City, N.Y.: Doubleday, 1964.

Autobiography of General Motors' Chief Executive
Officer for twenty-three years. Chapter 16,
"Distribution and the Dealers" details franchise
distribution at G. M.

I. M. SINGER & CO.

262.   Brandon, Ruth. A CAPITALIST ROMANCE. Philadelphia and
       New York: J. B. Lippincott, 1977.

       Biography of Isaac Merritt Singer, founder of I. M.
       Singer & Co. Singer's marketing techniques were among
       the earliest forms of franchising.

V.   TAX PREPARATION SERVICES

H & R BLOCK

263.   Goldwasser, Thomas. FAMILY PRIDE: PROFILES OF FIVE OF
       AMERICA'S BEST-RUN FAMILY BUSINESSES. New York:
       Dodd, Mead & Co., 1986.

       Among family-owned corporations studied is the
       franchise, H & R Block which offers consumers tax-
       preparation assistance.

APPENDIX I
ORGANIZATIONS AND ASSOCIATIONS

A. GOVERNMENT AGENCIES

Government agencies assist and counsel franchise owners regarding management, financing, and marketing assistance. Information is disseminated through pamphlets, periodicals, books, and personal consultation. Government agencies covered in this section are the Small Business Administration, the Minority Business Development Agency, and the Federal Trade Commission. The U.S. Government Printing Office's address is also provided as a source of distribution of publications.

The Small Business Administration offers assistance to present and future entrepreneurs through counseling and financial aid. The SBA also publishes a series of publications on small business including franchising. Seminars or courses are also conducted by SBA members. Field offices of the SBA are listed in this section.

The Minority Business Development Agency or MBDA was established to promote the expansion of minority-owned businesses. The MBDA, established within the Department of Commerce is responsible for: the provision of management, marketing, and technical assistance; the dissemination of information in the form of reports and statistics; and provision of grants and funds. Regional offices of the MBDA are also listed in this section.

SMALL BUSINESS ADMINISTRATION FIELD OFFICES

REGIONAL OFFICES:

Region 1--(Connecticut, Maine, Massachusetts, New Hampshire, Rhode Island, Vermont)

60 Batterymarch Street, Boston, Massachusetts   02110,
Telephone: 617-223-3204

Region 2--(New Jersey, New York, Puerto Rico, Virgin Islands)
26 Federal Plaza, Room 29-118, New York, N.Y.   10278,
Telephone: 212-264-7772

Region 3--(Delaware, District of Columbia, Maryland,
Pennsylvania, Virginia, West Virginia)
231 St. Asaphs Road, Suite 640-W, Bala Cynwyd, Pennsylvania
19004, Telephone: 215-596-5889

Region 4--(Alabama, Florida, Georgia, Kentucky, Mississippi,
North Carolina, South Carolina, Tennessee)
1375 Peachtree Street, N.E., Atlanta, Georgia   30367
Telephone: 404-347-2797

Region 5--(Illinois, Indiana, Michigan, Minnesota, Ohio,
Wisconsin)
230 South Dearborn Street, Room 510, Chicago, Illinois   60604,
Telephone: 312-353-0359

Region 6--(Arkansas, Louisiana, New Mexico, Oklahoma, Texas)
8625 King George Drive, Dallas, Texas   75235
Telephone: 214-767-7643

Region 7--(Iowa, Kansas, Missouri, Nebraska)
911 Walnut Street, 13th Floor, Kansas City, Missouri   64106
Telephone: 816-374-5288

Region 8--(Colorado, Montana, North Dakota, South Dakota,
Utah, Wyoming)
1405 Curtis Street, 22nd Floor, Denver, Colorado   80202
Telephone: 303-844-5441

Region 9--(Arizona, California, Hawaii, Nevada, Pacific Islands
Federal Building, 450 Golden Gate Avenue, Room 15307, San
Francisco, California   94102
Telephone: 415-556-7487

Region 10--(Alaska, Idaho, Oregon, Washington)
2615 4th Avenue, Room 440, Seattle, Washington   98104
Telephone: 206-442-5676

DISTRICT OFFICES:

Region 1

10 Causeway Street, Boston, Massachusetts   02222, Telephone: 617-565-5590

Federal Building, 40 Western Avenue, Room 512, Augusta, Maine 04330, Telephone: 207-622-8378

55 Pleasant Street, Room 209, Concord, New Hampshire   03301 Telephone: 603-225-1400

330 Main Street, Hartford, Connecticut   06106, Telephone: 203-722-3600

Federal Building, 87 State Street, Room 205, Montpelier, Vermont   05602, Telephone: 802-828-4474

380 Westminister Mall, Providence, Rhode Island   02903 Telephone: 401-528-4586

Region 2

Carlos Chardon Avenue, Hato Rey, Puerto Rico   00918 Telephone: 809-753-4002

60 Park Place, Newark, New Jersey   07102, Telephone: 201-645-2434

100 State Street, Room 601, Rochester, New York   14614 Telephone: 716-263-6700

Federal Building, Room 1071, 100 South Clinton Street, Syracuse, New York   13202, Telephone: 315-423-5383

111 West Huron Street, Room 1311, Federal Building, Buffalo, New York   14202, Telephone: 716-846-4301

333 E. Water Street, Elmira, New York   14901, Telephone: 607-734-8130

445 Broadway, Albany, New York   12207, Telephone: 518-472-6300

Region 3

168 W. Main Street, Clarksburg, West Virginia   26301
Telephone: 304-623-5361

960 Penn Avenue, Pittsburgh, Pennsylvania   15222
Telephone: 412-644-2780

Federal Building, 400 North 8th Street, Room 3015, Richmond,
Virginia   23240, Telephone: 804-771-2617

1111 18th Street, N.W., Washington, D.C.   20417, Telephone:
202-634-4950

100 Chestnut Street, Harrisburg, Pennsylvania   17101
Telephone: 717-782-3840

20 N. Pennsylvania Avenue, Wilkes-Barre, Pennsylvania   18702
Telephone: 717-826-6497

844 King Street, Federal Building, Room 5207, Wilmington,
Delaware   19801, Telephone: 302-573-6294

600 Federal Place, Louisville, Kentucky   40202, Telephone:
503-582-5976

Region 4

2121 8th Avenue, N., Suite 200, Birmingham, Alabama   35203
Telephone: 205-731-1344

222 S. Church Street, Room 300, Charlotte, North Carolina
28202, Telephone: 704-731-6563

1835 Assembly Street, Columbia, South Carolina   29202
Telephone: 803-765-5376

100 West Capitol Street, Jackson, Mississippi   39269
Telephone: 601-965-4378

Federal Building, 400 West Bay Street, Room 261, Jacksonville,
Florida   32202, Telephone: 904-791-3782

2222 Ponce de Leon Boulevard, 5th Floor, Miami, Florida
33184, Telephone: 305-536-5521

404 James Robertson Parkway, Nashville, Tennessee   37129
Telephone: 615-736-5881

700 Twiggs Street, Suite 607, Tampa, Florida   33602
Telephone: 813-228-2594

1720 Peachtree Road, N.W., 6th Floor, Atlanta, Georgia   30309
Telephone: 404-347-4749

Region 5

Four North Old State Capital Plaza, Springfield, Illinois
62701, Telephone: 217-492-4416

1240 East 9th Street, Room 317, Cleveland, Ohio   44199
Telephone: 216-522-4180

85 Marconi Boulevard, Columbus, Ohio   43215, Telephone: 614-
469-6860

Federal Building, 550 Main Street, Cincinnati, Ohio   45202
Telephone: 513-684-2814

477 Michigan Avenue, McNamara Building, Detroit, Michigan
48225, Telephone: 313-226-6075

575 N. Pennsylvania Avenue, Century Building, Indianapolis,
Indiana   46204, Telephone: 317-269-7272

212 East Washington Avenue, Room 213, Madison, Wisconsin
53703, Telephone: 608-264-5261

100 North 6th Street, Minneapolis, Minnesota   55403
Telephone: 612-349-3550

220 W. Washington Street, Marquette, Michigan   49855
Telephone: 906-225-1108

Federal Building, 517 East Wisconsin Avenue, Room 246,
Milwaukee, Wisconsin   53202, Telephone: 414-291-3941

500 South Barstow Street, Room 16, Federal Office Building &
U.S. Courthouse, Eau Claire, Wisconsin   54701
Telephone: 715-834-9012

Region 6

5000 Marble Avenue, N.E., Patio Plaza Building, Albuquerque,
New Mexico   87100, Telephone: 505-262-6171

2525 Murworth, Houston, Texas   77054, Telephone: 713-660-4401

320 West Capitol Avenue, Little Rock, Arkansas   72201
Telephone: 501-378-5871

1611 Tenth Street, Lubbock, Texas   79401, Telephone: 806-762-7466

222 East Van Buren Street, Harlingen, Texas   78550 Telephone: 512-423-8934

100 South Washington Street, Marshall, Texas   75670
Telephone: 214-935-5257

1661 Canal Street, New Orleans, Louisiana   70113
Telephone: 504-589-6685

200 N.W. 5th Street, Suite 670, Oklahoma City, Oklahoma
73102, Telephone: 405-231-4301

727 E. Durango, Room A-513, San Antonio, Texas   78206
Telephone: 512-229-6250

1100 Commerce Street, Dallas, Texas   75242, Telephone: 214-767-0605

10737 Gateway W., Suite 320, El Paso, Texas   79902
Telephone: 915-541-7586

400 Main Street, Corpus Christi, Texas   78401, Telephone: 512-888-3331

Region 7

New Federal Building, 210 Walnut Street, Room 749, Des Moines,
Iowa   50309, Telephone: 515-284-4422

11145 Mill Valley Road, Omaha, Nebraska   68154, Telephone:
402-221-4691

815 Olive Street, St. Louis, Missouri   63101, Telephone: 314-425-6600

110 East Waterman, Wichita, Kansas   67202, Telephone: 316-269-6571

Region 8

Room 4001, Federal Building, 100 East B Street, Casper,
Wyoming   82601, Telephone: 307-261-5761

301 S. Park, Room 528, Helena, Montana   59626, Telephone:
406-449-5381

Federal Building, 657 2nd Avenue, North, Room 218, Fargo,
North Dakota   58102, Telephone: 701-237-5771

Federal Building, 125 South State Street, Room 2237, Salt Lake
City, Utah   84138, Telephone: 801-524-5800

101 South Main Avenue, Sioux Falls, South Dakota   57102
Telephone: 605-336-2980

Region 9

300 Ala Moana Boulevard, Honolulu, Hawaii   96850, Telephone:
808-546-8950

350 S. Figueroa Street, Los Angeles, California   90071
Telephone: 213-688-2956

211 Main Street, San Francisco, California   94105, Telephone:
415-974-0642

2005 N. Central Avenue, Phoenix, Arizona   85004, Telephone:
602-261-3732

880 Front Street, San Diego, California   92101, Telephone:
619-293-5440

301 E. Stewart, Las Vegas, Nevada   89121, Telephone: 702-388-
6611

2202 Monterey Street, Fresno, California   93721, Telephone:
209-487-5189

Region 10

1020 Main Street, Boise, Idaho   83702, Telephone: 208-334-
1696

1220 S.W. Third Avenue, Portland, Oregon   97205, Telephone:
503-423-5221

W. 920 Riverside Avenue, Spokane, Washington   99201,
Telephone: 509-456-3783

8th & C Streets, Anchorage, Alaska   99501, Telephone: 907-
271-4022

MINORITY BUSINESS DEVELOPMENT AGENCY

Atlanta Regional Office

Carlton Eccles
Atlanta Region
MBDA Regional Director
1371 Peachtree Street, N.W., Suite 505
Atlanta, Georgia   30309
Telephone: 404-881-4091

Rudy Suarez
MBDA District Officer
930 Federal Building
Miami, Florida   33130
Telephone: 305-350-5054

Chicago Regional Office

David Vega
Chicago Region
MBDA Regional Director
55 E. Monroe St., Room 1440
Chicago, Illinois   60603
Telephone: 312-353-0182

Dallas Regional Office

Melda Cabrera
Dallas Region
MBDA Acting Regional Director
1100 Commerce, Room 7B19
Dallas, Texas   75242
Telephone: 214-767-8001

New York Regional Office

Georgina Sanchez
MBDA Regional Director
26 Federal Plaza, Suite 37-20
New York, New York   10278
Telephone: 212-264-3262

R. K. Schwartz
MBDA District Officer
441 Stuart Street, 9th Floor
Boston, Massachusetts   02116
Telephone: 617-223-3726

San Francisco Regional Office

Xavier Mena
San Francisco Region
MBDA Regional Director
221 Main Street, Room 1280
San Francisco, California   94102
Telephone: 415-974-9597

Rudy Guerra
MBDA District Officer
2500 Wilshire Boulevard, Room 908
Los Angeles, California   90057
Telephone: 213-688-7157

OTHER GOVERNMENT AGENCIES

THE FEDERAL TRADE COMMISSION
Bureau of Enforcement
Sixth Street and Pennsylvania Avenue, N.W.
Washington, D.C.   20580

Provides information about legal aspects of franchising
specifically on disclosure regulations and contracts.

SUPERINTENDENT OF DOCUMENTS
U.S. Government Printing Office
Washington, D.C.   20402

Publishes and distributes government documents including the
annual publications FRANCHISING IN THE ECONOMY and
FRANCHISE OPPORTUNITIES HANDBOOK.

B. NON-PROFIT ORGANIZATIONS

    The following organizations provide assistance concerning
the franchise industry:

AMERICAN BAR ASSOCIATION
FORUM ON FRANCHISING
750 North Lake Shore Drive
Chicago, Illinois   60611

Founded in 1977, the FORUM ON FRANCHISING is the preeminent
legal source on franchising. The FORUM provides current and
authoritative information on important developments in franchising including product and business format franchising and
offers its members the opportunity to study and discuss
significant issues with colleagues and experts from the
public and private sectors. Publishes the FRANCHISE LAW
JOURNAL, THE MONOGRAPH SERIES, and the FORUM MEMBERSHIP
DIRECTORY. Sponsors meetings and seminars. Provides sources
of information on all aspects of franchising law.

AMERICAN FRANCHISE ASSOCIATION
12077 Wilshire Boulevard
Suite 750
Los Angeles, California   90025
Telephone: 213-829-0841

Organization for franchise owners, accountants, attorneys, and
others involved in the franchiseing industry. Provides information on franchising trends.

COUNCIL OF BETTER BUSINESS BUREAUS, INC.
1515 Wilson Boulevard
Arlington, Virginia   22209

Maintains files on selected franchising firms. The Council
provides addresses of local Better Business Bureaus.

INTERNATIONAL FRANCHISE ASSOCIATION, see pages 125 and 126.

NATIONAL ASSOCIATION OF FRANCHISE COMPANIES
P.O. Box 6996
Hollywood, Florida   33081

Telephone: 305-966-1530
Executive Director: Edward J. Foley

Organization of franchised companies. Promotes the industry
through public information, business shows, and maintenance of
a speakers bureau.

INTERNATIONAL FRANCHISE ASSOCIATION AND ITS CODE OF ETHICS

INTERNATIONAL FRANCHISE ASSOCIATION
1350 New York Avenue
Suite 900
Washington, D.C.   20005
Telephone: 202-628-8000
President and Chief Operating Office: William B. Cherkasky

Founded in 1960 as a non-profit trade association by a
group of franchise company executives.

The IFA: speaks on behalf of the franchising industry
before government bodies and the general public; provides
services to member companies and others interested in franchising and licensed distribution; sets standards of business
practices through, among other means, a Code of Ethics; provides franchise data and information; offers educational programs to managers and executives; and provides a forum for
exchange of experiences among its member companies.

The IFA provides information on the industry through its
books, pamphlets, periodicals, educational forums, and conferences. Franchised companies must meet IFA standards for
membership by meeting the requirements involving financial
stability, length of time in business, and compliance with
state and federal dislcosure regulations.

The IFA Code of Ethics reads as follows:

I. In the advertisement and grant of franchises or dealerships
a member shall comply with all applicable laws and regulations
and the member's offering circulars shall be complete, accu-
rate and not misleading with respect to the franchisee's or
dealer's investment, the obligations of the member and the
franchisee or dealer under the franchise or dealership and all
material facts relating to the franchise or dealership.

II. All matters material to the member's franchise or
dealership shall be contained in one or more written
agreements, which shall clearly set forth the terms of the
relationship and the respective rights and obligations of the
parties.

III. A member shall select and accept only those franchisees or dealers who, upon reasonable investigation, appear to possess the basic skills, education, experience, personal characteristics and financial resources requisite to conduct the franchised business or dealership and meet the obligations of the franchisee or dealer under the franchise and other agreements. There shall be no discrimination in the granting of franchises based solely on race, color, religion, national origin, or sex. However, this in no way prohibits a franchisor from granting franchises to prospective franchisees as part of a program to make franchises available to persons lacking the capital, training, business experience, or other qualifications ordinarily required of franchisees or any other affirmative action program adopted by the franchisor.

IV. A member shall provide reasonable guidelines to its franchisees or dealers in a manner consistent with its franchise agreement.

V. Fairness shall characterize all dealings between a member and its franchisees or dealers. A member shall make every good faith effort to resolve complaints by and disputes with its franchisees through direct communication and negotiation. To the extent reasonably appropriate in the circumstances, a member shall give its franchisee or dealer notice of, and a reasonable opportunity to cure, a breach of their contractual relationship.

VI. No member shall engage in the pyramid system of distribution. A pyramid is a system wherein a buyer's future compensation is expected to be based primarily upon recruitment of new participants, rather than upon the sale of products or services.

C. FRANCHISING CONSULTING FIRMS

        Consulting firms offer the expertise of specialists in the field of franchising. The following consultants provide franchising information in various forms among which are seminars, publications, and personal consultation.

FRANCHISE CAPITAL CORPORATION (FCC)
1935 Camino Vida Roble
Carlsbad, California   92008
Telephone: 800-FCC-7899
             619-431-9100

Donna A. Feinhandler, Executive Vice-President

FCC was organized in 1984 to provide professional assistance
and competitive financing to experienced franchise entrepreneurs while simultaneously offering investors an opportunity
to become a part of the franchise industry. FCC's financing
program may be used to develop new locations, to remodel
existing establishments, to acquire new locations, and to
refinance existing locations.

FRANCHISE DEVELOPMENT SERVICES LTD.
Castle House
Castle Meadow
Norwich NR2 1PJ
England
Telephone: (0603) 62301/667024

Publishes the UNITED KINGDOM FRANCHISE DIRECTORY and THE
FRANCHISE MAGAZINE. Sponsors seminars on "How to Franchise
Your Business."

FRANCHISE RECRUITERS LTD.
Chicago: 3500 Innsbruck
                      Lincolnshire Country Club
                      Crete, Illinois   60417
                      Telephone: 312-757-5595

Washington, D.C.: 2201 Wisconsin Avenue, N.W.
                   Suite C-120
                   Washington, D.C.   20007
                   Telephone: 202-337-1277

Jerry C. Wilkerson, President

An executive search company dedicated exclusively to
franchising, representing franchisors. Publishes Franchise
Recruiters Ltd. NEWSLETTER.

FRANCHISE SYSTEMS INTERNATIONAL, INC.
1449 W. Littleton Blvd.
Suite 100
P.O. Box 1219
Littleton, Colorado   80160
Telephone: 303-730-0350

Carol B. Green, President

Provides franchise consulting and marketing.

FRANCORP
Chicago: 20200 Governors Drive
                      Olympia Fields, Illinois   60461
                      Telephone: 312-481-2900

Los Angeles: 6033 W. Century Boulevard
                      Los Angeles, California   90045
                      Telephone: 213-338-0600

Donald D. Boroian, Chairman and Chief Executive Officer
Patrick J. Boroian, President
Annette Knight, Vice-President, Western Region
Michael P. Boroian, Executive Vice-President

Presents "Franchise Your Business" seminars for business
owners and CEOs.

NATIONAL FRANCHISE SERVICES, INC.
1661 East Camelback Road
Suite 118
Phoenix, Arizona   85016
Telephone: 602-263-1225

Kenneth M. Hollowell, President/CEO

A professional franchise consulting company that specializes
in consulting with clients so that they can legally market
franchises and also teaches clients how to successfully market
their franchises.

SOMMERS RETAIL EXPANSION CONSULTANTS, INC.
50 East Palisade Avenue
Suite 322
Englewood, N.J.   07631
Telephone: 201-871-0370

Ronald Sommers, President

Designed to provide prospective franchisors with guidelines
for planning, designing, and implementing the total franchise
program.

D. INTERNATIONAL FRANCHISING ORGANIZATIONS

The following are overseas trade associations on franchising:

Association of Canadian Franchisors
44 Laird Dr.
Toronto, Canada   M4G 3T2

Belgian Franchising Association
rue saint-bernard, 60
b 1060-Brussels
Belgium

British Franchise Association
75a Bell Street
Henley-on-Thames
Oxon RG9 2BD
England

Danish Franchisor Association
Pilestrade 52
1112 Copenhagen K
Denmark

Dutch Franchise Association
Arubalaan 4
1213 VG Hilversum
The Netherlands

European Franchise Association
Home Tune House
Effingham, Leatherhead
Surrey
England

Franchisors Association of Australia
7/123 Clarence Street
Sydney, NSW 2000
Australia

French Franchise Federation
9 Boulevard des Italiens
75002 Paris
France

Irish Franchise Association
13 Frankfield Terrace
Summerhill South, Cork
Republic of Ireland

Italian Franchise Association
20121 Milano
c.so di porta nuova 3
Italy

Japan Franchise Association
Elsa Building, 3-13-12 Roppongi
Minato-ku
Tokyo
Japan

South African Franchise Association
P.O. Box 260722
Excom 2023
Johannesburg
South Africa

Swedish Franchise Association
Box 5039
S--181 05 Lidingo
Sweden

Swiss Franchise Association
5 Avenue du Maie
CH-1205 Geneva
Switzerland

APPENDIX II
JOURNALS, NEWSLETTERS, AND NEWSPAPERS

Listed are journals, newsletters, and newspapers with articles on franchising.

Some periodicals listed are exclusively devoted to the field of franchising, others cover other subjects such as marketing, management, small business management, the food service industry, and law. The latter titles such as MONEY MAGAZINE, BLACK ENTERPRISE, and VENTURE will feature articles on franchising as it relates to the scope of the periodical. In other examples, AUTOMOTIVE NEWS will treat franchised car dealerships and NATION'S RESTAURANT will discuss fast food chains. Other journal titles may be located by scanning periodical indexes and online databases which are listed in the appendixes.

ABA JOURNAL: THE LAWYER'S MAGAZINE
ABA Press
American Bar Association
750 N. Lake Shore Drive
Chicago, Illinois   60611
V. 1, 1915-   15/yr (ISSN 0747-0088), $36 to non-members
Includes articles on legal aspects of franchising.
Indexed: CURRENT CONTENTS, HISTORICAL ABSTRACTS, INDEX TO LEGAL PERIODICALS, PUBLIC AFFAIRS INFORMATION SERVICE, SOCIAL SCIENCES CITATION INDEX, AMERICAN BIBLIOGRAPHY OF SLAVIC AND EASTERN EUROPEAN STUDIES, AMERICA: HISTORY AND LIFE, CURRENT LAW INDEX, CRIMINAL JUSTICE PERIODICAL INDEX, PERSONNEL LITERATURE, RISK ABSTRACTS, CRIMINAL JUSTICE ABSTRACTS.

AMERICAN JOURNAL OF SMALL BUSINESS
University of Baltimore
School of Business
Charles at Mount Royal
Baltimore, Maryland   21201

V. 1, 1976-   Quarterly (ISSN 0363-9428), $16 per year,
individuals; $30 per year, institutions.
Articles are scholarly works of both an empirical and
conceptual nature.
Indexed: BUSINESS PERIODICALS INDEX, PUBLIC AFFAIRS
INFORMATION SERVICE, SCIENCE ABSTRACTS, BUSINESS INDEX,
BUSINESS PUBLICATIONS INDEX AND ABSTRACTS.

ANTITRUST AND TRADE REGULATION REPORT
Bureau of National Affairs (BNA)
1231 25th Street, N.W.
Washington, D.C.   20037
V. 1, 1961- Weekly (ISSN 0003-6021), $596 per year
Reports current antitrust and trade regulation developments
including current information on state and federal franchising
legislation and court decisions.   An Index-Summary is provided
with service.   Looseleaf format.   Also available online.
Vendors: Mead Data Central and Westlaw.

ANTITRUST BULLETIN
Federal Legal Publications, Inc.
157 Chambers Street
New York, N.Y.   10007
V. 1, 1955- (ISSN 0003-603x) Quarterly $72 per year for
academic and government personnel.
Features articles on franchising and antitrust law.
Indexed: INDEX TO LEGAL PERIODICALS, PUBLIC AFFAIRS
INFORMATION SERVICE, ABSTRACTS OF BOOK REVIEWS IN CURRENT
LEGAL PERIODICALS, BUSINESS PUBLICATIONS INDEX AND ABSTRACTS,
BUSINESS INDEX, CURRENT LAW INDEX, LEGAL RESOURCES INDEX,
TRADE AND INDUSTRY INDEX.

ANTITRUST LAW AND ECONOMICS REVIEW
Antitrust Law and Economics Review, Inc.
Beach P.O. Box 3532
Vero Beach, Florida   32964
V. 1, 1967- (ISSN 0003-6048) Quarterly, $77.50 per year
Articles on legal aspects of franchising included.
Indexed: BUSINESS PERIODICALS INDEX, PUBLIC AFFAIRS
INFORMATION SERVICE, BUSINESS PUBLICATIONS INDEX AND
ABSTRACTS, BUSINESS INDEX, CURRENT LAW INDEX, LEGAL RESOURCES
INDEX.

ANTITRUST LAW JOURNAL
American Bar Association
Antitrust Law Section
750 N. Lake Shore Drive
Chicago, Illinois   60611

V. 1, 1968- 4/yr. (ISSN 0003-6056) $22 per year to non-members of Section.
Features proceedings of meetings.
Indexed: INDEX TO LEGAL PERIODICALS, CURRENT LAW INDEX, LEGAL RESOURCES INDEX.

AUTOMOTIVE NEWS: ENGINEERING, MANUFACTURING, SALES, MARKETING, SERVICING
Crain Communications, Inc. (Detroit)
Automotive News
1400 Woodbridge Avenue
Detroit, Michigan 48207
V. 1, 1925- Weekly, (ISSN 0005-1551) $50 per year.
Features articles on franchised dealerships.
Indexed: BUSINESS PERIODICALS INDEX, BUSINESS INDEX, PROMT, TRADE AND INDUSTRY INDEX.

BARRON'S: THE WEEKLY BUSINESS NEWSPAPER FOR INFORMED INVESTORS
200 Liberty Street
New York, N.Y. 10281
Weekly, (ISSN 0005-6073), $92 per year
Features news items on franchising.

BLACK ENTERPRISE
Earl G. Graves Publishing Co., Inc.
130 Fifth Avenue
New York, N.Y. 10011
V. 1, 1970- Monthly (ISSN 0006-4165) $15 per year
Articles and reports on Black American entrepreneurs.
Features the "Black Enterprise Franchise 50" issue, a ranking of franchises based on the number of their black franchise units.
Indexed: BUSINESS PERIODICALS INDEX, BOOK REVIEW INDEX, BUSINESS INDEX, MAGAZINE INDEX, POPULAR MAGAZINE REVIEW, TRADE AND INDUSTRY INDEX, WORK RELATED ABSTRACTS.

BUSINESS WEEK
McGraw-Hill Publications Co.
1221 Avenue of the Americas
New York, N.Y. 10020
V. 1, 1929- Weekly (ISSN 0007-7135), $39.95 per year
Source of information on recent trends in franchising.
Indexed: BUSINESS PERIODICALS INDEX, CHEMICAL ABSTRACTS, OCEANIC ABSTRACTS, POLLUTION ABSTRACTS, READERS' GUIDE TO PERIODICAL LITERATURE, ABRIDGED READERS' GUIDE TO PERIODICAL LITERATURE, ABSTRAX, BMT ABSTRACTS (BRITISH MARITIME TECHNOLOGY), BUSINESS PUBLICATIONS INDEX AND ABSTRACTS, BANKING LITERATURE INDEX, BOOK REVIEW INDEX, BUSINESS INDEX, COMPUTER BUSINESS, COMPUTER INDUSTRY UPDATE, COMPUTER LITERATURE INDEX, CURRENT LITERATURE IN FAMILY PLANNING,

CURRENT PACKAGING ABSTRACTS, OPERATIONS RESEARCH/MANAGEMENT
SCIENCE, FUTURE SURVEY, HIGHER EDUCATION CURRENT AWARENESS
BULLETIN, KEY TO ECONOMIC SCIENCE, MANAGEMENT CONTENTS,
MICROCOMPUTER INDEX, MAGAZINE INDEX, POPULAR MAGAZINE REVIEW,
PERSONNEL LITERATURE, RESOURCE CENTER INDEX, MANAGEMENT AND
MARKETING ABSTRACTS, ROBOMATIX REPORTER, TRADE AND INDUSTRY
INDEX, TEXTILE TECHNOLOGY DIGEST.
Available online through: DIALOG, MEAD DATA CENTRAL

CHOICES: FOR ENTREPRENEURIAL WOMEN
Entrepreneur, Inc.
2311 Pontius Avenue
Los Angeles, California   90064
V. 1, 1985- Monthly (ISSN 0884-0989)
Magazine for women entrepreneurs and franchise buyers and
owners.

CONTINENTAL FRANCHISE REVIEW
National Research Publications, Inc.
P.O. Box 6360
Denver, Colorado   80206
V. 1, 1968- 26/yr. (ISSN 0045-8376) $135 per year
Source of information on legal and legislative developments,
new operational techniques, business trends affecting
franchise growth, financing, marketing methods, franchisor-
franchisee relations, etc. Features articles, reports on
seminars and legislative and regulatory hearings, book
reviews.

D & B REPORTS: THE DUN AND BRADSTREET MAGAZINE FOR SMALL
BUSINESS MANAGEMENT.
Dun & Bradstreet Credit Services
99 Church Street
New York, N.Y.   10007
V. 27, No. 3- May/June 1979- Bi-Monthly. (ISSN 0746-6110)
Articles on small business including franchising trends.
Indexed: BUSINESS INDEX, MANAGEMENT ABSTRACTS, MANAGEMENT
CONTENTS, PROMT, POPULAR MAGAZINE REVIEW.

ENTREPRENEUR MAGAZINE
Entrepreneur Group, Inc.
2311 Pontius Avenue
Los Angeles, California   90064
V. 1, 1973- Monthly (ISSN 0163-3341) $17.97 per year.
Magazine for entrepreneurs, prospective franchisees, and
investors. Features "Franchise News" section as well as
articles and case studies on franchising. Publishes the
annual "Franchise 500" issue, a ranking of franchises by such
variables as number of franchised units, start-up costs,

growth rate, etc. "Franchise 500" listing is indexed by
company name.
Indexed: PUBLIC AFFAIRS INFORMATION SERVICE, POPULAR MAGAZINE
REVIEW.

FORBES
Forbes, Inc.
60 Fifth Avenue
New York, N.Y.   10011
V. 1, 1917- Fortnightly (ISSN 0015-6914), $42 per year
Includes features on franchises.
Indexed: BUSINESS PERIODICALS INDEX, CHEMICAL ABSTRACTS, DATA
PROCESSING DIGEST, READERS' GUIDE ABSTRACTS, BUSINESS
PUBLICATIONS INDEX AND ABSTRACTS, BANKING LITERATURE INDEX,
BUSINESS INDEX, COMPUTER LITERATURE INDEX, COMPUTER BUSINESS,
KEY TO ECONOMIC SCIENCE, MAGAZINE INDEX, MANAGEMENT CONTENTS,
PROMT, REHABILITATION LITERATURE, ROBOMATIX REPORTER, TRADE
AND INDUSTRY INDEX.
Available online through: DIALOG, MEAD DATA CENTRAL.

FORTUNE MAGAZINE
Time, Inc.
Time & Life Building
1271 Avenue of the Americas
New York, N.Y.   10020
Subscriptions to:
Time Inc.
541 N. Fairbanks Ct.
Chicago, Illinois   60611
V. 1, 1930- Bi-Weekly, $39 per year
Includes studies of franchises.
Indexed: BUSINESS PERIODICALS INDEX, OPERATIONS
RESEARCH/MANAGEMENT SCIENCE, EXCERPTA MEDICA, INTERNATIONAL
MANAGEMENT INFORMATION BUSINESS DIGEST, EXECUTIVE SCIENCE
INSTITUTE, PAIS, READERS' GUIDE TO PERIODICAL LITERATURE,
SCIENCE ABSTRACTS, AMERICAN BIBLIOGRAPHY OF SLAVIC AND EAST
EUROPEAN STUDIES, INSTITUTE OF PAPER CHEMISTRY. ABSTRACT
BULLETIN, BMT ABSTRACTS (BRITISH MARITIME TECHNOLOGY),
BUSINESS PUBLICATIONS INDEX AND ABSTRACTS, BUSINESS INDEX,
COMPUTER INDUSTRY UPDATE, COMPUTER LITERATURE INDEX, COMPUTER
BUSINESS, FUEL AND ENERGY ABSTRACTS, INTERNATIONAL AEROSPACE
ABSTRACTS, OCEANIC ABSTRACTS, KEY TO ECONOMIC SCIENCE,
MAGAZINE INDEX, POLLUTION ABSTRACTS, MANAGEMENT CONTENTS,
MANAGEMENT AND MARKETING ABSTRACTS, POPULAR MAGAZINE REVIEW,
PROMT, RESOURCE CENTER INDEX, ROBOMATIX REPORTER, SELECTED
WATER RESOURCE ABSTRACTS, WORK RELATED ABSTRACTS, TEXTILE
TECHNOLOGY DIGEST, TRADE AND INDUSTRY INDEX.
Available online through: VU/TEXT INFORMATION SERVICES, INC.

FRANCHISE LAW JOURNAL
American Bar Association Press
750 North Lake Shore Drive
Chicago, Illinois   60611
V. 1, 1980- 4/yr. $30 to nonmembers
Articles on legal aspects of franchising.
Indexed: INDEX TO LEGAL PERIODICALS, CURRENT LAW INDEX, LEGAL
RESOURCE INDEX, LEGAL INFORMATION MANAGEMENT INDEX

FRANCHISE LAW REVIEW
International Franchise Association
1350 New York Avenue, N.W.
Suite 900
Washington, D.C.   20005
V. 1. Winter 1986- 2/yr.
Scholarly articles on franchise law published in law school
journals and business law and bar association publications are
reproduced in the FRANCHISE LAW REVIEW.

FRANCHISE LEGAL DIGEST
International Franchise Association
1350 New York Avenue, N.W.
Suite 900
Washington, D.C.   20005
V. 1, 1973- Monthly, looseleaf format.
Reports on recent developments in franchise law.

THE FRANCHISE MAGAZINE
Franchise Development Services Ltd.
Castle House
Castle Meadow
Norwich NR2 IPJ
England
V. 1, 1985- Quarterly,   (ISSN 0268-8395)
Articles on franchise opportunities with emphasis on the
industry in the United Kingdom. Describes current trends,
franchise success stories and includes book reviews and
advertisements of new opportunities.

FRANCHISE: THE MAGAZINE
P.O. Box 591005
Houston, Texas   77259
V. 1, 1985- Bi-Monthly
Forum for discussion of all aspects of franchise industry.

FRANCHISE WORLD
Franchise Publications
James House

37 Nottingham Road
London SW17 7EA
England
No. 1, 1978-   Quarterly (ISSN 0144-0543)
Articles about new franchises, workshops with franchise
directory in each issue (by product), emphasis on United
Kingdom franchises.

FRANCHISING WORLD
International Franchise Association
1350 New York Avenue, N.W.
Suite 900
Washington, D.C.   20005
V. 1, 1960-   6/yr.
News of conferences, legislation, calendar of events.
Features case studies, recent developments in the United
States and overseas, and advertisements of new opportunities.

HOTEL & MOTEL MANAGEMENT
Harcourt Brace Jovanovich Inc.
7500 Old Oak Blvd.
Cleveland, Ohio   44130
Subscriptions to:
One E. First Street
Duluth, Minnesota   55802
V. 1, 1875-   18/yr. (ISSN 0018-6082) $25 per year
Case studies of hotel and motel chains, advertisements of new
opportunities in franchised hotels and motels; and news of
food, beverage, and restaurant industry.
Indexed: BUSINESS PERIODICALS INDEX, TRADE & INDUSTRY INDEX,
BUSINESS INDEX.

IFA FRANCHISE INSIDER
International Franchise Association
1350 New York Avenue, N.W.
Suite 900
Washington, D.C.   20005
Monthly
New information on laws, conferences, legislation, etc.

IN BUSINESS
J.G. Press, Inc.
Box 351
Emmaus, Pennsylvania   18049
V. 1, 1979-   Bi-Monthly (ISSN 0190-2458)
Articles on small business management, including franchise
information.
Indexed: BUSINESS INDEX, SCIENCE ABSTRACTS.

INC.
Inc. Publishing Co.
38 Commercial Wharf
Boston, Massachusetts   02109
Subscriptions to:
Box 2538
Boulder, Colorado   80321
V. 1, 1979-   Monthly (ISSN 0612-8968)
Articles on business ventures, including franchise
opportunities.
Indexed: BUSINESS INDEX, BUSINESS PERIODICALS INDEX, CIS
ABSTRACTS, MAGAZINE INDEX, PROMT, REHABILITATION LITERATURE,
TRADE AND INDUSTRY INDEX.

INCOME OPPORTUNITIES
Davis Publications, Inc.
380 Lexington Avenue
New York, N.Y.   10017
Subscriptions to:
Box 1931
Marion, Ohio   43305
V. 1, 1952-   Monthly, (ISSN 0019-3429) $7.95 per
year. Features monthly column, "Franchise Roundtable," by
Bryce Webster.

INFO FRANCHISE NEWSLETTER
Info Press, Inc.
736 Center Street
Lewiston, N.Y.   14092
or
11 Bond Street
St. Catharines
ONT L2R 4Z4
Canada
V. 1, 1977- Monthly (ISSN 0147-5924) $80 per year
Issues contain news reports on franchises including
litigation, legislation, new franchise listings, announcements
of courses and conferences, new publications. Info Press is
the publisher of the FRANCHISE ANNUAL (see DIRECTORIES OF
FRANCHISING OPPORTUNITIES chapter).

JOURNAL OF INTERNATIONAL FRANCHISING AND DISTRIBUTION LAW
International Franchise Association
1350 New York Avenue, N.W.
Suite 900
Washington, D.C.   20005
V. 1, 1986-   Quarterly (ISSN 0950-365X), $90 per year
Sold and distributed in North America and Mexico exclusively
by the International Franchise Association. Articles concern

international franchising and distribution, with emphasis on
legal and tax issues.

JOURNAL OF SMALL BUSINESS MANAGEMENT
International Council for Small Business
West Virginia University
Bureau of Business Research
Box 6025
Morgantown, West Virginia   25405
V. 1, 1963- Quarterly (ISSN 0047-2778)
Includes articles on recent developments in franchising.
Indexed: BUSINESS PERIODICALS INDEX, PUBLIC AFFAIRS
INFORMATION SERVICE, BUSINESS PUBLICATIONS INDEX AND
ABSTRACTS, MANAGEMENT CONTENTS, MAGAZINE INDEX, PERSONNEL
MANAGEMENT ABSTRACTS, TRADE AND INDUSTRY INDEX.

MONEY
Time, Inc.
Time & Life Building
New York, N.Y.   10020
Subscriptions to:
P.O. Box 54429
Boulder, Colorado   80322
V. 1, 1972 -   Monthly   (ISSN 0149-4953)
Magazine on investment opportunities features articles on
franchising.
Indexed: BUSINESS PERIODICALS INDEX, PUBLIC AFFAIRS
INFORMATION SERVICE, READERS GUIDE TO PERIODICAL LITERATURE,
ABSTRAX, BUSINESS PUBLICATIONS INDEX AND ABSTRACTS, BOOK
REVIEW INDEX, BANKING LITERATURE INDEX, BUSINESS WEEK,
CONSUMERS INDEX, MAGAZINE INDEX, POPULAR MAGAZINE INDEX, TRADE
AND INDUSTRY INDEX.

NATION'S BUSINESS
Chamber of Commerce of the United States
1615 H Street, N.W.
Washington, D.C.   20062
V. 1, 1912- Monthly (ISSN 0028-047X), $22 per year
Features franchise case histories, "how-to" articles on
finding franchises, classified advertisements on franchise
opportunities.
Indexed: BUSINESS PERIODICALS INDEX, BUSINESS PUBLICATIONS
INDEX AND ABSTRACTS, BUSINESS INDEX, BANK LIT. INDEX,
MANAGEMENT CONTENTS, PERSONNEL LITERATURE, MICROCOMP. IND.
MAGAZINE INDEX, PMR, PROMT, WORK RELATED ABSTRACTS, TRADE &
INDUSTRY INDEX, R.G. ABSTRAX.

NATION'S RESTAURANT NEWS
Lebhar-Friedman Inc.

425 Park Avenue
New York, N.Y.   10022
Weekly, $59 per year
Includes articles on fast food franchises.
Indexed: PROMT, TRADE AND INDUSTRY INDEX; available online
through DIALOG.

OCCUPATIONAL OUTLOOK QUARTERLY
    see U.S. BUREAU OF LABOR STATISTICS. OCCUPATIONAL OUTLOOK
    QUARTERLY

RESTAURANT BUSINESS
Bill Communications, Inc.
633 Third Avenue
New York, N.Y.   10017
V. 1, 1902-   (ISSN 0097-8043) Monthly (except semi-monthly in
March, May, and September), $54 per year
Features articles on fast food chains; good source for case
history of chain restaurants.
Indexed: FOOD SCIENCE AND TECHNOLOGY ABSTRACTS, BUSINESS
INDEX, BUSINESS PERIODICALS INDEX, PROMT, TRADE AND INDUSTRY
INDEX

RESTAURANT HOSPITALITY: THE RESTAURANT PEOPLE MAGAZINE
Penton Publishing
1100 Superior Avenue
Cleveland, Ohio   44114
V. 1, 1919-   (ISSN 0147-9989) Monthly, $40 per year
Features news on fast food industry.
Indexed: BUSINESS INDEX, TRADE AND INDUSTRY INDEX, PROMT

RESTAURANTS USA
National Restaurant Association
311 First Street, N.W.
Washington, D.C.   20001
V. 1, 1919- 11/yr.   (ISSN 0465-7004), $125 per year
News items on fast food franchises. Publishes the
"Statistical Appendix to Foodservice Trends" article on
franchise restaurants, which appears each March. The
"Appendix" gives up-to-date sales and operations data of a
generic nature on franchises in various food service segments.
The cost of the "Appendix" is $15 to members and $30 to non-
members.
Indexed: PROMT

SECRETS OF WINNERS
Successful Publishing Co.
P.O. Box 157
Whooping Loop
Altamonte Springs, Florida   32701

V. 1, 1985- (ISSN 0883-8941), $36 per year
With section, "The Franchise Advisor," on case histories of
companies.

SMALL BUSINESS USA
National Small Business United
1155 15th Street, N.W.
Suite 710
Washington, D.C.   20005
Telephone: 202-293-8830
V. 1, 1988-   Monthly, $30 per year (subscription rate for
members, included in the annual dues)
Official publication of National Small Business United, an
organization dedicated to the economic improvement of small
companies. Features occasional articles on franchising and
announces conferences and seminars that feature franchising.

SYLVIA PORTER'S PERSONAL FINANCE
Davis Publications
P.O. Box 1928
Marion, Ohio   43306
V. 1, 1983- Monthly, except for combined issues in January &
February and July & August (ISSN 0738-4173), $19.97 per year
Magazine concerns advice on personal finance and investments;
franchises are among topics included.
Indexed: ACCESS: THE SUPPLEMENTARY INDEX TO PERIODICALS

U.S. BUREAU OF LABOR STATISTICS. OCCUPATIONAL OUTLOOK
QUARTERLY
U.S. Bureau of Labor Statistics
441 G Street, N.W.
Washington, D.C.   20212
Orders to:
Superintendent of Documents
Washington, D.C.   20402
V. 1, 1957-   Quarterly, September - June (ISSN 0029-7968)
$5 per year.
Includes articles on opportunities in franchising.
Indexed: PAIS, BUSINESS INDEX, CIJE, INDEX TO U.S. GOVERNMENT
PERIODICALS, MAGAZINE INDEX, PERSONNEL LITERATURE, TRADE AND
INDUSTRY INDEX, WORK RELATED ABSTRACTS

VENTURE
Venture Magazine, Inc.
521 Fifth Avenue
New York, N.Y.   10175
V. 1, 1979- Monthly (ISSN 0191-3530), $18 per year
Current information and case studies of franchises.

Indexed: BUSINESS PERIODICALS INDEX, PAIS, BUSINESS
PUBLICATIONS INDEX AND ABSTRACTS, MANAGEMENT CONTENTS, POPULAR
MAGAZINE REVIEW

VENTURE CAPITAL JOURNAL
Venture Economics, Inc.
16 Laurel Avenue
Wellesley Hills, Massachusetts   02181
Orders to:
Box 348
Wellesley Hills, Massachusetts   02181
V. 1, 1961-   Monthly (ISSN 0883-2773), $495 per year
Provides financial analysis of small business investment
companies and venture capital companies. Venture Economics,
Inc. also publishes PRATT'S GUIDE TO VENTURE CAPITAL SOURCES.

WALL STREET JOURNAL
Dow Jones & Co., Inc.
200 Liberty Street
New York, N.Y.   10007
Subscriptions to:
Box 300
Princeton, New Jersey   08540
V, 1, 1889-   Daily (5/week), $101 per year
News items on franchising; listings of new franchise
opportunities.
Indexed: CHEMICAL ABSTRACTS, PAIS, BOOK REVIEW INDEX, BANKING
LITERATURE INDEX, CHILDREN'S BOOK REVIEW INDEX, FANATIC
READER, FUTURE SURVEY, MEDICAL CARE REVIEW, MUSIC INDEX,
PERSONNEL LITERATURE.
Available online through: DOW JONES/NEWS RETRIEVAL

WORLD FRANCHISE
Franchise Publications
James House
37 Nottingham Road
London SW17 7EA
England
V. 1, 198?-   (ISSN 0144-0543)
Reports on franchises, with emphasis on United Kingdom;
features "Magazine and Franchise Sales Directory."

ABSTRACTS AND INDEXES TO FRANCHISING LITERATURE

    Franchising literature may be found in a variety of journals and books on subjects ranging from the food industry to antitrust law. To access this material, it is necessary to use indexes and abstracts. It is important to note that many of the indexes and abstracts listed are available through on-line databases. WILSONLINE, for instance, is the vendor for the online editions of BUSINESS PERIODICALS INDEX, CUMULATIVE BOOK INDEX, BOOK REVIEW DIGEST, APPLIED SCIENCE & TECHNOLOGY INDEX, BIBLIOGRAPHIC INDEX, BIOGRAPHY INDEX, INDEX TO LEGAL PERIODICALS, and READERS' GUIDE TO PERIODICAL LITERATURE. See also the sections on the databases for listings and coverage. Following is a list of selected printed indexes and abstracts with references to franchising.

ACCOUNTANTS' INDEX
American Institute of Certified Public Accountants
1211 Avenue of the Americas
New York, N.Y.   10036
V. 1, 1920- Quarterly, with annual cumulation (ISSN 0748-7975), $160 per year. Indexes journal articles, accounting statements and publications. Available online through ORBIT Information Technologies.

AMERICAN STATISTICS INDEX (ASI): A COMPREHENSIVE GUIDE AND INDEX TO STATISTICAL PUBLICATIONS OF THE U.S. GOVERNMENT
Congressional Information Service, Inc.
4520 East-West Highway
Bethesda, Maryland   10814
V. 1, 1974- Monthly, with quarterly and annual cumulations (ISSN 0091-1658), price varies. Index to statistics published

by the Federal Government. Issued in two volumes, one for
Index and the other for Abstracts (with description of
statistical publication). Available online through ORBIT
Information Technologies and DIALOG.

APPLIED SCIENCE AND TECHNOLOGY INDEX
H.W. Wilson Co.
950 University Avenue
Bronx, N.Y.   10452
V. 46, 1958- (Monthly, except July, with periodic
cumulations) (ISSN 0003-6986) Subject index to approximately
300 journals in various fields including food and food
industry, transportation, and petroleum, all of which include
franchised companies.

BIBLIOGRAPHIC INDEX
H.W. Wilson Co.
950 University Avenue
Bronx, N.Y.   10452
V. 1, 1937/42- (Semiannual with annual cumulations), (ISSN
0006-1255) Index to bibliographies appearing in books,
pamphlets, and periodicals. BIBLIOGRAPHIC INDEX lists
bibliographies with 50 or more citations.

BIOGRAPHY INDEX
H.W. Wilson Co.
950 University Avenue
Bronx, N.Y.   10452
V. 1, 1949- (Quarterly, with annual cumulations), $95 per
year (ISSN 0006-3053) Indexes biographies appearing in books
and journals. Includes a Name Index, an alphabetical listing
of the biographies and an Index to Professions and Occupa-
tions, an alphabetical listing of professions. Outstanding
individuals in field of franchising are listed.

BOOK REVIEW DIGEST
H.W. Wilson Co.
950 University Avenue
Bronx, N.Y.   10452
V. 1, 1905- (Monthly, except February and July, with annual
cumulations). Index to book reviews appearing in journals,
with excerpts from the reviews. Covers reviews of current
adult and juvenile fiction and non-fiction.

BOOK REVIEW INDEX
Gale Research Co.
Book Tower

Detroit, Michigan   48226
V. 1, 1965- (Monthly, with quarterly and annual cumulations).
Indexes book reviews appearing in journals.

BUSINESS INDEX
Information Access Co.
11 Davis Drive
Belmont, California   94002   (Monthly microfilm reel).
Accessed by microfilm viewer; covers approximately 650
business periodicals plus articles from BARRON'S, WALL STREET
JOURNAL, the NEW YORK TIMES. Also available online through
BRS. DIALOG, MEAD DATA CENTRAL.

BUSINESS PERIODICALS INDEX
H.W. Wilson Co.
950 University Avenue
Bronx, N.Y.   10452
V. 1, 1958-   Monthly with quarterly and annual cumulations
(ISSN 0007-6961)
Covers approximately 300 periodicals in field of business and
management. To locate articles on franchising, look under
subject heading: "Franchise System." Cross references are
provided for specific industries such as "Restaurants,"
"Automobile Dealers," "Computer Stores," "Hotels and Motels,"
etc.

C I S INDEX
Congressional Information Service, Inc.
4520 East-West Highway
Bethesda, Maryland   20814
V. 1, 1970-   Monthly, with quarterly and annual cumulations
(ISSN 0007-8514) Indexes Congressional documents including
Committee hearings, reports, publications of joint committees
and subcommittees, etc. Issued in two sections: Index and
Abstracts (description of publication).
Available online through ORBIT Information Technologies.

COMMERCE CLEARING HOUSE. ACCOUNTING ARTICLES: DESCRIBING
ACCOUNTING ARTICLES PUBLISHED IN ACCOUNTING AND BUSINESS
PERIODICALS, BOOKS-PAMPHLETS
Commerce Clearing House, Inc.
4025 W. Peterson Avenue
Chicago, Illinois   60646
Monthly (ISSN 0007-7992)
Index to articles on franchising as they relate to accounting.

CUMULATIVE BOOK REVIEW INDEX
H.W. Wilson Co.
950 University Avenue

Bronx, N.Y.   10452
V. 1, 1899-   Eleven monthly paperbound issues (no issues in
August) including quarterly cumulations in March, June,
September, and December, plus a permanent annual clothbound
cumulation (ISSN 0011-300x) Permanent record of information
on approximately 50,000 English-language books indexed by
author, title, and subject.

INDEX TO INTERNATIONAL STATISTICS
Congressional Information Inc.
4520 East-West Highway
Bethesda, Maryland   20814
V. 1, 1983-   Monthly with quarterly and annual cumulations
(ISSN 0737-4461) Descriptive guide and index to statistical
publications compiled by international agencies. Issued in
Abstracts and Index volumes.

INDEX TO LEGAL PERIODICALS
H.W. Wilson Co.
950 University Avenue
Bronx, N.Y.   10452
V. 1, 1908- Eleven monthly paperbound issues (no issue in
September), including quarterly cumulations published in
February, May, August, and November, plus a permanent
clothbound annual cumulation. $180 per year. (ISSN 0019-4077)
Index to legal periodicals published in the U.S., Canada,
Great Britain, Ireland, Australia, and New Zealand. Also
offers a Table of Cases arranged alphabetically by name of
plaintiff and defendant; Table of Statutes, arranged by
jurisdiction and listed alphabetically by name; and Book
Reviews of current books relevant to the legal profession.

INDEX TO U.S. GOVERNMENT PERIODICALS
Infordata International, Inc.
Suite 4602
175 E. Delaware Pl.
Chicago, Illinois   60611
V. 1, 1970-   Quarterly plus annual cumulation, $400 per year.
(ISSN 0098-4604) Indexes over 180 periodicals produced by
agencies of the U.S. government including the U.S. Department
of Commerce, Bureau of Economic Analysis, and Economic
Research Service. Indexed by subject and author. Also
available online through BRS and WILSONLINE.

THE LODGING AND RESTAURANT INDEX
American Hotel and Motel Association
Continuing Education Business Office

110 Stewart Center
Purdue University
West Lafayette, Indiana   47907
V. 1, 1985-   Quarterly, with annual cumulation, $95 per year. Published in cooperation with the Restaurant, Hotel, and Institutional Management Institute at Purdue University, and the Hospitality, Lodging & Travel Research Foundation, an affiliate of the American Hotel and Motel Association. Indexes journals with restaurant and hotel franchising articles. Among journals indexed are: HOTEL AND RESORT INDUSTRY, LODGING, LODGING HOSPITALITY, PIZZA TODAY, RESTAURANT BUSINESS, RESTAURANTS USA, and RESTAURANT HOSPITALITY.

MANAGEMENT CONTENTS
FIND SVP
500 5th Avenue
New York, N.Y.   10110
V. 1, 1975- Bi-Weekly, $95 per year (ISSN 0360-2400)
Copies tables of contents from approximately 300 management related journals.   Subject index is included with each issue.

MONTHLY CATALOG OF UNITED STATES GOVERNMENT PUBLICATIONS
U.S. Government Printing Office
Superintendent of Documents
Washington, D.C.   20402
V. 1, 1895-   Monthly, $141 per year (ISSN 0362-6830)
Indexes publications of federal government agencies by author, title, subject, series/report, stock number, and title keyword.   Each publication entry includes author, title, subject headings, Superintendent of Documents call number, and item number.   Also available online through BRS and DIALOG.

PREDI-BRIEFS
Predicasts Inc.
200 University Circle Research Center
11001 Cedar Avenue
Cleveland, Ohio   44106
V.1, 1973-   Monthly, $225 per year (ISSN 0551-9276)
Abstracts articles from business and trade publications. Abstracts articles that offer in-depth coverage of a particular industry.   Organization is by industry subject heading.   Each entry lists publication name, date of issue, and page number.

PREDICASTS BASEBOOK
Predicasts Inc.
200 University Circle Research Center

11001 Cedar Avenue
Cleveland, Ohio   44106
V. 1, 1973-   Annual, $550 per year (ISSN 0093-8025)
Provides historical data on U.S. business and economic
activities. Consists of over 26,000 statistical time series,
each of which features SIC code of subject, description of
event (e.g. production), numeric data covering the previous
fourteen years, unit of measure, title of original source,
and percent annual growth. Data compiled from over three
hundred statistical publications issued by the U.S. government, national trade associations and agencies. Covers
specific industries with emphasis on products and markets.
Entries are arranged by modified SIC system.

PREDICASTS F & S INDEX EUROPE
Predicasts Inc.
200 University Circle Research Center
11001 Cedar Avenue
Cleveland, Ohio   44196
V. 1, 1978-   Monthly with quarterly and annual cumulations
(ISSN 0270-4536), $825 per year. Covers company, product, and
industry information in and Europe. Covers business
activities in the Common Market, Scandinavia, other regions of
Western Europe, the USSR, and Eastern Europe. Entries are
arranged by product using a modified Standard Industrial
Classification (SIC) coding system; by company, with an
alphabetical listing; and by name of country.

PREDICASTS F & S INDEX INTERNATIONAL
Predicasts Inc.
200 University Circle Research Center
11001 Cedar Avenue
Cleveland, Ohio   44196
V. 1, 1967- Monthly, with quarterly and annual cumulations,
$825 per year
(ISSN 0270-4528) Includes information on business activities
in Canada, Latin America, Africa, the Mid East, Asia, and
Oceania. Entries are arranged by product (through modified
SIC code); by company name, in an alphabetical listing; and by
name of country.

PREDICASTS F & S INDEX OF CORPORATE CHANGE
Predicasts Inc.
200 University Circle Research Center
11001 Cedar Avenue
Cleveland, Ohio   44106
V. 1, 1972-   Quarterly plus annual cumulations, $275 per
year, (ISSN 0744-2785) Index to business literature which
covers changes in ownership of U.S. corporations, both public
and private. The one or two line index entries identify the
companies involved, the nature of the change, and include a

complete source citation. Covers over 1500 international
business sources. Provides information on mergers and
acquisitions, reorganizations, bankruptcies, foreign
operations, company formations, etc. Entries are organized
by company (alphabetically), by industry (modified SIC codes),
and by type of event (e.g. mergers and acquisitions).

PREDICASTS F & S INDEX UNITED STATES
Predicasts Inc.
200 University Circle Research Center
11001 Cedar Avenue
Cleveland, Ohio   44106
V. 1, 1960- Monthly, with quarterly and annual cumulations,
$875 per year, $1000 with weekly supplements (ISSN 0270-4544)
Indexes U.S. company, product, and industry information from
approximately 750 journals and newspapers. Industries may be
searched by seven-digit industry codes in "green pages"
section; companies may be searched by name index in "white
pages" section. Available online through BRS and DIALOG.

PREDICASTS FORECASTS
Predicasts Inc.
200 University Circle Research Center
11001 Cedar Avenue
Cleveland, Ohio   44196
V. 1, 1960-   Annual, $775 per year (ISSN 0278-0135)
Economic and market forecast abstracts arranged by product.
Each entry includes forecast subject and SIC code, the event
(e.g. consumption, employment, etc.), quantitites for a Base
Year, Short-Term Projection and Long-Term Projection, unit of
measure, complete source citation and projected annual growth.
Entries are organized by product and industry (modified SIC
code) and an alphabetical cross-reference to SICs is provided
with each issue. The annual volume provides a source section
which includes full bibliographic data and identifies the
specific authority and organizational affiliations for the
respective statistic.

PREDICASTS OVERVIEW OF MARKETS AND TECHNOLOGIES (PROMT)
Predicasts Inc.
200 University Circle Research Center
11001 Cedar Avenue
Cleveland, Ohio 44196
V. 1977-   Monthly, with monthly index; cumulative quarterly
and annual indexes, $925 per year (ISSN 0161-8032) A multi-
industry reference source for finding information on domestic
and international company, product and industry activities.
Provides, each month, over 4000 abstracts of industrial

activities as reported in international business and trade
literature. Abstracts are grouped into 28 major industry
sections. Each abstract is indexed alphabetically by subject
(product, industry, and company) with descriptive co-terms
(production, sales, etc.) listed under each main entry.

PUBLIC AFFAIRS INFORMATION SERVICE BULLETIN (PAIS). New York
(semimonthly, Public Affairs Information Service, Inc.
11 W. 40th Street
New York, N.Y.   10018
V. 1, 1915-   Monthly, $295 per year
Indexes periodical articles, books, pamphlets, government
publications, reports of public and private agencies.

READERS' GUIDE TO PERIODICAL LITERATURE
H.W. Wilson Co.
950 University Avenue
Bronx, N.Y.   10452
V. 1, 1901-   Seventeen paperbound issues plus a permanent
annual clothbound cumulation, $140 per year (ISSN 0034-0464)
Indexes selected U.S. general interest journals. Source of
information on franchising from journals such as TIME,
NEWSWEEK, BUSINESS WEEK, FORBES, etc.

STATISTICAL REFERENCE INDEX (SRI)
Congressional Information Service, Inc.
4520 East-West Highway
Bethesda, Maryland   20814
V. 1, 1980-   Monthly with quarterly and annual cumulations.
(ISSN 0278-694X) Guide to U.S. statistical publications
available from sources other than Federal Government Agencies.
Sources described include trade, professional, and other
nonprofit organizations, state government agencies, commercial
publishers, and university research centers. Issues in
two volumes: one for Index and the other for Abstracts (with
description of statistical publication).

VERTICAL FILE INDEX
H.W. Wilson Co.
950 University Avenue
Bronx, N.Y.   10452
V. 1, 1932/34- (Monthly, except August with annual
cumulations), $42 per year (ISSN 0042-4439) Index to pamphlet
material including selected government publications, selected
university publications, and inexpensive paperbacks.
Offers subject access with bibliographic information and
ordering instructions.

WORLDCASTS
Predicasts Inc.
200 University Circle Research Center
11001 Cedar Avenue
Cleveland, Ohio   44106
V. 1, 1964-   Eight volumes, published annually, $1300 per
year. Abstracts over 60,000 forecasts for products and
markets in countries outside the United States. Each entry
consists of subject and SIC code, the event being forecast,
base period, short- and long-range forecasts, complete source
information and projected annual growth rate. Covers international publications sponsored by government agencies and
bureaus, private industry and trade associations. The eight
volumes issued each year are divided into four distinct
product volumes and four distinct regional volumes.

APPENDIX IV
ONLINE DATABASES

The literature of franchising in book, periodical, and pamphlet form may be located by scanning online databases. The following vendors offer access to databases that provide franchising information:

BRS INFORMATION TECHNOLOGIES

CLASS

COMPUSERVE

DATA-STAR

DIALOG INFORMATION SERVICES, INC.

DOW JONES NEWS/RETRIEVAL

MEAD DATA CENTRAL

NEWSNET, INC.

OCLC ONLINE COMPUTER CENTER, INC.

ORBIT SEARCH SERVICE see under PERGAMON ORBIT INFOLINE

RLIN see under CLASS

THE SOURCE

VU/TEXT INFORMATION SERVICES, INC.

WESTLAW

WILSONLINE

BRS INFORMATION TECHNOLOGIES
1200 Route 7
Latham, New York   12110
Telephone: 800-227-5277
800-345-4277
914-783-1161

The following databases with franchising information are
available through BRS. The names of databases are followed by
acronyms which are used in accessing each file.

ABI/INFORM (INFO). Source: UMI/DATA COURIER. For description
see listing in section on DIALOG INFORMATION SERVICES, INC.

ABSTRACTS OF WORKING PAPERS IN ECONOMICS (AWPE). Source: HAL
WHITE, UNIVERSITY OF CALIFORNIA, SAN DIEGO, DEPARTMENT OF
ECONOMICS.   Contains records from 1982 to the present.
Abstracts economics papers produced by over 60 organizations
including economics departments, graduate business schools,
etc.

BOOKS IN PRINT (BBIP). Source: R.R. BOWKER. For description
see listing in section on DIALOG INFORMATION SERVICES, INC.

BOOKSINFO (BOOK). Source: BRODART. Contains current listings
with monthly updates. Provides citations of English language
monographs currently available from approximately 10,000 U.S.
publishers, including academic and small presses and foreign
publishers.

BOWKER'S INTERNATIONAL SERIALS DATABASE (ULRI). Source: R.R.
BOWKER.   Contains current records, with monthly updates.
Formerly: ULRICH'S INTERNATIONAL PERIODICALS DIRECTORY and
IRREGULAR SERIALS AND ANNUALS.   Directory of periodicals and
serials published in the U.S. and worldwide.

CORPORATE & INDUSTRY RESEARCH REPORTS ONLINE INDEX (CIRR).
Source: J.A. MICROPUBLISHING INC. Contains records from
January 1982 to the present, with quarterly updates.   Indexes
company and industry research reports by major U.S. and
Canadian securities and institutional investment firms.

DISCLOSURE/HISTORY DATABASE (DSCH). Source: DISCLOSURE
INFORMATION GROUP. Contains records from 1978-1985, with
monthly updates. Historical data for corporations from
information filed with the Securities and Exchange
Commission. Company descriptions are from 10-K, 10-Q, 8-K
reports, annual reports, proxy statements, and registration
statements.

DISCLOSURE ONLINE DATABASE (DSCL). Source: DISCLOSURE
INFORMATION GROUP. Contains current information with weekly
updates. Provides financial data from reports filed with the
Securities and Exchange Commission. Information for
approximately 11,000 public companies from U.S. and foreign
companies includes: name, address, exchange, ticker symbol,
balance sheets, income statements, etc.

DISCLOSURE/SPECTRUM OWNERSHIP DATABASE (OWNR). Source:
DISCLOSURE INFORMATION GROUP. Contains current information
with quarterly updates. Indexes corporate and stock ownership
information for approximately 5,000 publicly held U.S.
companies. Provides data on name, address, exchange, ticker
symbol, SIC codes, names of stockholders, etc.

DISSERTATION ABSTRACTS ONLINE (DISS). Source: UNIVERSITY
MICROFILMS INTERNATIONAL. For description see listing under
DIALOG INFORMATION SERVICES, INC.

FEDERAL AND STATE BUSINESS ASSISTANCE (FSBA). Source: CENTER
FOR UTILIZATION OF FEDERAL TECHNOLOGY, NTIS, U.S. DEPARTMENT
OF COMMERCE. Contains current information with updates every
two years. Directory of assistance programs from federal and
state for businesses. Lists name, address, telephone number,
summary of service, and eligibility requirements, where
applicable.

GPO MONTHLY CATALOG (GPOM). Source: SUPERINTENDENT OF
DOCUMENTS, U.S. GOVERNMENT PRINTING OFFICE. For description
see listing under DIALOG INFORMATION SERVICES.

GUIDE TO MICROFORMS IN PRINT (MFIP). Source: MECKLER
PUBLISHING. Contains current records with quarterly updates.
Print equivalent is: GUIDE TO MICROFORMS IN PRINT. Lists
publications available in microform including books, journals,
newspapers, government publications, etc.

HARVARD BUSINESS REVIEW DATABASE (HBRO). Source: JOHN WILEY &
SONS, INC. For description see listing under DIALOG
INFORMATION SERVICES.

INDEX TO FROST & SULLIVAN MARKET RESEARCH REPORTS (FSIS).
Source: FROST & SULLIVAN, INC. Contains records from 1978 to
present, with monthly updates. Indexes reports published by
FROST & SULLIVAN, a market research company. Reports analyze
various industries and project trends.

INDEX TO U.S. GOVERNMENT PERIODICALS (GOVT). Source: INFORDATA
INTERNATIONAL INCORPORATED. Contains records from 1980 to the

present, with monthly updates. Indexes articles, book
reviews, conference proceedings, etc. from approximately 185
U.S. Government published periodicals.

INDUSTRY DATA SOURCES (HARF). Source: INFORMATION ACCESS
COMPANY. Contains records from 1979 to the present, with
monthly updates. Source of directory and statistical
information on U.S., Canadian, and Western European industry.
Materials listed include market research reports, investment
studies, special issues of trade journals, forecasts, industry
newsletters, databases, etc.

INVESTEXT (INVT). Source: TECHNICAL DATA INTERNATION. For
description see listing under DIALOG INFORMATION SERVICES.

INVESTOR'S DAILY (IVDA). Source: JA MICROPUBLISHING INC.
Contains records from 1986 to the present, with monthly
updates. Indexes and abstracts the INVESTOR'S DAILY, a
financial newspaper. INVESTOR'S DAILY features sections:
"Inside the Market," "Industries in the News," "Stock Quotes,"
"Today's News Digest," etc.

LEGAL RESOURCE INDEX (LAWS). Source: INFORMATION ACCESS
COMPANY. For description see listing under DIALOG INFORMATION
SERVICES.

MAGAZINE ASAP III (MSAP). Source: INFORMATION ACCESS COMPANY.
For description see listing under DIALOG INFORMATION SERVICES.

MAGAZINE INDEX (MAGS). Source: INFORMATION ACCESS COMPANY.
For description see listing under DIALOG INFORMATION SERVICES.

MANAGEMENT CONTENTS (MGMT) AND BACKFILE (MGMB). Source:
INFORMATION ACCESS COMPANY. MGMT contains records from August
1984 to present; MGMB contains records from 1974 to July 1984.
For description see listing under DIALOG INFORMATION SERVICES.

NATIONAL NEWSPAPER INDEX (NOOZ). Source: INFORMATION ACCESS
COMPANY. For description see listing under DIALOG INFORMATION
SERVICES.

NEWSEARCH (DALY). Source: INFORMATION ACCESS COMPANY. For
description see listing under DIALOG INFORMATION SERVICES.

NTIS BIBLIOGRAPHIC DATABASE (NTIS). Source: NATIONAL TECHNICAL
INFORMATION SERVICE (NTIS). Contains records from 1970 to the
present with monthly updates. For description, see listing
under DIALOG INFORMATION SERVICES.

OCLC EASI REFERENCE (OCLC). Source: ONLINE COMPUTER LIBRARY
CENTER, INC. (OCLC). Contains records with imprint dates
falling within current four-year period, with quarterly and
annual updates. Indexes by author, title, subject, and other
fields to subset of the OCLC Online Union Catalog. Materials
are in formats for books, serials, sound recordings, software,
musical scores, maps, manuscripts, and audiovisual materials.

PAIS INTERNATIONAL (PUBLIC AFFAIRS INFORMATION SERVICE)
(PAIS). Source: PUBLIC AFFAIRS INFORMATION SERVICE, INC. For
description see listing under DIALOG INFORMATION SERVICES.

POPULAR MAGAZINE REVIEW ONLINE (PMRO). Source: DATA BASE
COMMUNICATIONS CORP. Contains records from 1984 to the
present, with weekly updates. Indexes and abstracts articles
from popular periodical literature. Articles on franchising
from general interest magazines such as TIME and NEWSWEEK may
be accessed.

PREDICASTS ANNUAL REPORTS ABSTRACTS (PTSA). Source:
PREDICASTS, INC. For description see listing under DIALOG
INFORMATION SERVICES.

PTS/F & S INDEXES (PTSI). Source: PREDICASTS, INC. For
description see listing under DIALOG INFORMATION SERVICES.

PTS/PROMT and PTS F & S INDEXES, Concatenated File (PTSL).
Source: PREDICASTS, INC. For description see listing under
DIALOG INFORMATION SERVICES.

PTS/PROMT (PTSP). Source: PREDICASTS, INC. For description
see listing under DIALOG INFORMATION SERVICES.

TRADE AND INDUSTRY ASAP III (TSAP). Source: INFORMATION ACCESS
COMPANY. For description see listing under DIALOG INFORMATION
SERVICES.

UMI ARTICLE CLEARINGHOUSE (UMAC). Source: UMI ARTICLE
CLEARINGHOUSE. Contains records from 1978 to present, with
monthly updates. Records are for articles and reports from
more than 9000 periodicals and conference proceedings.
Subject coverage includes business.

CLASS
COOPERATIVE LIBRARY AGENCY FOR SYSTEMS AND SERVICES
1415 Koll Circle
Suite 101
San Jose, California   95112
Telephone: 408-289-1756

CLASS, founded in 1976, is a membership based public
agency dedicated to promoting library cooperation, automation
and resource sharing among all types of information centers
and libraries. Among the services available to CLASS members
is RLIN (RESEARCH LIBRARIES INFORMATION NETWORK), a database
of over 25 million bibliographic records. The database contains records for books, serials, visual materials, musical
scores, sound recordings, maps, machine-readable data files,
and archival and manuscript collections. RLIN records have
been entered by over 140 institutions including many of the
major research libraries in the United States. Any library
that is not eligible for membership in RLG may use RLIN
through CLASS.
     Records in RLIN may be searched by author, title, and
subject. Through searching the RLIN database, subject
bibliographies may be prepared. CLASS offers two types of
RLIN services: Search and Cataloging. CLASS RLIN Search
Service provides search access to RLIN database for bibliographic verification, holdings, interlibrary loan, and
cataloging information. CLASS RLIN Cataloging Service has the
same features as the RLIN Search Service and also includes
access to online cataloging, acquisitions, archival and
manuscripts control, and interlibrary loan systems.

COMPUSERVE
INFORMATION SERVICE
5000 Arlington Centre Boulevard
P.O. Box 20212
Columbus, Ohio   43220
Telephone: 800-848-8199
            614-457-0802 (in Ohio)

COMPUSERVE offers a variety of services including electronic shopping; communications software; communications &
bulletin boards; and access to a selection of databases
covering various subjects. Their business databases are:

AP NEWS AND SPORTS WIRES: THE ASSOCIATED PRESS NEWS service
covers international, state, national, Washington business,
political, entertainment, and other wires. THE AP SPORTS WIRE
covers news and scores in sports.

EXECUTIVE NEWS SERVICE (ENS): An electronic clipping service
of news on business, current events, entertainment, etc. from
the ASSOCIATED PRESS and THE WASHINGTON POST.

BUSINESS NEWS: Features the files: THE BUSINESS WIRE, AP
BUSINESS NEWS, and IQUEST. THE BUSINESS WIRE prints news and
press releases from hundreds of companies each day. AP
BUSINESS NEWS emphasizes industry and corporate issues, with
updates on Wall Street developments and changes in the Dow
Jones Industrial Average. IQUEST covers archives and current
articles from the AP service, the British Broadcasting Company
and major European resources.

DATA-STAR
Suite 110
485 Devon Park Drive
Wayne, Pennsylvania   19087
Telephone: 1-800-221-7754
215-687-6777

Business databases available through Data-Star are as follc

ABI/INFORM (INFO). Source: UMI/DATA COURIER. For description
see listing under DIALOG.

AMERICAN BANKER (BANK). Source: American Banker, Inc.
Contains records from 1981 to date, with weekly updates.   The
online version of the newspaper, AMERICAN BANKER, database
covers banking and financial services including small business
loans.

BUSINESS (BUSI). Source: Online GmbH. Contains records from
1983 to date with monthly updates. A European database on
international trade opportunities, business contacts for
manufacturing, marketing sales, etc.

FAIRBASE (FAIR). Source: INTAG, Hanover, West Germany.
Contains current information, updated every two months.
Reports on international trade fairs, exhibitions, and
conferences. Announces forthcoming events and describes past
events from the current year. Source to locate dates of
upcoming franchise exhibits and/or conferences.

FINANCIAL TIMES COMPANY INFORMATION (FNTL). Source: D-S
Production Ltd., Trowbridge, U.K. Contains records from
January 1981 with updates every working day. Source of
European company information comprises all articles in the
London and Frankfurt editions of the FINANCIAL TIMES.

FOREIGN TRADE AND ECONOMIC ABSTRACTS (IEAB). Source: Ministry
of Economic Affairs, The Hague, Netherlands. Contains records
from 1978 with monthly updates. Provides information on
foreign markets, market trends, economic developments, etc.
Database abstracts articles from approximately 2,000 English,
French, German, and Dutch source.

FOOD SCIENCE AND TECHNOLOGY ABSTRACTS (FSTA). Source:
International Food Information Service, Frankfurt, West
Germany. Contains records from 1985 to present, with monthly

updates. Provides international coverage of subject of food
science and technology, including information on chain
restaurants.

FROST & SULLIVAN MARKET RESEARCH REPORTS (FSFS). Source: Frost
& Sullivan Ltd., London, U.K. Contains records for reports
currently available from Frost & Sullivan. Reports are
indexed and summarized. Reports analyze and make projections
for various industries internationally.

FROST & SULLIVAN POLITICAL RISK (FSRI). Source: Frost &
Sullivan, London and New York. Contains current information,
with updates as new data becomes available or conditions
change. Assesses the political and economic conditions in 85
countries most important to international business with
projections for finance, investment, operations, and trade.
Each report describes political and economic data, current and
expected regime stability, political turmoil, trade restrictions, economic policies, and international investment
restrictions. Good source for analyzing possible opportunities for international franchises.

HARVARD BUSINESS REVIEW/ONLINE (HBRO). Source: John Wiley &
Sons, Inc. Contains records from 1971 to the present. For
description, see listing under DIALOG INFORMATION SERVICES.

HOPPENSTEDT AUSTRIA (HOAU). Source: Verlag Hoppenstedt,
Darmstadt, West Germany. Contains current records, with
updates once a year in September. Provides detailed
descriptions of all branches and all business enterprises of
over 2,000 major companies in Austria. Online version of
printed directory, OESTERREICH 2000.

HOPPENSTEDT NETHERLANDS (HONL). Source: ABC Voor Handel en
Industrie, Harlem, Netherlands. Contains current records,
with updates once a year in August/September. Provides
company information of approximately 20,000 companies in the
Netherlands. Online version of directory NEDERLANDS ABC VOOR
HANDEL EN INDUSTRIE.

HOPPENSTEDT (HOPE). Source: Verlag Hoppenstedt Co., Darmstadt,
West Germany. Contains current records, updated three times a
year in January, July, and September. Provides company
descriptions of 35,000 major companies in the Federal Republic
of Germany and West Berlin. Online version of directory:
HANDBUCH DER GROSSUNTERHEHMEN UND HANDBUCH DER
MITTELSTAENDISCHEN UNTERNEHMAN.

ICC CANADIAN COMPANIES (ICCA). Source: The ICIS-LOR Group
Ltd., London, U.K. Contains records from September 1987 with
daily updates. Furnishes detailed profile, financial, and
performance date for approximately 5,000 leading Canadian
companies.

ICC KEY NOTES (ICKN). Source: ICC Database, London, U.K.
Contains current information. Provides market information on
approximately 175 United Kingdom industry sectors. Features
full-text of ICC published KEY NOTE reports.

ICC STOCKBROKER RESEARCH (ICBR). Source: ICC Database, London,
U.K. Contains information from 1985, with weekly updates.
Reports are retained for at least eighteen months. Full-text
of international stockbroker reports with detailed comparisons, assessments and projection of company performance and
industry trends.

ICC UK COMPANIES DATABASE (ICUK). Source: ICC Database,
London, U.K. Contains current records, with weekly updates.
Directory of all limited liability companies in the U.K. with
financial data for over 60,000 organizations.

INDUSTRY DATA SOURCES (HARF). Source: Information Access
Company. For description, see listing under DIALOG
INFORMATION SERVICES.

INVESTEXT (INVE). Source: Business Research Corporation. For
description, see listing under DIALOG INFORMATION SERVICES.

KYODO NEWS SERVICE (KYOP). Source: Kyodo Service, Tokyo,
Japan. Contains records from October 1986 with daily updates.
Database describes news of business activity in Japan and of
Japanese companies outside Japan.

MANAGEMENT CONTENTS (MGMT). Source: Management Contents/
Information Access Co. For description, see listing under
DIALOG INFORMATION SERVICES.

NTIS (NTIS). Source: National Technical Information Service.
For further description, see listing under DIALOG INFORMATION
SERVICES.

PREDICASTS. (PTZZ--acronym to search simultaneously multiple
Predicasts files) Source: Predicasts International, Inc.
Files contain information from 1978. Files are: PREDICASTS
PROMT (PTSP), PREDICASTS FORECASTS (PTFC), PREDICASTS TIME
SERIES (PTTS), PREDICASTS INDEXES (PTIN), PREDICASTS ANNUAL

REPORTS (PTAR), PREDICASTS MARKETING AND ADVERTISING SERVICE (PTMA), PREDICASTS NEW PRODUCT ANNOUNCEMENTS (PTNP), and PREDICASTS DEFENSE MARKETS AND TECHNOLOGY (PTDT). For description, see listings under DIALOG INFORMATION SERVICES.

PUBLIC AFFAIRS INFORMATION SERVICE (PAIS). Source: Public Affairs Information Service. For description, see listing under DIALOG INFORMATION SERVICES.

SELL - SALES OPPORTUNITIES (SELL). Source: Company Line UK Ltd., Northampton, U.K. Contains current information with daily updates. A business opportunities database which lists details of products or services on a worldwide basis for which suppliers are required now. The organization Company Line receives inquiries from data centers throughout the world for companies interested in buying products and services. A manufacturer or provider of product or service can review inquiries, contact nearest SELL/Company Line office who will provide more details and put manufacturer or provider in touch with the buying company.

DIALOG INFORMATION SERVICES, INC.
Marketing Department
3460 Hillview Avenue
Palo Alto, California   94304
Telephone: 800-3-DIALOG

Franchising information may be located by searching the
following databases available through DIALOG.

ABI/INFORM (File 15). Source: UMI/DATA COURIER. Contains
records from August 1971 to the present, with weekly updates.
Covers approximately 680 publications in field of business.
Journal articles on franchising may be searched by company
name and/or industry.

BOOK REVIEW INDEX (File 137). Source: GALE RESEARCH COMPANY.
Contains records from 1969 to the present, with updates three
times per year. Covers over 380 journals. Source of
information on recent books on franchising.

BOOKS IN PRINT (File 470). Source: R.R. BOWKER. Contains
records for books currently in print, with monthly updates.
Books may be located by author, title, and subject. Each
record includes author, title, publisher, date, LC card
number, International Standard Book Number (ISBN), and price.

BRITISH BOOKS IN PRINT (File 430). Source: J. WHITAKER & SONS,
LTD. Contains records currently published in the United
Kingdom and other books from other countries printed in the
English language that are available in the United Kingdom.
Updated monthly.

BUSINESS DATELINE (File 635). Source: UMI/DATA COURIER.
Contains records from 1985 to the present, with weekly updates. Includes full text of articles from regional business
publications of U.S. and Canada. Source of information on
case histories of companies and recent trends in franchises.

CIS (File 101). Source: CONGRESSIONAL INFORMATION SERVICE,
INC. Contains records from 1970 to the present, with montly
updates. Printed form is CIS INDEX TO PUBLICATIONS OF THE
UNITED STATES CONGRESS. Indexes hearings, special publications, reports, etc. of U.S. Congress. Source of current
government hearings regarding franchise legislation.

CONGRESSIONAL RECORD ABSTRACTS (File 135). Source: NATIONAL
STANDARDS ASSOCIATION. Contains records from 1981 to the

present, with weekly updates. Provides abstracts of
CONGRESSIONAL RECORD, the journal of proceedings of the
United States Congress. Information on franchising in regard
to public laws, bills and resolutions, committee and
subcommittee reports, etc. may be scanned.

D & B-DONNELLEY DEMOGRAPHICS (File 575). Source: DONNELLEY
MARKETING SERVICES. Contains current demographic data based
on 1980 census and to estimates and projections of the
DONNELLEY MARKETING INFORMATION SERVICES. For U.S. states,
counties, towns, cities, and zip code areas, demographic data
on age, sex, race, industry, households, families, income,
etc. may be examined. Source of information for investigation
of possible franchise locations.

D & B-DUN'S FINANCIAL RECORDS (File 519). Source: DUN'S
MARKETING SERVICES and DUN & BRADSTREET CREDIT SERVICES.
Contains up to three years of financial statements for
approximately 700,000 public and private companies. Records
for companies include: balance sheet, income statement,
primary and secondary SIC (Standard Industrial Classification)
Codes, number of employees, etc. Source of finding out how
much financial security there is in an exisiting franchise.

DISCLOSURE (File 100). Source: DISCLOSURE INFORMATION GROUP.
Contains current financial records on over 10,000 publicly
owned companies. Compiled from reports filed with the U.S.
Securities and Exchange Commission, company records include
financial information, new developments, listings of chief
executive officers, etc. Source of financial information on
franchised companies.

DISSERTATION ABSTRACTS ONLINE (File 35). Source: UNIVERSITY
MICROFILES INTERNATIONAL. Contains records of American dis-
sertations from 1861 to the present, with monthly updates.
Source of research in field of franchising.

ECONOMIC LITERATURE INDEX (File 139). Source: AMERICAN
ECONOMIC ASSOCIATION. Contains records from 1969 to the
present, with quarterly updates. Index of journal articles
and book reviews, with abstracts for selected recent titles.

ENCYCLOPEDIA OF ASSOCIATIONS (File 114). Source: GALE RESEARCH
COMPANY. Contains current directory information for trade
associations, professional societies, labor unions, fraternal
and patriotic associations, etc. Each record includes name,
address, phone number, size of organization, purpose of
organization, publications, and location and time of annual

conferences. Names and addresses of organizations related to
franchising and small business may be scanned.

FEDERAL REGISTER ABSTRACTS (File 136). Source: NATIONAL
STANDARDS ASSOCIATION. Contains records from March 1977 to
the present, with weekly updates. Provides abstracts of
FEDERAL REGISTER, the U.S. Government publication of
regulations, proposed rules, and legal notices of federal
agencies. Current source of information on franchise
regulations.

FINANCIAL TIMES COMPANY ABSTRACTS (File 560). Source:
FINANCIAL TIMES BUSINESS INFORMATION, LTD. Contains records
from 1981 to the present, with weekly updates. Contains
abstracts of articles about companies published in London and
Frankfurt editions of THE FINANCIAL TIMES newspaper. Source
of information on international franchising.

FINANCIAL TIMES FULLTEXT (File 622). Source: FINANCIAL TIMES
BUSINESS INFORMATION, LTD. Contains records from 1986 to the
present, with daily updates. Provides full text of articles
published in the London and International editions of the
FINANCIAL TIMES newspaper. Subjects covered include company
information, government regulation, industry data, etc.
Source of information on international franchising.

FINDEX REPORTS AND STUDIES (File 196). Source: NATIONAL
STANDARDS ASSOCIATION. Contains records from 1977 to the
present, with quarterly reloads. Corresponds to printed
source, FINDEX: THE DIRECTORY OF MARKET RESEARCH REPORTS,
STUDIES, AND SURVEYS. Locator of industry and market research
reports. Prospective franchisors and franchisees may study
industry and/or company by examining market research studies.

GPO MONTHLY CATALOG (File 66). Source: U.S. GOVERNMENT
PRINTING OFFICE. Contains records from July 1976 to the
present, with monthly updates. Corresponds to printed source,
MONTHLY CATALOG OF UNITED STATES GOVERNMENT PUBLICATIONS.
Index of reports, studies, hearings, conference proceedings, handbooks, etc. issued by U.S. federal government
agencies. Source of current government publications on
franchising.

GPO PUBLICATIONS REFERENCE FILE (File 166). Source: U.S.
GOVERNMENT PRINTING OFFICE. Contains records from 1971 to the
present, with biweekly updates. Indexes publications for sale
by Superintendent of Documents, U.S. Government Printing
Office. Also furnishes records of forthcoming and recently
out-of-print publications.

HARVARD BUSINESS REVIEW (File 122). Source: JOHN WILEY & SONS, INC. Contains records from 1971 to the present, with bimonthly updates. Includes full text of articles from HARVARD BUSINESS REVIEW from 1976 to present.

INDUSTRY DATA SOURCES (File 189). Source: INFORMATION ACCESS COMPANY. Contains records from 1979 to the present, with monthly updates. Index to information sources on approximately 65 industries for United States and foreign countries. Records listed include marketing research reports, economic forecasts, trade journal special issues, etc. Source for market studies and forecasts on franchises.

INVESTEXT (File 545). Source: TECHNICAL DATA INTERNATIONAL. Contains records from July 1982 to the present, with weekly updates. Features full text of financial research reports from investment banking firms in United States, Canada, Europe, and Japan. The financial research reports describe over 1000 publicly traded corporations in the U.S., Canada, Germany, France, Great Britain, Switzerland, Sweden, Japan, etc.

LC MARC (Files 426, 427). Source: U.S. LIBRARY OF CONGRESS. Contains records from 1968 to the present, with monthly updates. Index to books cataloged by the United States Library of Congress since 1968. Book records can be searched by author, title, subject, series, publication date, etc.

LEGAL RESOURCE INDEX (File 150). Source: INFORMATION ACCESS COMPANY. Contains records from 1980 to the present, with monthly updates. Indexes approximately 750 law journal and law newspapers. Also indexes selected legal monographs. Indexes articles, book reviews, case notes, obituaries, editorials, letters to the editor, etc. Also includes law articles from MAGAZINE INDEX, NATIONAL NEWSPAPER INDEX, and TRADE AND INDUSTRY INDEX. Source for locating court cases and legislation on franchising.

MAGAZINE INDEX (File 47).Source: INFORMATION ACCESS COMPANY. Contains records from 1959 to March 1970 and 1973 to the present, with monthly updates. Indexes over 400 general interest magazines including TIME, NEWSWEEK, U.S. NEWS & WORLD REPORT, all of which have had featured articles on franchising. Selected business periodicals are also included.

MANAGEMENT CONTENTS (File 75).Source: INFORMATION ACCESS COMPANY. Contains records from September 1974 to the present, with monthly updates. Indexes articles from approximately 120 U.S. and international journals and proceedings, transactions, business course materials, newsletters, and research reports.

MCGRAW-HILL NEWS (File 600).Source: MCGRAW-HILL INFORMATION
NETWORK. Contains records from June 18, 1987 to the present.
Features complete text of news stories of business events
throughout the world. Source of stock market information,
economic indicators, and economic forecasts.

MOODY'S CORPORATE NEWS--INTERNATIONAL (File 557).Source:
MOODY'S INVESTOR SERVICES, INC. Contains records from 1983 to
the present, with weekly updates. Provides financial
information for over 3900 major corporations.

MOODY'S CORPORATE NEWS--U.S (File 556).Source: MOODY'S
INVESTOR SERVICES, INC. Contains records from 1983 to the
present, with weekly updates. Provides financial information
for approximately 13,000 publicly held U.S. corporations.

MOODY'S CORPORATE PROFILES (File 111).Source: MOODY'S INVESTOR
SERVICES, INC. Contains records from 1979 to the present.
Access to LOS ANGELES TIMES and WASHINGTON POST is from 1982
to the present. Indexes articles, news reports, obituaries,
etc. from newspapers including NEW YORK TIMES and WALL STREET
JOURNAL. Provides current items and developments in franchising.

NEWSEARCH (File 211). Source: INFORMATION ACCESS COMPANY.
Contains current month, with daily updates. Indexes articles,
news items, book reviews, etc. from approximately 1700
newspapers, magazines, and periodicals. At the end of each
month, indexed items are transferred to the databases:
MAGAZINE INDEX, NATIONAL NEWSPAPER INDEX, LEGAL RESOURCE
INDEX, MANAGEMENT CONTENTS, and TRADE AND INDUSTRY INDEX.

NEWSPAPER ABSTRACTS (File 603). Source: UMI, INC. Contains
records from 1984 to the present, with weekly updates.
Indexes 19 major newspapers including BOSTON GLOBE, NEW YORK
TIMES, WALL STREET JOURNAL, USA TODAY, LOS ANGELES TIMES, etc.

NEWSWIRE ASAP (File 649). Source: INFORMATION ACCESS COMPANY.
Contains PR NEWSWIRE from January 1985 to the present; KYODO
from July 1987 to the present; and REUTERS from June 1987 to
the present, with daily updates for each. Furnishes full text
and indexing of news releases and wire stories from the news
organizations: PR NEWSWIRE, KYODO, and REUTERS. All cover
industry, financial, and business news.

NTIS (File 6). Sources: NATIONAL TECHNICAL INFORMATION SERVICE
(NTIS), U.S. DEPARTMENT OF COMMERCE. Contains records from
1964 to the present, with biweekly updates. Indexes reports

on government-sponsored research, development and engineering; subjects include business and economics.

PAIS INTERNATIONAL (File 49). Source: PUBLIC AFFAIRS INFORMATION SERVICE, INC. Contains records from 1972 to the present, with monthly updates. Indexes public policy literature of business, political science, law, international relations, etc. Format of materials indexed are: books; state, local, federal, and non-U.S. government documents; pamphlets; committee hearings; and reports of public and private organizations. PAIS publishes print indexes: PAIS BULLETIN and PAIS FOREIGN LANGUAGE INDEX.

PR NEWSWIRE (File 613). Source: PR NEWSWIRE. Contains records from May 1, 1987 to the present, with updates every 15 minutes. Full text of news releases prepared by companies, public relations agencies, trade associations, city, state, federal and foreign government agencies, etc. Source of business and financial developments.

PTS ANNUAL REPORTS ABSTRACTS (File 17). Source: PREDICASTS. Contains current records, with monthly updates. Provides coverage of over 3000 publicly held corporations in the U.S. and internationally located.

PTS F & S INDEXES (FUNK & SCOTT) (Files 18, 19). Source: PREDICASTS. Contains records from 1972 to the present, with weekly updates. Provides coverage of U.S. and international company, industry, and product information. Additionally, the database indexes a bibliography of over 5000 publications cited; complete publication citation includes title, publisher, address, cost, frequency, description of publication, and Predicasts codes for product, country, and event.

PTS F & S INTERNATIONAL FORECASTS (File 83). Source: PREDICASTS. Contains records from 1971 to the present, with monthly updates. Covers industry and product information and economic data.

PTS MARKETING & ADVERTISING REFERENCE SERVICE (PTS MARS) (File 570). Source: PREDICASTS. Contains records from 1984 to the present, with daily updates. Covers information on marketing and advertising of consumer goods and products.

PTS NEW PRODUCT ANNOUNCEMENTS/PLUS (File 621). Source: PREDICASTS. Contains records from 1985 to the present, with weekly updates. Full text coverage of press releases from industries regarding product announcements, descriptions, prices, distribution channels, etc.

PTS PROMT (File 18). Source: PREDICASTS. PROMT or PREDICASTS
OVERVIEW OF MARKETS AND TECHNOLOGY contains records from 1972
to the present, with weekly updates. Indexes trade journals,
business magazines, government reports, bank letters, special
reports, and abstracts of corporate and industry research
reports. The corporate and industry research reports are made
available through J.A. Micropublishing.

PTS PROMT DAILY (File 602). Source: PREDICASTS. Contains
records for current week, with daily updates; at end of week
records are transferred to PTS PROMT file. Indexes and
abstracts articles appearing in newspapers, business
magazines, trade journals, government reports, bank letters,
brokerage reports, etc.

PTS U.S. FORECASTS (File 81). Source: PREDICASTS. Contains
records from July 1971 to the present, with monthly updates.
Provides abstracts of published forecasts from newspapers,
journals, government reports, business publications, etc.
Records from the CENSUS OF MANUFACTURERS from 1967, 1972, and
1977 are also listed.

PTS U.S. TIME SERIES (File 82). Source: PREDICASTS. Years of
records vary for time series data; earliest recorded date is
1957. PTS U.S. TIME SERIES is divided into two subfiles:
PREDICASTS COMPOSITES and PREDICASTS BASEBOOK. The COMPOSITES
file is updated with quarterly replacements. COMPOSITES
contains approximately 500 time series on U.S. providing
historical data since 1957 and projected consesnsus of
published forecasts through 1990. Provides data on
population, GNP, per capita income, employment, price series,
etc. BASEBOOK contains data from 1957 to date for 47,000
series on U.S. production, prices, wages, foreign trade, etc.
BASEBOOK is updated quarterly, with yearly replacements.

REMARC (Files 421, 422, 423, 424, 425). Source: CARROLLTON
PRESS. Contains records of collections of U.S. Library of
Congress from 1897 to 1980. Books may be searched by author,
titles, subject, series, publication date, etc.

REUTERS (File 611). Source: REUTERS U.S., INC. Contains
records from January 1987 to present, with updates every 15
minutes. Provides full text of news releases from the news
wires: REUTER FINANCIAL REPORT and the REUTER LIBRARY
SERVICE. Subject coverage includes business and international
news.

STANDARD & POOR'S CORPORATE DESCRIPTIONS (File 133). Source:
STANDARD & POOR'S CORPORATION. Contains current records, with

biweekly updates. Provides descriptions of approximately
11,000 publicly traded U.S. corporations. File 133 and Files
132 and 134 (see records below) are equivalent of printed
STANDARD & POOR'S CORPORATION RECORDS.

STANDARD & POOR'S NEWS (File 132, 134). Source: STANDARD &
POOR'S CORPORATION. Contains records from June 1979 to the
present, with daily updates. Provides general news and
financial information on approximately 10,000 publicly owned
U.S. companies. Equivalent of printed source: STANDARD &
POOR'S CORPORATION RECORDS DAILY NEWS AND CUMULATIVE NEWS.

STANDARD & POOR'S REGISTER--BIOGRAPHICAL (File 526). Source:
STANDARD & POOR'S CORPORATION. Contains current records, with
semiannual updates. Profiles executives of public and private
corporations, U.S. and non-U.S., with sales of one million and
over. Equivalent of printed source: STANDARD & POOR'S
REGISTER OF CORPORATIONS, DIRECTORS, AND EXECUTIVES, Volume
Two.

STANDARD & POOR'S REGISTER--CORPORATE (File 527). Source:
STANDARD & POOR'S CORPORATION. Contains current records, with
quarterly updates. File includes records of approximately
45,000 public and private companies. Each record include
name, address, financial and marketing information, lists of
officers and directors, etc.

TRADE & INDUSTRY ASAP (File 648). Source: INFORMATION ACCESS
COMPANY. Contains records from 1983 to the present, with
monthly updates. File provides complete text and indexing for
approximately 85 journals from TRADE & INDUSTRY INDEX (see
below). Also includes news releases from PR NEWSWIRE.

TRADE & INDUSTRY INDEX (File 148). Source: INFORMATION ACCESS
COMPANY. Contains records from 1981 to the present, with
monthly updates. Indexes and abstracts business journals
related to trade, industry, and commerce. Covers newspapers
including WALL STREET JOURNAL and NEW YORK TIMES FINANCIAL
SECTION. File also offers PR NEWSWIRE from 1983 to the
present and AREA BUSINESS DATABANK.

TRINET COMPANY DATABASE (File 532). Source: TRINET INC.
Contains current records with quarterly updates. Provides
current address, financial and marketing information on U.S.
single and multi-establishment companies.

TRINET ESTABLISHMENT DATABASE (File 531). Source: TRINET INC.
Contains current records with quarterly updates. Provides
current address, financial and marketing information on U.S.
establishments with 20 or more employees.

ULRICH'S INTERNATIONAL PERIODICALS DIRECTORY (File 480).
Source: R.R. BOWKER. Contains current records with monthly
updates. Print equivalents: ULRICH'S INTERNATIONAL
PERIODICALS DIRECTORY, IRREGULAR SERIALS AND ANNUALS, SOURCES
OF SERIALS, and ULRICH'S QUARTERLY. Directory of serial
publications with information on address of publisher,
frequency of publication, International Standard Serial Number
(ISSN), circulation, abstracting and indexing services
covering publication, subject, etc. Source for compiling
subject list of publications covering franchising.

WASHINGTON POST ELECTRONIC EDITION (Files 146, 147). Source:
THE WASHINGTON POST COMPANY. Contains records from April 1983
to the present, with daily updates. Electronic edition of
morning daily and Sunday editions.

DOW JONES NEWS/RETRIEVAL
Dow Jones & Co.
P.O. Box 300
Princeton, New Jersey   08530
Telephone: 609-452-1511

Dow Jones News/Retrieval service provides up-to-the-minute business and financial information on companies and industries. In addition, Dow Jones News/Retrieval features national and international news from the Associated Press, Dow Jones News Service and broadcast media; sports news; weather forecasts, movie reviews, book reviews, college selection service, an encyclopedia, and shopping service. Business databases applicable to franchising and the access codes for these databases are listed below:

BUSINESS AND FINANCE REPORT (//BUSINESS). Continuously updated business and financial news compiled from THE WALL STREET JOURNAL, BARRON'S and the DOW JONES NEWS SERVICE and other newswires.

COMPANY AND INDUSTRY TRACKING SERVICE (//TRACK). Creates customized portfolios of up to 125 companies or industries. Automatically tracks news and stock price quotes.

DISCLOSURE ONLINE (//DISCLO). Contains 10K extracts, company profiles, and other detailed data on over 10,000 publicly held companies from reports filed with the Securities and Exchange Commission (SEC) and other sources.

DOW JONES NEWS (//DJNEWS). Contains records ranging from 90 days old to 90 seconds. Provides access to stories from the DOW JONES NEWS SERVICE (wire) and selected stories from THE WALL STREET JOURNAL and BARRON'S. May be searched by company, industry, or news category.

DOW JONES QUICKSEARCH (//QUICK). Provides a complete corporate report compiled from multiple Dow Jones/News Retrieval sources. Covers latest news, current stock quotes, financial overview, company vs. industry performance, income statements, market overview, etc.

DUN'S FINANCIAL RECORDS (//DB). Includes financial reports and business information from Dun & Bradstreet for over 750,000 public and private companies.

JAPANESE ECONOMIC DAILY (//KYODO). Same-day coverage of business, economic, financial market, and political developments in Japan from the KYODO NEWS SERVICE.

MEDIA GENERAL FINANCIAL SERVICES (//MG). Provides financial and statistical information on 5400 companies and 180 industries. Compares data on two companies, two industries, or a company versus its industry. For each company includes data on revenues, earnings, dividends, ratio, price changes, etc.

STANDARD & POOR'S ONLINE (//SP). Profiles 4700 companies with data on current and historical earnings and estimates, dividends and market figures from Standard & Poor's Corporation.

TEXT-SEARCH SERVICES (//TEXT). Database includes: THE WALL STREET JOURNAL FULL-TEXT VERSION, featuring the full text of all articles that appeared or were scheduled to appear in THE WALL STREET JOURNAL since January 1984; DOW JONES NEWS, containing selected DOW JONES NEWS SERVICE (wire) stories and selected, condensed stories from THE WALL STREET JOURNAL and BARRON'S since June 1979; BARRON'S, with the full text of all articles since January 1987; THE WASHINGTON POST, with the full text of selected articles since January 1984; THE BUSINESS LIBRARY, with the full text of selected articles from FORBES, FORTUNE, MONEY, INC., AMERICAN DEMOGRAPHICS, FINANCIAL WORLD and the full text of the JAPAN ECONOMIC NEWSWIRE and the PR NEWSWIRE; BUSINESS DATELINE, with the full text of selected articles from over 140 regional business journals since January 1985; DATATIMES, with regional news from 16 local newspapers including the CHICAGO SUN-TIMES, the SAN FRANCISCO CHRONICLE, and the HOUSTON CHRONICLE and national news from USA TODAY, the ASSOCIATED PRESS NEWSIRE, and the GANNETT NEWS SERVICE.

ZACKS CORPORATE EARNINGS ESTIMATOR (//EPS). Consensus earnings-per-share estimates and price/earnings ratio forecasts for over 4800 companies.

MEAD DATA CENTRAL
9443 Springboro Pike - DM
Post Office Box 933
Dayton, Ohio   45401
Telephone: 800-227-4908
513-865-6800

Mead Data Central is the vendor for LEXIS, NEXIS, and
LEXIS FINANCIAL INFORMATION SERVICE, all of which provide
franchising information. LEXIS includes files of legal
information sources such as Supreme Court rulings, biblio-
ographic citations of articles from law journals, and state
codes. NEXIS provides full text coverage of business publications among which are THE NEW YORK TIMES, LOS ANGELES
TIMES, HARVARD BUSINESS REVIEW, THE ECONOMIST, FORBES, and
THE JAPAN ECONOMIC JOURNAL. The LEXIS FINANCIAL INFORMATION
SERVICE provides company, business, and financial information. A description of LEXIS, NEXIS, and the LEXIS FINANCIAL
INFORMATION SERVICE follows:

LEXIS has the following file groups:

I. GENERAL LAW LIBRARIES

> A. GENERAL FEDERAL LIBRARY (GENFED) - Among files
> are UNITED STATES REPORTS AND UNITED STATES SUPREME
> COURT DECISIONS from 1790; COURTS OF APPEAL from
> January 1912; COURT OF APPEALS FOR THE FEDERAL
> CIRCUIT FROM October 1982; FEDERAL REGISTER from
> July 1, 1980; combined CONGRESSIONAL RECORD files;
> RULES OF PROCEDURE OF THE U.S.TAX COURT; FEDERAL
> JUDICIARY ALMANAC, etc.

> B. STATES LIBRARY (STATES) - Files available for
> each of the fifty states vary. Most include state
> Supreme Court and Court of Appeals decisions and
> attorney general opinions. States which include
> Florida, Kentucky, North Carolina, and Wyoming
> include statutes. Among the California files is
> CALIFORNIA FRANCHISE TAX BOARD RULINGS from June
> 1958.

> C. INDIVIDUAL STATE LAW LIBRARIES - Files available
> for each of the fifty states vary. Most files
> include state Supreme Court decisions, the state
> Constitution, statutes, codes, and attorney general
> opinions.

D. AMERICAN LAW REPORTS ANNOTATIONS LIBRARY (ALR) –
Files are: AMERICAN LAW REPORTS, FEDERAL
ANNOTATIONS, Volumes 1-82; LAWYERS' EDITION, SECOND
SERIES ANNOTATIONS, Volumes 1-85; AMERICAN LAW
REPORTS, FOURTH SERIES ANNOTATIONS, Volumes 1-55;
AMERICAN LAW REPORTS, THIRD SERIES ANNOTATIONS,
Volumes 1-100; AMERICAN LAW REPORTS, SECOND SERIES
ANNOTATIONS, Volumes 1-100; All series include
current supplements.

E. THE LAW REVIEW LIBRARY (LAWREV) – Among files
are: H.W. Wilson's INDEX TO LEGAL PERIODICALS,
IAC'S LEGAL RESOURCE INDEX, COMBINED FILE with
all law reviews, CATHOLIC UNIVERSITY LAW REVIEW
from Fall 1982, COLUMBIA LAW REVIEW from October
1982, HARVARD LAW REVIEW from November 1982, NEW
YORK UNIVERSITY LAW REVIEW from April 1982,
STANFORD LAW REVIEW from November 1982, ABA TAX
LAWYER from Fall 1981, and YALE LAW JOURNAL from
November 1982.

F. LEGAL REFERENCE LIBRARY (LEXREF) – Files are:
THE ALMANAC OF AMERICAN POLITICS, BIBLIOGRAPHY OF
AMERICAN BAR ASSOCIATION'S PUBLICATIONS, BILLCAST
LEGISLATIVE FORECASTS, BLCAST ARCHIVE, ENVIRONMENTAL
LAW INSTITUTES' ENVIRONMENTAL LAW REPORER'S LAW
REVIEW BIBLIOGRAPHY, FORENSIC SERVICES DIRECTORY,
FEDERAL JUDICIARY ALMANAC, H.W. WILSON'S INDEX TO
LEGAL PERIODICALS, NILS INSURANCE PERIODICAL
INDEX, NILS IPI THESAURUS, IAC'S LEGAL RESOURCE
INDEX, STATE GOVERNMENT TAX TELEPHONE NUMBERS, and
FEDERAL GOVERNMENT TAX TELEPHONE NUMBERS.

II. SPECIALIZED LAW LIBRARIES – Files contain selected
materials pertinent to selected topical areas.

A. ADMIRALTY LIBRARY (ADMRTY) – Among files are:
AMERICAN MARITIME CASES from 1923, THE MARITIME
LAWYER from Spring 1980, and SOCIETY OF
MARITIME ARBITRATORS AWARD DECISIONS from January
1965.

B. AMERICAN BAR ASSOCIATION LIBRARY (ABA) – Among
files are: ABA JOURNAL from January 1982, BUSINESS
LAWYER from November 1981, INTERNATIONAL LAWYER from
Fall 1981, LEGAL ECONOMICS from January 1982, TAX
LAWYER from Fall 1981, PATENT, TRADEMARK & COPYRIGHT
LAW from August 1981, and ABA FORUM from Fall 1981
to Summer 1985.

C. FEDERAL BANKING LIBRARY (BANKNG) - Among files
are: FEDERAL RESERVE BULLETIN from January 1980,
BNA'S BANKING DAILY, ABA BUSINESS LAWYER from
November 1981, and UNITED STATES REPORTS from
October 1926.

D. FEDERAL BANKRUPTCY LIBRARY (BKRTCY) - Files are:
UNITED STATES REPORTS from January 1925, Courts of
Appeal from January 1938, DISTRICT COURTS from
January 1948, BANKRUPTCY COURTS from October 1979,
and LEGISLATIVE HISTORY 98-2.

E. COMMERCE CLEARING HOUSE BLUE SKY LAW REPORTER
LIBRARY (CCHSKY) - Files are: REPORT LETTERS, LAWS
AND REGULATIONS, COURT & AGENCY DECISIONS, GUIDES TO
PRACTICE, ADMINISTRATIVE FEES BY STATE, INDUSTRY
STATEMENTS AND GUIDES, TOPICAL INDEX, UNIFORM
SECURITIES ACT, and COMBINED FILE OF ALL CCHSKY
FILES.

F. COMMERCE CLEARING HOUSE LIBRARY (CCH) - Files
are: CCH TAX DAY- FEDERAL from January 1985, CCH TAX
DAY from August 1983 to December 1984, CCH TAX DAY -
STATE from January 1985, CCH STATE TAX WEEK: THE
ELECTRONIC VERSION OF CCH STATE TAX LAW REVIEW from
January 1983 to December 1984, and COMBINED FILES:
TAXDAY & STATAX.

G. FEDERAL COMMUNICATIONS LIBRARY (FEDCOM) - Among
files are: UNITED STATES REPORTS from December 1936;
FEDERAL COMMUNICATIONS COMMISSION RECORD from
November 1986, and FEDERAL COMMUNICATIONS
COMMISSION REPORTS from 1939 to 1965.

H. CORPORATE LAW LIBRARY (CORP) - Files are: STATE
CASE LAW (Supreme Court and Courts of Appeal for the
fifty states), CORPORATE INFORMATION, CASES
CONSTRUING DELAWARE LAW, and JOURNALS (ABA BUSINESS
LAWYER from November 1981 and the DELAWARE JOURNAL
OF CORPORATE LAW from Fall 1982).

I. CORPORATE INFORMATION LIBRARY (INCORP) - Files
are: CALIFORNIA SECRETARY OF STATE CORPORATION
INFORMATION TAKEN FROM CORPORATE FILINGS, ILLINOIS
SECRETARY OF STATE CORPORATION INFORMATION TAKEN
FROM CORPORATE FILINGS, MISSOURI SECRETARY OF STATE
CORPORATION INFORMATION TAKEN FROM CORPORATE FILINGS
WITH THE DIVISION OF CORPORATIONS, and TEXAS SECRE-
TARY OF STATE CORPORATION INFORMATION TAKEN FROM
CORPORATE FILINGS.

J. STATE EMPLOYMENT LAW LIBRARY (EMPLOY) - Files
are: STATE CASE LAW, BUREAU OF NATIONAL AFFAIRS,
INC. PUBLICATIONS, and FEDERAL CASE LAW.

K. FEDERAL ENERGY LIBRARY (ENERGY) - Among files
Are: BNA ENVIRONMENT REPORTER from January 1982, BNA
CHEMICAL REGULATION REPORTER from January 1982,
FEDERAL ENERGY REGULATORY COMMISSION DECISIONS from
April 1931 to September 1977, and NUCLEAR
REGULATORY COMMISSION DECISIONS from January 1975.

L. ENVIRONMENTAL LAW LIBRARY (ENVIRN) - Among files
are: BNA ENVIRONMENT DAILY, BNA ENVIRONMENT REPORTER
from January 1982, PENNSYLVANIA ENVIRONMENTAL
HEARING BOARD from March 1972, and OCCUPATIONAL
SAFETY AND HEALTH REVIEW COMMISSION from November
1971.

M. HEALTH LAW LIBRARY (HEALTH) - Among files are:
STATE CASE LAW, FEDERAL CASE LAW, and JOURNALS AND
NEWSLETTERS (including HOSPITAL LAW from January
1984, HOSPITAL ADMITTING MONTHLY from July 1982).

N. INSURANCE LAW LIBRARY (INSRLW) - Files are: STATE
CASE LAW AND ATTORNEY GENERAL OPINIONS, NATIONAL
INSURANCE LAW SERVICE, and PROCEEDINGS AND JOURNALS.

O. FEDERAL LABOR LIBRARY (LABOR) - Among files are:
NATIONAL LABOR RELATIONS BOARD DECISIONS from
January 1972, BNA DAILY LABOR REPORT from January
1982, BNA PENSIONS & BENEFITS DAILY, and
OCCUPATIONAL SAFETY AND HEALTH REVIEW COMMISSION
from November 1971.

P. MILITARY JUSTICE LIBRARY (MILTRY) - Among files
are: COURT OF MILITARY APPEALS from August 1951,
MILITARY LAW REVIEW from Winter 1982, and COURTS OF
MILITARY REVIEW from June 1951. January 1948.

Q. FEDERAL PATENT, TRADEMARK & COPYRIGHT LIBRARY
(PATCORP) - Among files are: UNITED STATES REPORTS
from 1850; DISTRICT COURTS from January 1948;
TRADEMARK TRIAL & APPEAL BOARD DECISIONS from
January 1982; DECISIONS OF COMMISSIONER OF PATENT &
TRADEMARKS from January 1981; BNA PATENT, TRADEMARK
& COPYRIGHT JOURNAL from January 1982; and ABA
PATENT, TRADEMARK & COPYRIGHT LAW from August 1981.

R. FEDERAL PUBLIC CONTRACTS LIBRARY (PUBCON) - Among
files are: UNITED STATES REPORT from January 1925,
COURT OF APPEALS FOR THE FEDERAL CIRCUIT from
October 1982, DISTRICT COURTS from January 1948, and
VETERANS ADMINISTRATION BOARD OF CONTRACT APPEALS
from January 1960.

S. PUBLIC UTILITIES LAW LIBRARY (UTILITY) - Files
are: STATE CASE LAW and STATE ADMINISTRATIVE
DECISIONS.

T. STATE SECURITIES LAW LIBRARY (STSEC) - Files are:
STATE SECURITIES LAW LIBRARY and CCH BLUE SKY LAW
REPORTER.

U. FEDERAL TAX LIBRARY (FEDTAX) - Among files are:
FEDERAL COURT TAX CASES, FINAL & TEMPORARY TREASURY
REGULATIONS PUBLISHED IN FEDERAL REGISTER, TAX
ANALYSTS' WEEKLY TAX NOTES MAGAZINE from January
1982, ABA'S QUARTERLY TAX LAWYER from Fall 1981,
RIA'S COMPLETE ANALYSIS OF THE TAX REFORM ACT OF
1986, RIA FEDERAL TAX COORDINATOR 2d, PRACTICE
AIDS FOR RIA'S FEDERAL TAX COORDINATOR 2d, COMBINED
RIA TAX ALERT NEWSLETTERS, BNA'S DAILY TAX REPORT
from September 1986, IRS PRIVATE LETTER RULINGS from
January 1954, UNITED STATES SUPREME COURT REPORTS
from April 1913, COMBINED RIA TAX ALERT NEWSLETTERS,
STATE TAX CASES AND DECISIONS, and IRS TAXPAYER
INFORMATION PUBLICATIONS.

V. STATE TAX LIBRARY (STTAX) - Files are STATE CASE
LAW AND ADMINISTRATIVE DECISIONS for each of fifty
states.

W. INTERNATIONAL TRADE LIBRARY (ITRADE) - Among
files are: COURT OF INTERNATIONAL TRADE from
November 1980, BNA INTERNATIONAL TRADE REPORTER from
July 1984, BNA UNITED STATES IMPORT WEEKLY from
January 1982, BNA UNITED STATES EXPORT WEEKLY from
January 1982, TAX NOTES INTERNATIONAL from June
1984, ABA INTERNATIONAL LAWYER from Fall 1981,
INTERNATIONAL TRADE COMMISSION GENERAL COUNSEL
MEMORANDA from August 1975 to June 1986, and CUSTOMS
COURT from June 1962 to October 1983.

X. FEDERAL TRADE REGULATION LIBRARY (TRADE) - Among
files are: UNITED STATES REPORTS from 1890, FEDERAL
TRADE COMMISSION REPORTS from March 1950, BNA

ANTITRUST & TRADE REGULATION REPORT from January
1982, ABA ANTITRUST LAW JOURNAL from April 1981, and
ABA BUSINESS LAWYER from November 1981.

Y. FEDERAL TRANSPORTATION LIBRARY (TRANS) - Among
files are: NATIONAL TRANSPORTATION SAFETY BOARD
ORDERS AND DECISIONS from April 1967; UNITED STATES
REPORTS from January 1925; CIVIL AERONAUTICS BOARD
ORDERS, CERTIFICATES AND DECISIONS from March 1979;
and INTERSTATE COMMERCE COMMISSION DECISIONS,
OPINIONS AND ORDERS from January 1973.

III. UNITED KINGDOM LAW LIBRARIES - Files are made available
under an agreement with Butterworth (Telepublishing) Ltd.
Documents from the Immigration Appeal Reports, Industrial
Tribunal Reports, Reports of Patent Cases, Tax Cases, VAT
Tribunal Reports and Inland Revenue Publications are based on
British Crown copyright material with permission of the
Controller of Her Majesty's Stationery Office.

A. ENGLISH GENERAL LIBRARY (ENGGEN) - Among files
are: CURRENT PUBLIC GENERAL ACTS, CURRENT GENERAL
STATUTORY INSTRUMENTS, FINANCE AND OTHER CURRENT
BILLS, and REPORTED AND UNREPORTED CASES from 1980.

B. ENGLISH INDUSTRIAL LIBRARY (ENGIND) - Among files
are: CURRENT PUBLIC GENERAL ACTS, REPORTED CASES,
and CURRENT GENERAL STATUTORY INSTRUMENTS.

C. ENGLISH LOCAL GOVERNMENT LIBRARY (ENGLG) - Among
files are REPORTED AND UNREPORTED CASES, CURRENT
PUBLIC GENERAL ACTS, and CURRENT GENERAL STATUTORY
INSTRUMENTS.

D. EUROPEAN COMMUNITIES LIBRARY (EURCOM) - Among
files are REPORTED AND UNREPORTED CASES and
EUROPEAN COMMISSION DECISION ON COMPETITION POLICY
from 1972.

E. COMMONWEALTH CASES LIBRARY (COMCAS) - Among files
are ENGLISH GENERAL CASE LAW from 1945, CASES
REPORTED IN NEW ZEALAND LAW REPORTS from 1970, and
HEADNOTES OF CASES REPORTED IN AUSTRALIAN LAW
REPORTS & AUSTRALIAN CAPITAL TERRITORY REPORTS from
January 1973 to December 1980 & NORTHERN TERRITORY
REPORTS from January 1979 to December 1980.

F. NEW ZEALAND LIBRARY (NZ) - File is: CASES
REPORTED IN NEW ZEALAND LAW REPORTS from 1970.

G. AUSTRALIA LIBRARY (AUST) - File is: HEADNOTES OF
CASES REPORTED IN AUSTRALIAN LAW REPORTS &
AUSTRALIAN CAPITAL TERRITORY REPORTS from January
1973 to December 1980 & NORTHERN TERRITORY REPORTS
from January 1979 to December 1980.

H. UNITED KINGDOM INTELLECTUAL PROPERTY LIBRARY
(UKIP) - Among files are: REPORTED AND UNREPORTED
CASES, CURRENT PUBLIC GENERAL ACTS, and CURRENT
GENERAL STATUTORY INSTRUMENTS.

I. UNITED KINGDOM TAX LIBRARY (UKTAX) - Among files
are: REPORTED AND UNREPORTED CASES, CURRENT PUBLIC
GENERAL ACTS, CURRENT GENERAL STATUTORY AGREEMENTS,
CURRENT FINANCE BILL, and CURRENT DOUBLE TAXATION
AGREEMENTS.

J. IRELAND LIBRARY (IRELND) - Files include REPORTED
CASES.

K. SCOTLAND LIBRARY (SCOT) - Among files are
REPORTED AND UNREPORTED CASES.

L. ADMIRALTY LIBRARY (ADMRTY) - Among files are: THE
MARITIME LAWYER from Spring 1980, AMERICAN MARITIME
CASES from 1923, CURRENT PUBLIC GENERAL ACTS, and
CURRENT GENERAL STATUTORY AGREEMENTS.

IV. FRENCH LAW LIBRARY - Files made available under an
agreemtent with Tele Consulte.

A. INTERNATIONAL LIBRARY (INTNAT) - Among files are:
COUR DE JUSTICE DES COMMUNAUTES EUROPEENNES from
1954 and JOURNAL OFFICIEL DES COMMUNAUTES
EUROPEENES, SERIE L from 1952.

B. LAWS AND REGULATIONS LIBRARY (LOIREG) - Among
files are: JOURNAL OFFICIEL from 1955; BULLETIN
OFFICIEL DU TRAVAIL, DE L'EMPLOI from 1930; BULLETIN
OFFICIEL DU MINISTERE DE LA JUSTICE from 1981, and
REPONSES MINISTERIELLES from 1970.

C. PRIVATE CASES LIBRARY (PRIVE) - Among files are:
COUR DE CASSATION: CIVIL CASES from 1959; COUR DE
CASSATION: CRIMINAL CASES from 1970; and COURS
D'APPEL from 1983.

      D. PUBLIC CASES LIBRARY (PUBLIC) - Among files are:
      CONSEIL CONSTITUTIONNEL DECISIONS from 1958,
      TRIBUNEL DES CONFITS CASES from January 1964, and
      CONSEIL D'ETAT: CONTENTIEUX GENERAL and CONSEIL
      D'ETAT: CONTENTIEUX FISCAL CASES from October 1964.

      E. CASE INTERPRETATIONS LIBRARY (REVUES) - File is:
      LA SEMAINE SOCIALE LAMY from 1980.

V. THE AUTO-CITE SERVICE - Offered under agreement with
VERALEX INC., this service verifies the accuracy of case law
citations as well as IRS REVENUE RULINGS AND PROCEDURES by
providing the name and date of the case or ruling and the
official and unofficial citations including citations to
topical reporters. It also identifies cases that either
affect or validate a case's precedential value.

VI. SHEPARD'S CITATIONS SERVICE - Offered under agreement with
the Shepard's Division of McGraw-Hill, Inc., service provides
federal, state and regional case law citators giving for each
case cited the case history parallel citations and a
statement of subsequent history of the case.

VII. THE LEXTRACK SERVICE - Includes private and litigation
support libraries. Abbreviated text or the full text of work
product, litigation, or other materials can be created for a
subscriber or group of subscribers.

NEXIS provides the following files which cover business-
related topics:

I. NEXIS LIBRARY (NEXIS) - Following is a listing of NEXIS
Library files. The most recent documents from all files may
be searched at one time in the CURRNT file, which contains all
documents in the NEXIS library from 1986 to date. Documents
before 1986 may be accessed in the ARCHIV file. Documents
from all files may be searched in the OMNI file. Files provide
full-text coverage, with the exception of the BUSINESS
ABSTRACTS LIBRARY.

      A. GROUP FILES - Files are: CURRNT, with stories
      dated 1986 or later from all files of the NEXIS
      Library; ARCHIV, with stories dated prior to 1986
      from all files; and OMNI, all stories from all files
      of the NEXIS Library.

B. NEWSPAPER FILES - Among files are: PAPERS, a
group file of all newspapers; ADVERTISING AGE from
January 1986; the NEW YORK TIMES from June 1980;
the WASHINGTON POST from January 1977; LOS ANGELES
TIMES from January 1985; FINANCIAL TIMES from
January 1982; the NATIONAL LAW JOURNAL from January
1983; and BUSINESS TODAY from June 1987.

C. MAGAZINE FILES - Among files are: MAGS, a group
file of all magazines; BUSINESS WEEK from January
1975; FORBES from January 1975; FORTUNE from January
1977; HARVARD BUSINESS REVIEW from January 1976;
INC. from June 1981; MONEY from January 1982;
FINANCIAL WORLD from January 1982; and BUSINESS
MONTH from January 1975.

D. WIRES FILES - Among files are: WIRES, a group
file of all wire services; PR NEWSWIRE from January
1980; THE REUTER BUSINESS REPORT from May 1987; THE
ASSOCIATED PRESS WORLD, NATIONAL, BUSINESS AND
SPORTS WIRES from January 1977; THE INTER PRESS
SERVICE from April 1984; UNITED PRESS INTERNATIONAL
STATE AND REGIONAL WIRES from November 1980 through
December 1986; UNITED PRESS INTERNATIONAL STATE
AND REGIONAL WIRES from January 1987; and CENTRAL
NEWS AGENCY from April 1984.

E. NEWSLETTERS FILES - Among files are: NWLTRS, a
group file of all newsletters; AD DAY from January
1982; DAILY REPORT FOR EXECUTIVES from January 1982;
FEDWATCH from March 1984; BNA'S BANKING REPORT from
January 1982; THE EXPERT AND THE LAW from December
1981; and THE EXECUTIVE SPEAKER from June 1980.

F. BUSINESS DATELINE - This group file contains
selected full-text articles from over 120 regional
business publications among which are: CRAIN'S
DETROIT BUSINESS from January 1986; LOS ANGELES
BUSINESS JOURNAL from August 1987; THE BUSINESS
TIMES from February 1985; WASHINGTON BUSINESS
JOURNAL from January 1985; and BUSINESS RECORD
from May 1985.

G. BUSINESS FILES - This group file contains
publications and wire services that primarily cover
general business. Among these files are: BUS, a
group file; ADVERTISING AGE from January 1986; THE
REUTER BUSINESS REPORT from May 1987; CRAIN'S

DETROIT BUSINESS from January 1986; INC. from June
1981; FORBES from January 1975; FORTUNE from
January 1977; HARVARD BUSINESS REVIEW from January
1976; CRAIN'S NEW YORK BUSINESS from January 1986;
and THE BUSINESS TIMES from February 1985.

H. FINANCE FILES - This group file covers financial
markets and investing. Among these files are: FIN,
a group file; ABA BANKING JOURNAL from January 1980;
EUROMONEY from January 1985; SECURITIES WEEK from
January 1981; FEDWATCH from March 1984; and BANKING
EXPANSION REPORTER from January 1982.

I. GOVERNMENT FILES - This group file covers
publications and wire services that primarily cover
government and defense. Among these files are:
GOVT, a group file; LEGAL TIMES from January 1982;
THE WASHINGTON QUARTERLY from Winter 1982; and
FOREIGN AFFAIRS from 1981.

J. NEWS FILES - This group file covers publications,
wire services and broadcast transcripts with broad
coverage of nearly all subjects. Among these files
are: NEWS, a group file; BBC SUMMARY OF WORLD
BROADCASTS AND MONITORING REPORTS from January 1979;
CENTRAL NEWS AGENCY from April 1984; TIME from
January 1981; THE NEW YORK TIMES from June 1980; and
THE WASHINGTON POST from January 1977.

K. TRADE/TECHNOLOGY FILES - This group file covers
publications and wire services that primarily cover
a trade, science or technology. Among these files
are: TRDTEC, a group file; COAL WEEK from January
1981; DEFENSE ELECTRONICS from January 1982;
INFOWORLD from July 1983; OFFSHORE from January
1980; MINING JOURNAL from January 1981; and
NUCLEAR NEWS from January 1982.

II. ENCYCLOPAEDIA BRITANNICA LIBRARY (EB) - Among files are:
ENCYCLOPAEDIA BRITANNICA MICROPAEDIA 1982; ENCYCLOPAEDIA
MACROPAEDIA 1982; ENCYCLOPAEDIA BRITANNICA BOOK OF THE YEAR
1982, EVENTS OF 1981; and ENCYCLOPAEDIA BRITANNICA MEDICAL AND
HEALTH ANNUAL 1981-82.

III. THE INFORMATION BANK LIBRARY (INFOBK) - Among files are:
COMPLETE STORIES FROM THE NEW YORK TIMES from June 1980;
SELECTED BIOGRAPHICAL STORIES FROM THE NEW YORK TIMES from

June 1980; and ADVERTISING AND MARKETING INTELLIGENCE
ABSTRACTS FROM SELECTED TRADE AND PROFESSIONAL PUBLICATIONS
from January 1979.

IV. THE ASAP II LIBRARY (ASAPII) - Contains selected full-text
articles from over 160 publications from MAGAZINE ASAP II and
TRADE & INDUSTRY ASAP II produced by Information Access
Company. ASAP II does not contain the full text of any
publications currently available in the NEXIS Library. Group
files available are:

> A. MAGAZINE ASAP II - Among files are: MASAP, the
> group file; NATION'S BUSINESS from January 1983;
> BUSINESS AMERICA from January 1983; OCCUPATIONAL
> OUTLOOK QUARTERLY from June 1983; JOURNAL OF SMALL
> BUSINESS MANAGEMENT from July 1984; CANADIAN
> BUSINESS from January 1983; and WASHINGTON MONTHLY
> from July 1985.

> B. TRADE & INDUSTRY ASAP II - Among files are:
> TIASAP, the group file; CHAIN STORE AGE, EXECUTIVE
> EDITION from January 1983; BUSINESS AMERICA from
> January 1983; JOURNAL OF SMALL BUSINESS MANAGEMENT
> from July 1984; SURVEY OF CURRENT BUSINESS from
> February 1983; RESTAURANT BUSINESS from January
> 1983; NATION'S RESTAURANT NEWSPAPER from February
> 1983; and NATION'S BUSINESS from January 1983.

> C. UNITED STATES PATENT AND TRADEMARK OFFICE LIBRARY
> (LEXPAT) - Among files are: DESIGN PATENTS from
> December 1976; PLANT PATENTS from December 1976;
> MANUAL OF CLASSIFICATION as of June 1987; and
> UTILITY PATENTS from January 1975.

> D. BUSINESS ABSTRACTS LIBRARY (BUSABS) - Among files
> are: ABI/INFORM from 1971; BIS/INFOMAT NEWSFILE
> from January 1986; ADVERTISING AND MARKETING
> INTELLIGENCE ABSTRACTS FROM SELECTED TRADE AND
> PROFESSIONAL PUBLICATIONS from January 1979;
> FINANCIAL INDUSTRY INFORMATION SERVICE from January
> 1982; and THE INFORMATION BANK ABSTRACTS OF STORIES
> SELECTED FROM NEWSPAPERS, MAGAZINES, AND JOURNALS
> from January 1969.

> E. COMPUTERS AND COMMUNICATIONS LIBRARY (CMPCOM) -
> Among files are: INFOWORLD from July 1983; NETWORK
> WORLD from March 1986; DATAMATION from January 1983;
> PC MAGAZINE from January 1985; and PC WEEK from
> August 1983.

F. GOVERNMENT & POLITICAL NEWS LIBRARY (GOVNWS) –
Among files are: LEGAL TIMES from January 1982;
FINANCIAL TIMES from January 1982; FEDERAL RESERVE
BULLETIN from January 1980; and THE ECONOMIST from
January 1975.

LEXIS FINANCIAL INFORMATION SERVICE provides a comprehensive
Company Library (COMPNY) which contains over 75 files of
business and financial information. File groups include
SECURITIES AND EXCHANGE COMMISSION FILINGS, SEC LIMITED
PARTNERSHIPS, ECONOMIC INFORMATION, BUSINESS & FINANCE NEWS,
INTERNATIONAL BROKERAGE HOUSE RESEARCH REPORTS, U.S. NATIONAL
BROKERAGE HOUSE RESEARCH REPORTS, and COMPARATIVE COMPANY
LISTS. Among files are: ABI/INFORM from 1971; INSURANCE
PERIODICALS INDEX; FORBES ANNUAL DIRECTORY from 1984; SEC NEWS
DIGEST, and DISCLOSURE ONLINE DATABASE, CURRENT INFORMATION.

NEWSNET INC.
945 Haverford Road
Bryn Mawr, Pennsylvania   19010
Telephone: 800-345-1301
215-527-8030

NEWSNET offers a variety of databases on business
information including international developments, credit
ratings, corporate news, and stock prices. Among databases
available through NEWSNET are:

I. ADVERTISING AND MARKETING

MARKETING RESEARCH REVIEW. Source: HIGH TECH PUBLISHING CO.;
Coverage: 10/1/85 to present; Frequency: Monthly. Analyzes
and evaluates commercially available marketing research and
technology assessment reports. Helps readers identify,
appropriate, and adapt commercially available reports to their
own special and particular needs.

II. ASSOCIATED PRESS (AP)

AP DATASTREAM BUSINESS NEWS WIRE - AP01W. Source: PRESS
PUBLICATION INC. Provides up-to-the-minute information on
business and economic developments from major corporations and
the government.

III. CORPORATE COMMUNICATIONS (CC)

SID CATO'S NEWSLETTER ON ANNUAL REPORTS. Source: SID CATO
COMMUNICATIONS INC.; Coverage: 9/1/83 to present; Frequency:
Monthly. Contains SEC edicts; reviews of annual reports;
interviews with leading designers, printers, and executives;
latest survey results; and exclusive stories.

IV. GENERAL BUSINESS (GB)

CAMBRIDGE REPORTS TRENDS & FORECASTS. Source: CAMBRIDGE
REPORTS INC.; Coverage: 12/1/87 to present; Frequency:
Monthly. Discusses CAMBRIDGE REPORTS' exclusive national
consumer and public opinion surveys. It covers consumer
economic perceptions and behavior, financial services, energy,
etc.

C-STORE WEEK. Source: CAPITOL PUBLISHING GROUP; Coverage:
1/4/88 to present; Frequency: Weekly. Provides marketing
intelligence for the convenience store industry. Covers
marketing strategies, merchandising techniques, management
skills, etc.

V. GOVERNMENT AND REGULATORY (GT)

AMERICAN MARKETPLACE. Source: BUSINESS PUBLISHERS INC.;
Coverage: 1/19/82 to present; Frequency: Biweekly. Covers new
statistical data, with emphasis on demographic changes in the
consumer marketplace. Covers data issued by the Census
Bureau.

ANTITRUST FOIA LOG. Source: WASHINGTON REGULATORY REPORTING
ASSOCIATES; Coverage: 7/4/86 to present; Frequency: Weekly.
Provides reporting on Freedom of Information requests filed at
the U.S. Justice Department's Antitrust Division.

FTC FOIA LOG. Source: WASHINGTON REGULATORY REPORTING
ASSOCIATES; Coverage: 1/18/85 to present; Frequency: Weekly.
Provides a list of all Freedom of Information Act requests
received by the U.S. Federal Trade Commission.

FTC:WATCH. Source: WASHINGTON REGULATORY REPORTING ASSOCIATES;
Coverage: 1/8/82 to present; Frequency: Biweekly. Contains
information and details concerning policies, programs, and
personnel of the U.S. Federal Trade Commission.

THE INFORMATION REPORT. Source: WASHINGTON RESEARCHERS
PUBLISHING; Coverage: 5/1/85 to present; Frequency: Monthly.
Provides up-to-date coverage of new and little-known sources
of free and low-cost federal, state, local, international,
professional and trade information of interest to business
executives, corporate analysts, and others.

VI. INVESTMENT (IV)

BECHTEL SEC FILINGS INDEX. Source: BECHTEL INFORMATION
SERVICES; Frequency: Three-Six Times Daily--Annual Retention.
A listing of reports filed with the U.S. Securities and
Exchange Commission by over 18,000 publicly held companies
issuing investment securities in the U.S. The index covers
the three major exchanges: New York, American, and NASDAQ.

THE MONEYPAPER. Source: TEMPER OF THE TIMES COMMUNICATIONS;
Coverage: 7/1/87 to present; Frequency: Monthly. A financial
advisory letter featuring articles on business, investment,

taxation, consumer issues, and banking. Regular sections
include Smarts, Stocktrack, Financial News Digest, and Market
Outlook.

VII. INVESTEXT (IX)

INVESTEXT. Source: TECHNICAL DATA INTERNATIONAL; Frequency:
Weekly - 16 Week Retention. Includes company and industry
reviews by some of the top analysts from the leading brokerage
and investment-investing firms. Topics covered by analysts
include marketing strategies, new product introductions,
management changes, financial projections, etc.

VIII. LAW (LA)

BOWNE DIGEST-CORP/SEC ARTICLE ABSTRACTS. Source: LEGAL
ABSTRACT PUBLICATIONS; Coverage: 5/1/87 to present; Frequency:
Monthly. Contains summaries of important corporate and
securities law articles from over 250 legal periodicals,
including law reviews and journals, legal newspapers and
magazines, and bar journals.

REPORTS OF INTEREST TO LAWYERS. Source: MERTON ALLEN
ASSOCIATES; Coverage: 5/1/84 to present; Frequency: Bimonthly.
Presents reports related to regulations and law, and the
practice of business and law, from sources not normally
accessed by the legal profession.

IX. PUBLIC RELATIONS (PR)

PR NEWSWIRE. Source: PR NEWSWIRE ASSOCIATION INC.; Frequency:
Hourly-Annual Retention. Full text of press releases prepared
by corporations, public-relations agencies, labor unions,
civic and cultural organizations, government agencies, etc.

X. REUTER NEWS REPORTS (RN)

REUTER NEWS REPORTS. Source: REUTERS HOLDINGS, PLC. A high-
speed 24-hour newswire that provides breaking political and
economic news from 115 Reuter news bureaus around the world.

XI. TAXATION (TX)

CCH TAX DAY: FEDERAL. Source: COMMERCE CLEARING HOUSE INC.;
Coverage: 3/1/83 to present; Frequency: Daily. Coverage of

each day's developments in the federal tax area. Included are digests of final and proposed regulations, court decisions, IRS letter rulings, treasury releases, revenue rulings, etc.

CCH TAX DAY: STATE. Source: COMMERCE CLEARING HOUSE INC.; Coverage: 1/4/83 to present; Frequency: Daily. The electronic version of the STATE TAX REVIEW, a print publication that reports on tax developments in all 50 states. Included in the coverage are digests of pending legislation, regulations, court decisions, etc.

THE SMALL BUSINESS TAX REVIEW. Source: HOOKSETT PUBLISHING INC.; Coverage 10/1/83 to present; Frequency: Monthly. Provides the small business with vital news on changes in the tax laws, IRS rulings, court cases, and pending legislation in addition to in-depth analysis of changes that can help save taxes throughout the year.

TAX NOTES TODAY. Source: TAX ANALYSTS; Coverage: 6/29/82 to present; Frequency: Daily. Provides comprehensive daily coverage of all federal tax developments including Congressional hearings, court cases, etc.

XII. TRW BUSINESS PROFILES (TRW): A premium gateway service available exclusively via NEWSNET. Source: TRW BUSINESS CREDIT SERVICES; Frequency: Continuous updates. Profiles up-to-date payment histories on nearly 10 million business locations in the U.S. through a special gateway with NewsNet.

XIII. UNITED PRESS INTERNATIONAL (UP): Five individual services available through NEWSNET's NewsFlash. Source: UNITED PRESS INTERNATIONAL. NEWSNET monitors the national and international wires of United Press International on a 24-hour basis and automatically saves all relevant articles for NewsFlash delivery to NEWSNET users who have established NewsFlash profiles.

XIV. XINHUA NEWS AGENCY (XN). Source: XINHUA NEWS AGENCY. Provides 24-hour coverage of the important political, economic, social, and sporting events in the People's Republic of China.

OCLC ONLINE COMPUTER LIBRARY CENTER, INC.
6565 Frants Road
Dublin, Ohio   43017
Telephone: 614-764-6000

OCLC is a nonprofit membership organization that provides automation options to libraries. OCLC subsystems are available for library tasks such as acquisitions, cataloging, interlibrary loan, and serials control.   Included for each subsystem is the Online Union Catalog (OLUC), a bibliographic database representing records for monographs, serials, audiovisual media, machine-readable data files, manuscripts, maps, music scores, and sound recordings.   The Online Union Catalog contains 18 million records representing French, English, Chinese, Japanese, and Korean languages.   Approximately 35,000 records per week are added to OLUC by OCLC member libraries.   Records may be accessed by title, author, author/title, ISBN, Library of Congress card number (LCCN), OCLC Control Number, CODEN, Music Publisher Number, and Government Document Number.   Location symbols of libraries owning OLUC materials are provided for each record.

PERGAMON ORBIT INFOLINE
ORBIT SEARCH SERVICE
8000 Westpark Drive
McLean, Virginia   22102
Telephone: 800-421-7229
703-442-0900

Pergamon ORBIT Infoline offers the ORBIT Search Service
which features a variety of databases on various topics among
which are science, technology, and business. Databases with
information on franchising are as follows:

ABI/INFORM. Source: UMI/DATA COURIER. For description, see
listing under DIALOG INFORMATION SERVICES.

ACCOUNTANTS. Source: AMERICAN INSTITUTE OF CERTIFIED PUBLIC
ACCOUNTANTS. Provides accounting, auditing, taxation, data
processing, investments, financial management, financial
reporting, and related legal information.

CONGRESSIONAL RECORD. Source: NATIONAL STANDARDS ASSOCIATION.
Covers the official journal of the U.S. Congress, including
the House, Senate, Extension of Remarks, and Digest sections.

FEDERAL REGISTER. Source: NATIONAL STANDARDS ASSOCIATION.
Covers rules, proposed rules, public law notices, meetings,
hearings, and Presidential proclamations on a wide variety of
subject areas.

MANAGEMENT. Source: INFORMATION ACCESS CORPORATION. Covers
business and management literature from U.S. and non-U.S.
journals, proceedings, and transactions.

NTIS. Source: NATIONAL TECHNICAL INFORMATION SERVICE (U.S.
DEPARTMENT OF COMMERCE). Covers U.S. government-sponsored
research and development from over 200 federal agencies.

THE SOURCE
Source Telecomputing Corporation
1616 Anderson Road
McLean, Virginia   22102
Telephone: 703-734-7500

THE SOURCE offers a variety of services in the field of
business. Among these services are: electronic mail, multi-
user real-time conferencing, bulletin boards, and access to
business and investment databases. Databases included are:

ASSOCIATED PRESS - An electronic edition of the AP Newswire
with news, sports, and weather reports.

DONOGHUE MONEY LETTER - Biweekly report on investment
opportunities.

INVESTEXT BUSINESS RESEARCH - Research and opinions by over 40
domestic and international investment research and banking
firms. Reports information on corporations including
financial statistics, stock performance, earnings, historical
analysis, etc.

PROFESSIONAL BOOK CENTER - Online book-ordering center
specializing in technical and business books published or
distributed in the United States.

SCRIPPS-HOWARD NEWS SERVICE - A keyword searchable edition of
the last seven days' stories, provided by publications such as
PROVIDENCE JOURNAL, SCIENCE NEWS, and THE DETROIT NEWS.

UPI BUSINESS WIRE - Up-to-the-minute national business wire by
United Press Internation.

UNITED PRESS INTERNATIONAL - Up-to-the-minute reports on news,
sports, and weather.

THE WASHINGTON POST CAPITAL EDITION - A keyword searchable
edition of selected sections from the Monday-Friday editions
of THE WASHINGTON POST.

VU/TEXT INFORMATION SERVICES, INC.
325 Chestnut Street
Suite 1300
Philadephia, Pennsylvania   19106
Telephone: 800-323-2940
215-574-4409

VU/TEXT is a vendor that provides access to full text of
thirty-seven regional newspapers, the full text of selected
articles from over one hundred fifty regional business
journals and newspapers from the United States and Canada,
business summaries from over 1500 publications including
FORBES, BUSINESS WEEK, and THE WALL STREET JOURNAL, full text
of articles from journals including MONEY and FORTUNE, and
newswires including the Associated Press, PR Newsire, and
Business Wire. Databases with information on franchises are:

FULL TEXT NEWSPAPERS DATABASES:

ANCHORAGE DAILY NEWS (ALASKA). Contains records from October
1985 to present with daily updates.

ARIZONA REPUBLIC (ARIZONA). Contains records from May 1986 to
present with daily updates.

PHOENIX GAZETTE (ARIZONA). Contains records from May 1986 to
present with daily updates.

FRESNO BEE (CALIFORNIA). Contains records from March 1986 to
present with updates every 24 to 48 hours.

(LOS ANGELES) DAILY NEWS   (CALIFORNIA). Contains records from
October 1985 to present with daily updates.

LOS ANGELES TIMES (CALIFORNIA). Contains records from January
1985 to present with updates every 72 hours.

SACRAMENTO BEE (CALIFORNIA). Contains records from March 1984
to present with daily updates

SAN JOSE MERCURY NEWS (CALIFORNIA). Contains records from June
1985 to present with daily updates.

WASHINGTON POST (DISTRICT OF COLUMBIA). Contains records from
April 1983 to present with daily updates.

EL NUEVO HERALD (FLORIDA). Contains records from November 1982 to present with updates every 24 to 48 hours.

FORT LAUDERDALE NEWS (FLORIDA). Contains records from January 1985 to present with updates every 48 hours.

FORT LAUDERDALE SUN-SENTINEL (FLORIDA). Contains records from January 1985 to present with updates every 48 hours.

MIAMI HERALD (FLORIDA). Contains records from January 1983 to present with daily updates.

MIAMI NEWS (FLORIDA). Contains records from September 1983 to present with daily updates.

ORLANDO SENTINEL (FLORIDA). Contains records from April 1985 to present with daily updates.

ATLANTA CONSTITUTION (GEORGIA). Contains records from January 1988 to present with updates every 48 to 72 hours.

ATLANTA JOURNAL (GEORGIA). Contains records from January 1988 to present with updates every 48 to 72 hours.

CHICAGO TRIBUNE (ILLINOIS). Contains records from January 1985 to present with daily updates.

(GARY) POST-TRIBUNE (INDIANA). Contains records from November 1986 to present with updates every 24 to 72 hours.

WICHITA EAGLE-BEACON (KANSAS). Contains records from October 1984 to present with updates every 48 to 72 hours.

LEXINGTON HERALD-LEADER (KENTUCKY). Contains records from January 1983 to present with daily updates.

(ANNAPOLIS) CAPITAL (MARYLAND). Contains records from June 1986 to present with updates every 24 to 48 hours.

BOSTON GLOBE (MASSACHUSETTS). Contains records from January 1980 to present with updates every 48 to 72 hours.

DETROIT FREE PRESS (MICHIGAN). Contains records from January 1982 to present with daily updates.

ST. LOUIS POST-DISPATCH (MISSOURI). Contains records from January 1987 to present with daily updates.

(ALBANY) TIMES-UNION (NEW YORK). Contains records from March 1986 to present with updates every 48 to 72 hours.

KNICKERBOCKER NEWS (NEW YORK). Contains records from March 1986 to present with daily updates.

NEWSDAY (NEW YORK). Contains records from January 1986 to present with daily updates.

CHARLOTTE OBSERVER (NORTH CAROLINA). Contains records from July 1985 to present with daily updates.

AKRON BEACON JOURNAL (OHIO). Contains records from January 1985 to present with updates every 24 to 48 hours.

COLUMBUS DISPATCH (OHIO). Contains records from July 1985 to present with updates every 48 to 72 hours.

(ALLENTOWN) MORNING CALL (PENNSYLVANIA). Contains records from January 1984 to present with updates every 48 to 72 hours.

PHILADELPHIA DAILY NEWS (PENNSYLVANIA). Contains records from January 1978 to present with updates every 48 hours.

PHILADELPHIA INQUIRER (PENNSYLVANIA). Contains records from January 1981 to present with daily updates.

(COLUMBIA) STATE (SOUTH CAROLINA). Contains records from December 1987 to present with daily updates.

HOUSTON POST (TEXAS). Contains records from January 1985 to present with updates every 24 to 48 hours.

RICHMOND NEWS LEADER (VIRGINIA). Contains records from August 1985 to present with daily updates.

RICHMOND TIMES-DISPATCH (VIRGINIA). Contains records from August 1985 to present with daily updates.

SEATTLE POST-INTELLIGENCER (WASHINGTON). Contains records from January 1986 to present with updates every 24 to 48 hours.

NEWS AND CURRENT EVENTS DATABASES:

ASSOCIATED PRESS. Contains records from January 1985 to present with daily updates.   Full text of national, international, business, and sports news.

TIME. Contains records from January 1985 to present, with
weekly updates. Full text of articles on international and
national events, business, current trends, etc.

BUSINESS AND FINANCE DATABASES:

ABI/INFORM. Contains records from 1977 to present, with weekly
updates. Article summaries on industry, management, and
company information from 650 business publications worldwide.

BUSINESS DATELINE. Contains records from January 1985 to
present, with weekly updates. Full text of articles from over
150 regional publications in U.S. and Canada. Reports
business activities and trends.

BUSINESS WIRE. Contains records from June 1987 to present,
with daily updates. Full text of press releases issued by
over 9000 corporations and organizations.

DISCLOSURE. Contains records from past 18 months to three
years with weekly updates. Full text of reports of over
10,000 publicly owned companies including information on stock
ownership, balance sheet, income statement, corporate profile,
president's letter, etc.

FORTUNE. Contains records from January 1985 to present, with
biweekly updates. Full text of articles from business
journal, FORTUNE.

KNIGHT-RIDDER FINANCIAL NEWS. Contains records from January
1987 to present, with daily updates. Full text coverage of
financial market information including banking, economic
issues, etc.

MONEY. Contains records from August 1986 to present, with
monthly updates. Full text of articles from MONEY MAGAZINE, a
journal specializing in consumer finance.

PR NEWSWIRE. Contains records from January 1985 to present,
with daily updates. Full text of press releases from over
12,000 companies, government agencies, and other national news
sources. Reports corporate and industry developments.

PREDICASTS OVERVIEW OF MARKETS AND TECHNOLOGY (PROMT).
Contains records from January 1986 to present with weekly
updates. Article summaries of product, company, and industry
information from approximately 1500 trade and business
publications and daily newspapers.

WARNDEX (WALL STREET TRANSCRIPT). Contains records from July
1981 to present with weekly updates. Full text coverage of
the WALL STREET TRANSCRIPT, with company and industry
information as well as brokers' reports.

BUSINESS WEEK. Contains records from January 1985 to present
with weekly updates. Full text coverage of articles on latest
business trends.

WESTLAW
West Publishing Co.
P.O. Box 64526
St. Paul, Minnesota   55164
Telephone: 800-328-0109
612-688-3654

WESTLAW provides access to databases which cover the
U.S. CODE, federal regulations, case law from all federal
courts and specialized subjects such as tax, labor, antitrust,
banking, and international trade. WESTLAW files are as
follows:

I. GENERAL MATERIALS:

A. FEDERAL DATABASES - Among files are: COMBINED
FEDERAL CASES, which includes cases from U.S. Su-
preme Court, Courts of Appeals, District Courts,
U.S. Bankruptcy Court, etc.; STATUTES AND REGULA-
TIONS, which includes CODE OF FEDERAL REGULATIONS,
CONGRESSIONAL RECORD, FEDERAL REGISTER, UNITED
STATES CODE, etc.; ADMINISTRATIVE LAW, including
PRESIDENTIAL DOCUMENTS and U.S. ATTORNEY GENERAL
OPINIONS; and SPECIALIZED MATERIALS, including U.S.
LAW WEEK, U.S. LAW WEEK - DAILY EDITION, and
BICENTENNIAL OF THE CONSTITUTION.

B. STATE DATABASES - Covers Case law from all 50
states and the District of Columbia; Attorney
General Opinions from all available states, public
utilities reports from all states, and statutes from
all available states.

II. TOPICAL MATERIALS:

A. ADMINISTRATIVE LAW - File covers Law Reviews,
Texts, and Bar Journals.

B. ADMIRALTY - Files cover: FEDERAL CASE LAW,
FEDERAL STATUTES AND REGULATIONS, and TEXTS AND
PERIODICALS.

C. ANTITRUST AND BUSINESS REGULATION - Files cover:
FEDERAL CASE LAW; FEDERAL STATUTES AND REGULATIONS;
FEDERAL STATUTES AND REGULATIONS; SPECIALIZED (in-
cluding BNA ANTITRUST AND BUSINESS REGULATION DATA-
BASE; ANTITRUST & TRADE REGULATION REPORT; BNA'S
BANKING REPORT; DAILY REPORT FOR EXECUTIVES; SE-
CURITIES REGULATION & LAW REPORT; BNA BANKING
DAILY; and WESTLAW TOPICAL HIGHLIGHTS, ANTITRUST);
and TEXTS AND PERIODICALS.

D. BANKRUPTCY - Files cover: FEDERAL CASE LAW;
FEDERAL STATUTES AND REGULATIONS; SPECIALIZED (including WESTLAW TOPICAL HIGHLIGHTS, BANKRUPTCY
and DIRECTORY OF BANKRUPTCY ATTORNEYS); and TEXTS
AND PERIODICALS.

E. COMMUNICATIONS - Files cover: FEDERAL CASE LAW,
FEDERAL STATUTES AND REGULATIONS, FEDERAL ADMINIS-
TRATIVE LAW, and TEXTS AND PERIODICALS.

F. COPYRIGHT, PATENT AND TRADEMARK - Files cover:
FEDERAL CASE LAW; FEDERAL STATUTES AND REGULATIONS;
SPECIALIZED (including BNA'S PATENT, TRADEMARK &
COPYRIGHT JOURNAL); and TEXTS AND PERIODICALS.

G. CORPORATIONS - Files cover STATE CASE LAW;
DELAWARE CASE LAW; STATE ADMINISTRATIVE LAW (in-
cluding VIRGINIA CORPORATION COMMISSION DECI-
SIONS); SPECIALIZED (including WESTLAW TOPICAL
HIGHLIGHTS, CORPORATIONS AND SECURITIES); and TEXTS
AND PERIODICALS.

H. CRIMINAL JUSTICE - Files cover FEDERAL STATUTES
AND REGULATIONS and TEXTS AND PERIODICALS.

I. EDUCATION - File covers STATE CASE LAW.

J. ENERGY AND UTILITIES - Files cover: FEDERAL CASE
LAW; FEDERAL STATUTES AND REGULATIONS; FEDERAL
ADMINISTRATIVE LAW; SPECIALIZED (including PUBLIC
UTILITIES REPORTS and WESTLAW TOPICAL HIGHLIGHTS,
UTILITIES); and TEXTS AND PERIODICALS.

K. ENVIRONMENTAL LAW - Files cover: FEDERAL CASE
LAW; FEDERAL STATUTES AND REGULATIONS; FEDERAL
ADMINISTRATIVE LAW; and SPECIALIZED (including BNA
ENVIRONMENT DATABASE and WESTLAW TOPICAL HIGHLIGHTS,
ENVIRONMENTAL LAW).

L. FAMILY LAW - Files cover: STATE CASE LAW and
TEXTS AND PERIODICALS.

M. FINANCIAL SERVICES - Files cover: FEDERAL CASE
LAW; FEDERAL STATUTES AND REGULATIONS; FEDERAL
ADMINISTRATIVE LAW; SPECIALIZED (including BNA'S
FINANCIAL DATABASE and WESTLAW TOPICAL HIGHLIGHTS,
FINANCIAL SERVICES); and TEXTS AND PERIODICALS.

N. FIRST AMENDMENT - Files cover: FEDERAL CASE LAW
and FEDERAL STATUTES AND REGULATIONS.

O. GOVERNMENT CONTRACTS - Files cover: FEDERAL CASE
LAW; FEDERAL ADMINISTRATIVE LAW (including SMALL
BUSINESS ADMINISTRATION OFFICE OF HEARINGS AND AP-
PEALS DECISIONS); SPECIALIZED (including FEDERAL
CONTRACTS REPORT), and TEXTS AND PERIODICALS.

P. INSURANCE - Files cover: STATE CASE LAW, STATE
STATUTES, and TEXTS AND PERIODICALS.

Q. INTERNATIONAL LAW - Files cover: INTERNATIONAL
CASES; FEDERAL ADMINISTRATIVE LAW; and SPECIALIZED
(including INTERNATIONAL TRADE REPORTER, BNA INTER-
NATIONAL TRADE DAILY, and TAX NOTES INTERNATIONAL).

R. JURISPRUDENCE & CONSTITUTIONAL THEORY - File
covers TEXTS AND PERIODICALS.

S. LABOR - Files cover: FEDERAL CASE LAW; FEDERAL
STATUTES AND REGULATIONS; FEDERAL ADMINISTRATIVE
LAW; SPECIALIZED (including BNA PENSIONS & BENEFITS
DAILY and BNA LABOR DATABASE); and TEXTS AND
PERIODICALS.

T. LEGAL SERVICES - File covers TEXTS AND
PERIODICALS.

U. LITIGATION - File covers TEXTS AND PERIODICALS.

V. MILITARY LAW - File covers FEDERAL STATE LAW and
FEDERAL ADMINISTRATIVE LAW.

W. PROPERTY - File covers TEXTS AND PERIODICALS.

X. SECURITIES AND BLUE SKY LAWS - Files cover:
FEDERAL CASE LAW; FEDERAL STATUTES AND REGULATIONS;
FEDERAL ADMINISTRATIVE LAW; SPECIALIZED (including

BLUE SKY LAW REPORTER; BNA SECURITIES LAW DAILY;
BNA SECURITIES REGULATION & LAW REPORT, and WESTLAW
TOPICAL HIGHLIGHTS, CORPORATIONS AND SECURITIES);
and TEXTS AND PERIODICALS.

Y. TAXATION - Files cover: FEDERAL CASE LAW; FEDERAL
STATUTES AND REGULATIONS; FEDERAL ADMINISTRATIVE
LAW; STATE CASE LAW; STATE ADMINISTRATIVE LAW;
SPECIALIZED (including ALL TAX MANAGEMENT JOURNALS,
TAXSOURCE DIRECTORY; BNA HIGHLIGHTS & CONTENTS, TAX
NOTES, and TAX REFORM ACT OF 1986 SUMMARIES); and
TEXTS AND PERIODICALS.

Z. TORT LAW - Files cover: SPECIALIZED (including
WESTLAW TOPICAL HIGHLIGHTS, PRODUCTS LIABILITY) and
TEXTS AND PERIODICALS.

AA. TRANSPORTATION - Files include: FEDERAL
ADMINISTRATIVE LAW and TEXTS AND PERIODICALS.

III. TEXTS AND PERIODICALS - Contains selected articles from
over 200 law reviews and bar journals. TEXTS AND PERIODICALS
database is broken down into the following topics: ADMINISTRA-
TIVE LAW, ADMIRALTY, ANTITRUST & BUSINESS REGULATION, BANK-
RUPTCY, COMMUNICATIONS, COPYRIGHT & PATENT, CORPORATIONS,
CRIMINAL JUSTICE, ENERGY AND UTILITIES, FAMILY LAW, FINANCIAL
SERVICES, GOVERNMENT CONTRACTS, INSURANCE, JURISPRUDENCE &
CONSTITUTIONAL THEORY, LABOR, LEGAL SERVICES, LITIGATION,
PROPERTY, SECURITIES & BLUE SKY LAW, TAXATION, TORT LAW, and
TRANSPORTATION. Among periodicals covered are: BUSINESS
LAWYER, DELAWARE JOURNAL OF CORPORATE LAW, HARVARD LAW REVIEW,
INTERNATIONAL LAWYER, JOURNAL OF CORPORATION LAW, LITIGATION,
TAX LAWYER, and YALE LAW JOURNAL.

IV. CITATORS - Files include INSTA-CITE and SHEPARD'S
CITATIONS. INSTA-CITE displays: the direct case history
(prior and subsequent) for any federal or state case published
from 1938 to the present and precedential treatment for any
federal or state case affected by a case published from 1972
to the present. INSTA CITE may also be used to view parallel
citations and to validate citations. SHEPARD'S CITATIONS
contains citing case coverage of federal and state cases.

IV. SPECIALIZED MATERIALS - Among files available are: BNA
DATABASES (including BNA INTERNATIONAL TRADE DAILY, ANTITRUST
& TRADE REGULATION REPORTER, BNA'S BANKING REPORT, TAXSOURCE

DIRECTORY, and UNITED STATES LAW WEEK); CCH DATABASES (in-
cluding CCH BLUE SKY LAW REPORTER; CCH TAX DAY: FEDERAL; and
CCH TAX DAY: STATE); INDEX TO LEGAL PERIODICALS; LEGAL RE-
SOURCE INDEX; PRACTICING LAW INSTITUTE; TAX ANALYSTS DATABASES
(including TAX NOTES, TAX NOTES TODAY, and TAX MANAGEMENT
WEEKLY REPORT); WESTLAW HIGHLIGHTS (includes daily summaries
of recent cases and other legal news items of significance);
WESTLAW SERVICES (including BLACK'S LAW DICTIONARY and PER-
SONAL DIRECTORY OF QUERIES); PRACTICE AND TRAINING DATABASES;
GATEWAY SERVICES (gateway service to DIALOG, DOW JONES NEWS/
RETRIEVAL, INFORMATION AMERICA, PHINET and VU/TEXT); LIST
DATABASES (searchable list of WESTLAW database names and iden-
tifiers); and CURRENT AWARENESS MATERIALS (including CCH
MATERIALS, BNA MATERIALS, DOW JONES HIGHLIGHTS, IRS PUBLICA-
TIONS, PERSONAL DIRECTORY OF QUERIES, SEC NEWS DIGEST, TAX
NOTES HIGHLIGHTS, and WESTLAW TOPICAL HIGHLIGHTS.

WILSONLINE
THE H.W. WILSON COMPANY
950 University Avenue
Bronx, New York   10452
Telephone: 212-588-8400

WILSONLINE indexes articles from periodicals covering
topics of general interest, business, law, education, the
sciences, library and information science, the social sciences, and humanities. It also accesses book reviews, government publications, and Library of Congress book records.
Print equivalents of indexes below, with exception of Library
of Congress MARC records and Government Publications and
Periodicals, may be found in appendix on Indexes and Abstracts. WILSONLINE Data files applicable to franchising
information are:

APPLIED SCIENCE & TECHNOLOGY INDEX (AST) - Starting date:
October 1983. Indexes journals from various fields including
the food industry, transportation and petroleum, all of which
include franchised companies.

BIBLIOGRAPHIC INDEX (BIB) - Starting date: November 1984.
Indexes bibliographies in book and periodical format.

BIOGRAPHY INDEX (BIO) - Starting date: July 1984. Indexes
biographies published in book and periodical format. Includes
biographies of notable individuals in field of franchising.

BUSINESS PERIODICALS INDEX (BPI) - Starting date: June 1982.
Covers approximately 300 periodicals in field of business and
management. Subject and author listings.

BOOK REVIEW DIGEST (BRD) - Starting date: April 1983. Indexes
book reviews appearing in periodicals; excerpts from the
reviews are provided.

CUMULATIVE BOOK INDEX (CBI) - Starting date: January 1982.
Indexes book publications by subject, author, and title.

GOVERNMENT PRINTING OFFICE (GPO) - Starting date: July 1976.
Indexes publications of the U.S. Government Printing Office.

INDEX TO GOVERNMENT PERIODICALS (IGP) - Starting date: January
1980. Indexes articles appearing in U.S. Government published
periodicals.

INDEX TO LEGAL PERIODICALS (ILP) - Starting date: August 1981.
Index to law journal, includes articles on legal aspects of
franchising including recent legislation and court cases.

LIBRARY OF CONGRESS MARC BOOKS --FOREIGN (LCF) - Starting
date: January 1977. Indexes internationally published books.

LIBRARY OF CONGRESS MARC BOOKS (LCM) - Starting date: January
1977. Indexes by author, title, and published book records
from the Library of Congress.

READERS' GUIDE TO PERIODICAL LITERATURE (RDG) - Starting date:
January 1983. Indexes articles from selected U.S. general
interest periodicals.

VERTICAL FILE INDEX (VFI) - Starting date: December 1985.
Indexes pamphlet material.

AUTHOR INDEX

Numbers refer to entry numbers, not to page numbers.

Numbers refer to entry numbers, not to page numbers.

SUBJECT INDEX

Numbers refer to entry numbers, not to page numbers.